Indian Muslims against British Rule

About the Author

Dr. Aijaz Ahmad was born on 16th August, 1969, at Motipur village in Sant Kabir Nagar district of Uttar Pradesh. After completing his early education in Basti, he admitted in AMU Aligarh in 1985, for higher studies and completed B.A. (Hons), M.A. and M.Phil. in History. He also qualified NET and JRF test conducted by UGC from the same University. In 1994, he was appointed as a lecturer in History in YMD College Nuh in Mewat District of Haryana. In 2000, he obtained his Ph.D. degree as a teacher candidate from Jamia Millia Islamia, New Delhi. Now he is promoted as Associate Professor in History at the same college. During his service career in the same college he got published six research papers in national and international journals and proceedings of the Indian History Congress. In the same period he got published three books: (1) "Aligarh Muslim University: An Educational and Political History, 1920-47" Ghaziabad, 2005. (2) "Mewat: A Retrospective" Ghaziabad, 2013. (3) "Heritage of Mewat" Nuh, 2013. His current work is "Indian Muslims Against British Rule".

Indian Muslims against British Rule

Aijaz Ahmad

CONCEPT PUBLISHING COMPANY PVT. LTD.
NEW DELHI-110059

ISBN-13 : 978-93-5125-075-3

First Published 2014

Published and Printed by

Concept
Since 1974

Concept Publishing Company Pvt. Ltd.
A/15-16, Commercial Block, Mohan Garden
New Delhi-110059 (India)
T: 25351460, 25351794, *F*: 091-11-25357109
E: publishing@conceptpub.com, W: www.conceptpub.com
Editorial Office: H-13, Bali Nagar, New Delhi-110 015, India.

Cataloging in Publication Data—*Courtesy:* D.K. Agencies (P) Ltd. <docinfo@dkagencies.com>

Ahmad, Aijaz, 1969-
Indian Muslims against British rule / Aijaz Ahmad.
p. cm.
Includes bibliographical references (p.) and index.
ISBN 9789351250753

1. Muslims—Political activity—India—History. 2. Social movements—India. 3. India—History—Sepoy Rebellion, 1857-1858. 4. India—History—British occupation, 1765-1947. I. Title.

DDC 954.035 23

Dedicated

To the Memory of

My Father

Late Shafaat Mohammad

Preface

The present work, 'Indian Muslims Against British Rule' is a process to envelop all the events related to the Muslims and their religious duties of uprooting the British rule during the Uprising of 1857. A particular class within the Muslim society, the Ulema along with huge Muslim followers actively participated not only during the Uprising of 1857 but even before and after the same upheaval. For that very involvement, the heavy hand fell upon them, and they were brutally crushed in all over North India. I should not be misunderstood that only Ulema were the fighters of the Uprising, but they were having the leading role in a lot of fights against the British. They were the real instruments that mobilized not only the Muslims in the name of *Jihad* and martyrdom but also the Hindus for the sake of their religion and nation. It was the first time when even the Hindus frequently used the term *Jihad* to their fights against the British and in most of the places they arrayed under the green Islamic flag.

In my academic career and also in student's life, I had gone through a lot of books about the revolt of 1857 and most of which witness the role of various personalities who played leading role in the great upheaval. I was surprised that how Muslims, the second largest community of India, could be silent on this most burning episode. When I read the contemporary authors and some books written in Urdu script, I found that the matter was totally different then that which we were taught from school to college level. In the curricula of schools and college, there are no traces of the events in which the Ulema participated in the Uprising. The source materials which I have collected are full of narratives, which are enough to prove the active participation of the Muslims in the Uprising. Based on such findings, it would not be the exaggeration to say that the Muslim Ulema were the first torch bearers of the Indian freedom struggle which started on the eve of the Uprising of 1857. It is really unfortunate that the role of Muslims as a whole was ignored and deliberately not included in the syllabi or curricula of various standards of history.

This work is an attempt to prove the Muslim a true patriot and the real hero of the first war of independence, and remind the readers, what actually happened during the inordinate episode in 1857 and thereafter. This work is a humble submission of real tribute to the martyrdom of the religious clerics who taught a lesson of patriotism by their excessive sacrifice during the Uprising of 1857. It's the work of different historical dimension with independent analysis and research in the modern context. In this work, I have tried to do justice to the ideologically complex topic which was the need of the time. I seriously felt it necessary to my readers aware make about the Muslim torch bearers which always taught the lesson of love for the country and its people irrespective of caste and creed. They taught us that the patriotism or love of one's own nation is one of the true beliefs of Islam. They not only told the Muslims of that time but showed the fact by their martyrdom for the nation by the thousands in number.

I have divided the book into eight chapters, including the last one as conclusions. In these chapters, I have started from the overview of the Uprising and covered almost all the Muslim luminaries including rulers, clerics, soldiers, and general Muslim population. The role of the Wahabi Movement and Faraizi Movement also has been discussed in the context of the circumstances after a deep research and analysis. The role of the personalities like Bahadur Shah Zafar, General Bakht Khan, Sir Syed Ahmad Khan, Mirza Ghalib, and other related personalities have been very widely discussed. The print media or journalism of that time, particularly the Urdu Press which was the main source of inspiration to the common people has also been discussed in full detail.

I have started the writing of this book with the general happenings of the revolt from the greased cartridge issue which was suspected the mixture of the fat of swine and kine. I have fully covered that how the infanticide Rajput, the bigoted Brahmin; the fanatic Muslims had joined together in the cause. It was the first time, as Europeans generally quote; "cow-killer and the cow-worshiper, the pig-hater and the pig-eater," came forward and revolted together against the common enemy of their nation and religion. It was also the first time when the *Jawan* (Soldier) and *Kisan* (Farmer); *Dadhi-topi wala* (Muslim cleric) and *Tilakdhari* (Hindu cleric), joined the hands together in the national and religious passion. For the first time the world saw the miracle of the rainbow of Indian culture. The diversity of Indian culture greatly influenced the greatest social thinker of that time, such as, the great social thinker, Karl Marx, and Disraeli, the opposition leader of the British House of Commons.

I have much hope with this book that it would change the common mindset which has been developed about the Indian Muslim since the partition of India. For the Indian Muslims, the partition of India has been a curse resulting hatred and animosity between the two great religions of India. Following that very hatred, the political parties and the communal forces have time after time spread the poisonous ideology resulting in ill-feeling and communal riots among the people of this peace-loving nation. I hope that this book would give a lesson of fraternity, peace, and tranquility to the nation and avert the hatred ideology. This work would definitely prove much chagrin to the anti-national, communal, and separatist forces.

The Ulema or the Muslim theologians' role in the first war of independence was also unique of its kind in the history of India. It happened the first time in India or perhaps in the whole world when a religious class en mass rose against their tyrant ruler and happily met the boon of death for their nation and religion. They easily mixed the national struggle with their religion and appealed the mass participation; however, it is evident that their religion was not at all in danger. The main cause of their struggle was nothing more than the independence of their mother country, which had been enslaved about hundred years ere.

The Wahabi and Faraizi movements were a mixed reaction of the Muslims against the British rule which were not only attached to the national struggle of 1857, but had its beginnings much before the Sepoys' insurrection and lasted till the last quarter of the nineteenth century. The people associated with these movements were the worst sufferer and lose their lives uncountable for the cause of their beloved country and religion. The sacrifices of the people associated with these movements should be given the due importance rather than being considered merely a pan[2] Islamic propaganda.

This book also gives details of the Mughal Emperor Bahadur Shah Zafar, the only national symbol at that time, who met the brutal revenge of the British, which was the first of its kind in the history of India. The British Government in order to crush the Indian sentiment, transported him to Rangoon and massacred his kinsmen, and finally wiped out the Mughal dynasty from the Indian political scene. It's unfortunate to our Indian nationals that they have totally forgotten the sacrifices of that very dynasty, which did a lot for this country and its people, and also fought for the cause of the nation until their last breath.

It has been fully described that the ideology of Sir Syed Ahmad Khan is nothing but uneasiness for the people of his nation in order to save them from the clutches of the tyrant British rulers. Apart from being in the service of the British Government, Sir Syed Ahmad Khan was the first man in India who boldly abused the British policies which were the reasons for the great Uprising. His small bit support to the British was only to save his countrymen and advancement of his community. The other luminary Mirza Asadullah Khan Ghalib was openly praising the British for his pension, the means of his own livelihood. Apart from that he could not hide his pain when Delhi people were plundered, and mass level genocide waged by the British. His restless and anxious feelings could be observed through his letters and his book *Dastamboo*.

The whole history covered under different chapters within this book shows the real picture of the Uprising which was almost virtually ignored in the historical texts written about the topics of the Uprising of 1857. Almost all topics throughout this book are quite interesting, knowledgeable, and based on authentic sources with little hypothetical narrations. This book engaged me about two and half years and I accessed about twenty-five libraries and madarsas, met different individual scholars to get the research materials and information to complete this book. The topic in which I laboured a lot was the Ulema's participation in the Uprising. I am thankful for my Alim friends who provided me the relevant material and given related authentic information to complete that topic of my book. There is much scope to write on this topic as my work is not full and final, but I am sure that my readers would appreciate the work.

My purpose will be solved if the readers of both the communities, by forgiving the communal animosity, would embrace to each other with affection and fraternity. I would be delighted if the people of India would forsake the long hatred policies of divide and rule, which is still being followed by some communal forces. I have tried to remind that India would get freedom in a real sense if both the communities would unite for the sake of the nation, care for each other, feel the responsibility to run the nation jointly and maintain the long-cherished tradition of communal harmony. I am fully sure that this book may prove a boon to the millions of Indian nationals who are still living in the darkness and not even tasted the fruit of Indian unity and not smelled the flower of cultural diversity.

I am thankful to my esteemed teachers and well wisher Professor Mohammad Tariq, Professor Ali Athar, Professor Ali Mohammad, Professor Ateeque Ahmad, Professor Farhat Hasan, Mr. S.M. Javed, Dr. Mohammad Isa Gauhar, Dr. Hasan Imam, Dr. Basheer Hasan, etc. for boosting my will power and encouraging me whenever I lose my hope. My acknowledgements are due to my ever loving friends Dr. Mohd Imitiaz Khan,

Dr. Waseem Raja, Mr. Wahid Ali, Mr. Mazharul Haq, etc. for the support, they rendered me in every step of completing this book. My heartiest thanks are due to my wife Imrana Anjum, my kids Lubna, Iram, Anam, and Sadaf whose sweet smiles and happiness encouraged me to work constantly to complete the book; and freed me from all domestic assignments.

Aijaz Ahmad
Associate Professor in History
YMD College, Nuh, Mewat, Haryana

Contents

CHAPTER 1

Uprising: An Overview

After the downfall of the Mughal Empire, a British company of traders, with the Government of England as a sort of sleeping partner, started gaining control all over India. This company known as East India Company with an army of some thirty to forty thousand Europeans, permanently and peacefully maintained an oppressive system of domination and monopoly over the country of such a vast extent, inhabited by one hundred and fifty million of people of different religion, race, language, manner and custom. Up to 1856, the year before the outbreak of the Uprising, there had been for a whole century a continuous aggressive advance of the British power until it completed the ring fence of the Empire by the annexation of Awadh. It does not mean that Indians had no idea of governance, as claimed by the British, but history proves that the Indians either Hindus or Muslims were not only great rulers but great conquerors as well. The great masses of India, both Hindus and Muslims were strongly attached to their native system of Government and devoted to their modes of faith with an obstinate and inveterate bigotry which has no parallel in the British system of Government.

The Company's Government which was uniformly oppressive, treacherous, and unjust, not even tried to win over the inhabitants of this country, rather it economically handicapped the Indian subjects through their trade and commerce. They also attacked their religion and social customs, which had tied them since long into uniformity. Their political and economic policies further crushed aristocracy and general masses. The Christian Missionary activity further infuriated the Indian population and ultimately united them against the British East India Company. The British were fully aware of the discontents slowly developing in the native minds, but they did not care seriously. They were also afraid of the unknown danger of military dissatisfaction.

Malleson mentions that Lord Dalhousie on his journey homewards have written a minute, in which he painted in roseate hues the condition of India, the contentment of the Sepoys, and the improbability of disturbance from any cause whatever. However, this minute itself shows the doubt of disturbance, apart from the positive clarification of Dalhousie. In August, 1855, Lord Canning, at the farewell banquet given by the Directors, gave a warning, "We must not forget that in the sky of India, serene as it is, a small cloud may arise, at first no bigger than a man's hand, but which growing bigger and bigger may at last threaten to overwhelm us with ruin." The Indian atmosphere was also filled with many exciting rumours such as Russia was to avenge the Crimea by the invasion of India and the re-establishment of the Mughals. Persia will also help the Indians in establishing the Mughal rule and in this connection a proclamation, illustrated with a naked sword and shield, posted at the gates of the Great Mosque in March, 1857, announcing that the King of Persia was marching to the destruction of the British Raj, and that it behoved the faithful to be ready to fight the infidels.[1]

In the year 1857 there was a whispering among the Indian people about the old Indian prophecy. The prophecy was made by a Punjab Fakir of the twelfth century, seven hundred years ago, so the people were informed. It had been foretold that after various dynasties of Muslims had ruled for some centuries, the Nazarenes, or Christians, should hold power in India for one hundred years; that the Nazarenes would then be expelled. The prophecy was clearly indicating the hundred year's gap, dating from 1757 to 1857. According to prophesy there would be a change of Government in 1857 after a hundred years. Plassey had been in 1757 and in the hundredth year after the battle, it seemed everyone was waiting for a change.[2]

The British were well informed by their secret agents about the rumours and daily happenings and public grievances; however, they made little response and rather mistrusted their informers and avoided in the pretext that the natives have an unfortunate habit of sending anonymous information to the authorities with the view of injuring some personal enemy. Sir Syed Ahmad Khan says that for a long period, many grievances had been rankling in the hearts of the people. In the course of time, a vast store of explosive material was collected. It wanted a match to light it, and that match was applied by the mutinous army. The English were living over a volcano ready to burst into deadly violence at any moment, but they could not, or would not, apprehend their danger.[3]

After a hundred-year oppressive British rule, the Uprising broke out on 10th May 1857 from Meerut. The Uprising of 1857 provided a chance of revenge to the Indian masses for which they were waiting since long. This war mobilized all sections irrespective of race and religion and gradually converted the revolt into the war of independence. The Hindus and Muslims rose simultaneously to protect their '*Dharma*' and '*Din*' and to 'save their country'. The Sepoys (taken from Persian term *Sipahi*, meaning native infantry but the term Sepoy was generally used for every native troop, whether they belonged to infantry, artillery or cavalry) sparked at Meerut and proved the prophecy true.

The Indian Uprising of 1857 occurred as the result of the accumulation of factors over time, rather than any single event. Although the factors were political, socio-religious, economic, administrative, military etc. but these were the Sepoys or native troops which refused to use the cartridges allegedly greased with animal fat and dared enough to raise their arms against the East India Company's rule. The Sepoys were in the superiority complex and according to Karl Marx, 200,000,000 natives were being curbed by a native army of 200,000 men, officered by Englishmen, and that native army, in its turn, was being kept in check by an English army numbering 40,000, only.[4]

There was a discontent among the Sepoys regarding the service rules such as overseas service, promotions, pensions and the newly General Service Enlistment Act. Many Indian officers did not reach commissioned rank until they were too old to be effective. The final spark of unrest was due to the new Enfield rifle introduced in the Indian army in 1853. The cartridges of the Enfield rifle were heavily greased with wax and tallow made of cow and in certain lots swine fat. The grease was necessary in order to improve loading speed and so that during firing, the gases did not escape ahead of the bullet thereby reducing the range and accuracy of the weapon. The cartridges had to be bitten by teeth or opened by finger nails before being loaded.

The new rifles began to be manufactured at Damdam, Ambala, and Sialkot. When the complaints and suspicions of the Sepoys were made known firstly, from Damdam, inquiries were sent to England for exact particulars relating to the obnoxious missiles. It was ascertained that the new cartridges were made at the Royal Laboratory at Woolwich; and that Captain Boxer, the superintendent of that department, was accustomed to use for lubrication a composition formed of five parts tallow, five parts stearin and one part wax containing, therefore, ox or cow's fat, but none from pigs. He had no prejudices on the matter to contend against in England, and used therefore just such a composition as appeared to him most suitable for the purpose. The cartridges were not sent out to India ready greased for use; as, in a hot country, the grease would soon be absorbed by the paper. Therefore, a part of the process was left to be accomplished when the cartridges reached their destination. In January 1857, when the new weapon was to be issued to the Sepoys, rumours started spreading about the swine/cow fat in the cartridges.[5]

The story of greased cartridges goes back to January 1857, when a Khallasi or workman of a low caste attached in the Arsenal at Damdam (Artillery Station near Calcutta, where the school for musketry practice with the new Enfield rifle was then established), asked a Brahmin Sepoy of the 3rd Native Infantry (on some accounts 2nd Bengal Granadier) for a drink of water from his "lotah" or water-vessel. The Sepoy refused, saying, "You will defile my lotah by your touch." The classic answered, "You think much of your caste! Wait a little; the Sahib-logue will make you bite cartridges soaked in cow and pork fat! And where will your caste be then?" The Brahmin, alarmed, spread the report;

and the native troops, as is alleged, were afraid that when they went home their friends would refuse to eat with them. At that place, there was depot of musketry where the native soldiers were instructed to the use of Enfield rifle.[6]

When the rumour spread the native commissioned officer and Captain Wright at Damdam assured the soldiers that the grease was composed of mutton-fat and wax but the soldiers were not satisfied. They replied, "It may be so, but our friends will not believe it; let us obtain the ingredients from the bazaar and make it up ourselves; we shall then know what is used, and be able to assure our fellow soldiers and others that there is nothing in it prohibited by our caste." Captain Wright also observed that some of the depot men in conversing with him on the subject had stated, "the report had spread throughout India, and when they went to their homes their friends would refuse to eat with them." This rumour of greased cartridges soon spread like wild fire all over the Bengal Army from Calcutta to Peshawar. Matter was immediately reported to the Government on 22nd January. Major General J.B. Hearsay commanding the Presidency Division Barrackpur, immediately responded and reported the matter to the Governor General with some suggestions. On the 27th, the Governor General in Council not only approved General Hearsey's recommendation, but issued special orders to the Inspector-General of Ordnance that, "with the least possible delay, he was to submit any suggestions for removing the objections raised by the Sepoys, that means must be taken to satisfy them that nothing which may interfere with their caste was used". It was also ordered that in the meantime the cartridges were to be issued without any grease at all. On the morning of the 28th, the order of the Government, allowing the Sepoys to choose for themselves the grease required for their ammunition, was made known to every regiment in the cantonment. A modification was also made with the drill for loading so that the cartridge was torn from the hands and not bitten. The officers also attempted to convince the Sepoys. However, the damage had been done, and the Sepoys now started suspecting everyone and everything.[7]

Another military station which was badly affected by greased cartridge issue was Barhampur, near Murshidabad. The military cantonments were large and striking; the grand square, the excellent parade-ground, the quarters of the European officers all were handsome. Before the Revolt, Berhampore was included within the presidency division in military matters, and was usually occupied by a body of infantry and another of artillery. Barhampur, a few years before the Uprising, was a manufactorer of the silk bandana handkerchiefs once so popular in England. At that time, there were cantoned in it the 19th Regiment Native Infantry, a corps of irregular cavalry, and two 6-pounder guns manned by native gunners under Colonel Mitchell. On 25th of February, a portion of the 34th regiment of Bengal infantry changed its station from Barrackpur to Barhampur, where it was greeted and feasted by the men of the 19th Native Infantry, the only Native regiment stationed there at that time. During their feasting, the new-comers narrated all the news from Damdam and Barrackpur concerning the greased cartridges. Next day at the parade, when ordered to exercise with blank cartridge, the men all refused to touch the unclean thing! In the night of 27th February, the Sepoys rose and seized their arms, drumming and shouting defiance. As a result, they were warned and ordered for the 19th Native Infantry to march to Barrackpur where they were disbanded, but before they reached that station, the first blood had been shed in the Indian Mutiny.[8]

The next station which was caught by the cartridge fire was Barrackpur. It was situated at the banks of the Hooghly, sixteen miles from Calcutta. It was at that time the headquarters of the Presidency Division of the army, and four native regiments were quartered there; the 2nd Grenadiers, the 34th Native Infantry, the 43rd Light Infantry, and the 70th Native Infantry. The station was commanded by Brigadier Charles Grant; and the general of the Division was John Hearsey. On the 24th of January 1857, the telegraph office at Barrackpur was burnt down and this was the first act of open insubordination in the events of the Uprising 1857. It followed the burning of the Sergeants bungalow at Raniganj. On the 29th March 1857, Mangal Panday of the 34th Native Infantry at Barrackpur having intoxicated himself with bhang openly mutinied and fired at European Sergeant Major but his fire was missed. Mangal Panday also fired at Regiment

Adjutant Lieutenant Baugh and killed his horse with his second shot. This was followed by a hand to hand sword fight in which Baugh was wounded. Mangal Panday meanwhile was over powered by a Sepoy, Shaikh Paltoo. This enabled the wounded European Sergeant Major and the Adjutant to escape. Mangal Panday tried to commit suicide with his musket but was only wounded. In due course, Mangal Panday and his sympathizer Jamadar Ishwary Panday were court marshaled and hanged on 8th and 10th of April, 1857. The seven companies of the 34th Native Infantry were disbanded in the presence of all the troops. Shaikh Paltu was promoted and rewarded with proprietorship of a confiscated village.[9]

The next station, where the Sepoys mutinied, and continued their struggle for about one and half years, was Meerut. Here rumours were afloat in the markets and among the native troops, regarding the use of polluting grease in the preparation of the new cartridges about to be issued for the troops. The other rumour which added more hatred against the British was the mixture of ground bones in the flour sold in the markets. It was presumed that the British Government was intended to destroy caste and the religion of the Indian people.[10]

At Meerut cantonment, both Hindu and Muslim bound themselves by an oath not to use the cartridges when called out for exercise. On 24th April, the 3rd Bengal Light Cavalry was ordered to parade and perform firing drills. Only five (3 Muslims and 2 Hindus) obeyed and remaining 85 refused to accept their cartridges. All the 85 troops (49 Muslims and 36 Hindus) were ordered to return to their barracks. General Officer Commanding, Major General Hewitt ordered a Court of Inquiry composed of six members, four of whom were Native officers of the Infantry and two Native officers of the Cavalry. Based on the findings of this Court of Inquiry a General Court Martial was assembled. The tribunal before which they were to be brought up for trial was composed of fifteen native officers, of whom six were Muslims and nine were Hindus. Ten of these members were furnished by the regiments at Meerut Artillery, Cavalry, and Infantry; five came from the Infantry regiments at Delhi. The Court, by a vote of fourteen members against one, found the eighty-five guilty, and sentenced them to imprisonment and hard labour for ten years. Eventually, on mercy request of Major General Hewitt the sentence of 11 men who had less than five years service were reduced to five years hard labour. The sentence was to be carried into effect at daybreak on the 9th of May.[11]

It was decided to revenge the torture and humiliation of their brethren. On 10th of May, when most of the Europeans were attending the Church prayers on Sunday evening, the Indian troops led by the 3rd Cavalry together with the two native regiments, the 11th and 20th, seized the weapons, burnt the barracks and attacked and killed many of their officers. They galloped to the jail and broke it open releasing all the prisoners, including their 85 comrades. The markets soon thronged with crowds armed with sticks, staves, spears, and swords eager for the coming carnival of riot, plunder, and unrestrained licence.[12] A total of about 50 European men (including soldiers), women and children were killed in Meerut by Sepoys and local crowds.[13]

The Sepoys mutinied, and along with the civilian rioters, released their 85 fellows and other prisoners from jail of Meerut. It was followed by looting and plundering and massacring British men, women, and children. The Sepoys of Meerut mostly troopers of Malcolm's regiment, with some other Sepoys who had stolen ponies on the way, crossed the Yamuna, some going straight to the palace by way of a bridge of boats, while others forded the river came to Delhi and asked the Emperor to give his blessing to their war against the British. As a letter sent out by the rebels' leaders subsequently put it: "The English are people who overthrow all religions... As the English are the common enemy of both (Hindus and Muslims), we should unite in their slaughter... By this alone will the lives and faiths of both be saved."[14]

The mutineers entered Delhi without any pre-planning and shocked the Europeans as they could not take any defensive measure. Their occupation of Delhi on 11th May, proved to be the decisive general signal for the whole army to revolt. It is also said that the date of revolt was fixed by the revolutionaries on Sunday the 31st of May in their council, but the circumstances forced the Sepoys to explode several days before. John Kaye quotes the report of Mr. Cracroft Wilson, who was selected by the Supreme Government to fill the post of Special Commissioner, after the suppression of rebellion, with a view to the punishment of the guilty and the reward of the deserving, has placed upon record his full belief in this story of a general conspiracy for a simultaneous rising. The quote is as follows:[15]

> "Carefully collating oral information with facts as they occurred, I am convinced that Sunday, 31st of May, 1857, was the day fixed for mutiny to commence throughout the Bengal Army; that there were committees of about three members in each regiment which conducted the duties, if I may so speak, of the mutiny; that the Sipahis, as a body, knew nothing of the plans arranged; and that the only compact entered into by regiments, as a body, was, that their particular regiments would do as the other regiments did. The committee conducted the correspondence and arranged the plan of operations, viz., that on the 31st of May parties should be told off to murder all European functionaries, most of whom would be engaged at church; seize the treasure, which would then be augmented by the first installment of the rubbie harvest; and release the prisoners, of which an army existed in the North-western Provinces alone of upwards of twenty-five thousand men. The regiments in Dehli and its immediate vicinity were instructed to seize the magazine and fortifications.... From this combined and simultaneous massacre on the 31st of May, 1857, we were, humanly speaking, saved by Lieutenant-Colonel Smyth commanding the 3rd Regiment of Bengal Light Cavalry, and the frail ones of the Bazaar.... The mind had been prepared, and the train had been laid, but it was not intended to light the slow match for another three weeks. The spark, which fell from female lips, ignited it at once, and the night of the 10th of May, 1857, saw the commencement of a tragedy never before witnessed since India passed under British sway."

Meerut Sepoys of the three Native regiments and rioters numbering more than two thousand from the Meerut city and other nearby places reached to Delhi in the morning of 11th May. They admitted in the Red Fort, killed all white men and women they found within the fort wall. They cut down the Commissioner of Delhi, Mr. Fraser, Captain Douglas, Mr. Hutchinson, the Collector, the Chaplain Mr. Jennings, his daughter, and Miss Clifford. The fury soon spread from the palace to the city. Delhi bank was attacked first, its manager, Mr. Beresford was slain, and the bank was stormed and gutted. The church and every house occupied by Christian or Europeans were attacked and rifled, and no quarter was given to age or sex. They not even left the Indians who were converted to Christianity. The revolutionaries, in the city, were greeted with lotus flowers and chapatis and were urged to clear Delhi of the British. A slogan of '*Prithvi Raj Ki Jai*' was again raised after many hundred years.[16]

On the morning of the 11th of May, many of the Europeans, hearing that the mutineers were crossing the bridge, gathered themselves in one of the "largest and strongest houses" occupied by the Christian people, and there barricaded themselves. Nevertheless, the defence was not possible for long; the house was stormed, and the defenders were dragged to the Palace and thrust into an underground chamber. According to John Kaye, the Palace-guards came to the prison-door and told them to come forth, as they were to be taken to a better residence. They were taken to a courtyard; where great crowds of people were gathered together to witness the massacre of the Christians. So on 16th May, they were killed in spite of the objections of the Emperor. Their bodies were taken away in carts and pitched into the muddy flowing Jumna. After that 16th of May, there were no more Christians left in Delhi.[17]

After a large massacre of the Europeans and in the late hours of 11th May, two Subedars were admitted to a private audience to the Emperor Bahadur Shah as the representatives of the crowds of soldiery and asked the Emperor to give his blessing to their war against the British. As a letter sent out by them subsequently put it: "The English are people who overthrow all religions... As the English are the common enemy of both (Hindus and Muslims), was the thin spur of high ground in the north to the city of Delhi, and a continuous fight started from June to September, 1857. The British forces drove the revolutionaries within the walls, with a loss to them about 350 men, twenty-six guns, and some serviceable ammunition. The gain of the British under Henry Bernard, in the battle of Badli ki Sarai, was the occupation of the Ridge, the finest base of operations against the city, a position open at the rear to the reinforcements which he hoped to receive, whilst commanding the plain right up to the walls.[22]

After setting up of European forces at Ridge, a daily fight started at places like Alipur, Badli ki Sarai, Hindu Rao's House, Metcalfe's house, Flagstaff Tower, Shabzi Mandi, Kisangunj, Najafgarh, Paharipur, Eidgah, Teliwara, etc. with heavy loss from both the sides.

These were the very challenging days for the British in the history of their occupation of Indian Territory. On 23rd June, the centenary of Plassey, the revolutionary came out with all their available men and guns for the final battle as there was a prophecy which had long been quoted that on this day, they were destined to overthrow the Firangi rule. However, unfortunately, Sikh corps arrived from the Punjab on the same day and gave the specimen of their fighting powers to the revolutionaries. All day long, the fight went on under a burning sun which knocked over many officers and men; Hodson was in the saddle most of the day and bears testimony to the conduct of his old Guides and his new Sikhs and Gorkhas. In this, the British suffered a lot from this fierce sortie. The revolutionaries were also met a heavy loss. In the village Shabzi Mandi around 400 dead bodies were found. The total loss of the revolutionaries was about 1600 men.[23]

Fortunately, on 1st July 1857, a very experienced Bareilly leader, field battery commander Mohammad Bakht Khan, arrived in Delhi with a large military contingent and joined the revolutionaries. He assured the Emperor that he shall drive away the English out of Delhi and Meerut. A shield, a sword, and the title of General were bestowed on Mohammad Bakht Khan, and he was appointed Commander-in-Chief of the whole native forces. General Bakht Khan also received the title of *Farzand* later. A proclamation was issued ordering the attendance of all officers rebelled on 25th July, 1857 and joined Kunwar Singh of Jagdishpur. The 12th Irregular Cavalry at Segowlee on the Nepal border rebelled in June, 1857 and 32 Native Infantry in Orissa also rebelled in June, 1857.[20]

According to one estimate one-fifth of the Indian population in 1857 directly or indirectly participated in the Uprising. By popular support, different centres like Dehri, Patna, Arrah, Azamgarh, Allahabad, Gorakhpur, Faizabad, Fatehpur, Jhansi, Lucknow, Kanpur, Etawah, Fategarh, Gwalior, Shahjahanpur, Agra, Bharatpur, Rohilkhand, Mathura, Agra, Hatras, Delhi, Meerut, Bareilly and Roorki, etc. emerged as storm-centres of the Revolt. In this entire region, the dispossessed talluqdars and impoverished peasants and artisans, including Muslim fanatics known as *Jihadi, Ghazi,* and *Mujahideen* joined the Sepoys to contest the English authority. Almost all the areas of North and Central India were burning in the flames of Uprising. Massacre of Europeans, looting and plundering of their property was common throughout the period of Uprising. According to Karl Marx, "It is the first time that Sepoy regiments have murdered their European officers; that Musalmans and Hindus, renouncing their mutual antipathies, have combined against their common masters." He continues, "disturbances beginning with the Hindus, have actually, ended in placing on the throne of Delhi a Mohammadan Emperor."[21]

The loss of Delhi was a crushing blow to British prestige and the symbolic associations of the capital of the Mughals becoming the center of the revolt was something the British could not ignore. It took British nearly two months to regroup, and then they set out to reclaim Delhi. They reached Delhi with heavy enforcement. After reaching over Delhi on 7th of June, the European forces set their camp at Alipur, a few miles away from the revolutionary establishments. The British troops met with tough resistance from the revolutionaries of Delhi in the battle of Badli ki Sarai, on the 8th June. Henry Barnard moved towards the Ridge overlooking Delhi, drove thence the revolutionaries posted there, and encamped in the position whence he could best direct his attacks on Delhi. Thus, the British forces found the Ridge the most suited place, firmly established a base camp on the Ridge. The Ridge

Delhi a flag of *Jihad* was raised in the Jama Masjid, and many of the insurgents described themselves as *Mujahideenn* or *Jihadis*. Indeed, by the end to the siege, after a significant proportion of the Sepoys had melted away, hungry and dispirited, the proportion of *Jihadis* in Delhi grew to be about half of the total revolutionary force, and included a regiment of "suicide *Ghazis*" from Gwalior who had vowed never to eat again and to fight until they met death at the hands of the *Kafirs*, "for those who have come to die have no need for food". Under the command of Major Nicholson and with support of Sikh and Gorkha army, British could reclaim Delhi, breaking the walls with heavy guns and a bitter street-to-street fight afterwards. The first attempt to storm the city through the breaches and the Kashmiri Gate was launched on 14th September. The attackers gained a foothold within the city but suffered heavy casualties, including John Nicholson. After a week of street fighting, the British reached the Red Fort on 20th of September and occupied the whole city of Delhi. Bahadur Shah Zafar already fled to Humayun's tomb. During the street fighting, artillery had been set up in the Jama Masjid in the city, and the neighbourhoods within range were bombarded. These included the homes of the Muslim nobility from all over India, and contained innumerable cultural, artistic, literary, and monetary riches. Colonel John wrote to General Wilson announcing the capture of the palace in these words, "Blown open the gate, and got possession of the Palace."[27]

In the siege of Delhi, the grand total was nearly 4,000 including European and their faithful Sepoys, officers and men who were killed and wounded during the siege of Delhi (Julius George estimates 8,637). Another casualty of fully 1,200, perished by cholera and other diseases, during their stay on the Ridge, these were additional to those of the killed and wounded during the encounter of the revolutionaries. H.C. Fanshawe narrates that the killed and wounded were 992 killed and 2845 wounded, besides hundreds who died of disease and exposure. John Kaye remarks that the total loss to the army, from the 30th May to the final capture on the 20th September, amounted to nine hundred and ninety-two killed, two thousand seven hundred and ninety-five wounded, and thirty missing. However, in addition to these, many died from disease and exposure.[28]

in command of regiments to receive instructions from Mohammad Bakht Khan. Mirza Mughal was appointed Adjutant General.[24]

Mohammad Bakht Khan inflicted strict law and order. He informed even the Emperor that if any of the Princes attempted to plunder the city, he would cut off their noses and ears. He also informed the Kotwal of the city that if any more plundering took place, he would be hanged. Soldiers plundering were to be arrested. The General Mohammad Bakht Khan ordered a proclamation, by beat of drum, that all shopkeepers were to keep arms, and that no one should leave his house unarmed. Persons having no arms to apply to headquarters for them, and they would be given them free of charge. Any soldier caught plundering was to have his arm severed from his body. The General ordered to fine all those plundering, and to give compensation to the plundered victims. He was also instructed to arrange for the civil administration, the police, and revenue departments. By order of the Emperor Bahadur Shah Zafar, the royal princes were relieved from all further duties connected with the army.[25]

Nevertheless, General Bakht Khan's ability proved injurious for him. Slowly, and gradually he began to be victimized as soldiers of many contingents began to conspire against him and raised their finger on his loyalty. According to Munshi Jeewan Lal, it was 23rd of August when the officers of the Nimach force accused Bakht Khan of negotiating with the English, and of withholding his soldiers until the English should receive sufficient reinforcements from England and suggested to the Emperor that they should be allowed to disarm the Bareilly troops. The Emperor gave no answer to this proposal, but later in the day he issued orders to all the officers to obey neither the orders of Mirza Mughal nor of any other General, inasmuch as His Majesty had appointed a Court (Court of Administration) of twelve members, six to be appointed by the King and six by the army, for the future conduct during the siege. The army was to obey all orders issued by the Court.[26]

Many attacks were made on British forces vigorously and simultaneously at Shabzi Mandi, Alipur, Mubarak Bagh, Bara Hindu Rao, etc. and dispersed their forces and lost thousands of lives. Although the great majorities of the Sepoys were Hindus, in

From the side with the revolutionaries of Delhi, it was estimated that the total Sepoys fought against the British were around 40,000. In addition to the Sepoys there were similar numbers of the undisciplined armed hoards of fanatics known as *Ghazis* and *Mujahideen* and the city patriots called by Europeans as rabbles. They were about 1,00,000 in the number. They all fought very bravely but, unfortunately, as the time passed the Sepoys due to unavailability of their salaries or wages, started mass level desertion from the city. On the decisive days from 14th to 20th of September, there were only 50,000 fighters, including 25,000 Sepoys and similar number of the *Mujahideen* and city fighters. In the last days, there were only the *Mujahideen* in the city to resist the disciplined British force. However, unfortunately, they could not do a lot of harm to the British soldiers and were martyred while fighting at the front and in the streets. The total loss of lives of the revolutionaries was innumerable and the property which was looted and burnt was estimated in hundreds of millions.

The Mughal Emperor Bahadur Shah along with his family took shelter in the Humayun's Tomb but on the persuasion of Hodson and his spy Maulvi Rajab Ali, the Emperor and his family surrendered peacefully. Most of the Emperor's 16 sons and grandsons were tried and hanged, while two sons, Mirza Mughal, Mirza Khizr Sultan, with the grandson, the son of Mirza Mughal, by name Mirza Abu Bakr, were shot in cold blood, having first freely given up their arms, then been told to strip naked. Captain William Hodson wrote to his sister the following day. "In 24 hours I disposed off the principal members of the house of Taimur the Tartar, I am not cruel, but I confess I did enjoy the opportunity of ridding the earth of these wretches. I intended to have had them hung, but when it came to a question of 'they' or 'us,' I had no time for deliberation."[29]

Allahabad was another important place, which clung into the Uprising after Meerut and Delhi. Here, the garrison consisted of two regiments—one, the 6th Native Infantry, in the cantonment; the other, an Irregular Regiment of Sikhs, under Captain Brasyer, in the fortress. On the night of the 6th of June, the Sepoys at Allahabad which, the previous day, had been thanked by the

Government for its profession of unswerving loyalty, mutinied and murdered nearly all its officers, including some young boys just arrived from England. The fortress of Allahabad, occupying a most commanding position on the Jumna, considered the gateway to the North-West India.[30]

The next important centre of the Uprising was Lucknow, the capital of Awadh, where the Nawab Wajid Ali Shah dethroned and the territory was annexed by the British. Nawab Wajid Ali Shah was exiled to Garden Reach (Matia Burj) in the suburb of Calcutta with the pension of 12 lakh rupees per annum. At Lucknow, on 7th May some happening of disobedience was appeared, but it soon recovered. However, there were a constant anxiety and resentment among the Sepoys of Lucknow, which lasted through the end of this month. This was truly felt by the military officers and the Chief Commissioner Henry Lawrence and the civilian Europeans, and the British officers were advised for their defence arrangements. On 30th May 1857, Sepoys of the 71st Native Infantry and 7th Light Cavalry, in the area of Mudkipur mutinied. They burnt all the houses and bungalows in the cantonment except of Henry Lawrence, which was highly protected. It followed the murder and mass level destruction of the properties. Another fight took place in Husainabad area between the combined forces of mutineers and city people and British forces, but the attack of the revolutionaries was repulsed with some losses, and about forty in the number were arrested and lodged in Machhi Bhawan (old small Sikh fort). The defeated Sepoys were dispersed in the countryside especially to Sitapur and many more fled towards Delhi. The arrested mutineers were at Machhi Bhawan were Court Marshalled and hanged. On 30th of May out of four mutinous regiments no more than 437 i.e. 13th N.I. 200, 48th N.I. 57, 71st N.I. 120, 7th L.C. 60, remained loyal to the British. Most of the suspected regiments were disarmed, which reduced the Sepoys two-third in the British troops. The rebellion was quelled and the Sepoys were dispersed over countryside and the Lucknow remained calm throughout the June but again rose on 30th of June with full vigour and force.[31]

When the Uprising re-started on 30th of the June 1857, the combined fighting force comprising Sepoys and the masses from the general rural populace fought to oust the British. It is more than probable that it was the ties of loyalty that existed in the rural areas of Awadh, which resulted the thousands of men supplied by the talluqdars were not all just their retainers but also drawn from tenants, peasants and clansmen which lived in their land. The English were very much surprised that even the peasants whom the talluqdars oppressed should have joined the rebel cause under the leadership of their respective talluqdars as they presumed that the peasants would appreciate the Company's anti-talluqdari measures, since these were supposed to be in the interests of the peasants. However, the British had perhaps forgotten that if the talluqdars were an oppressor, then the new British rule was defamed for its heavy taxation and harsh mode of revenue collection.

It was reported to the British that revolutionaries were preparing to fight at Chinhat on the outskirt of Lucknow and the British soldiers moved accordingly with full preparation, but they met tough resistance near the village Ismailganj, near side of Chinhat. The battle of Chinhat fought on 30th of June and revolutionaries, including Sepoys, *Mujahideen* and common people, won a resounding victory. British officials and other European inhabitants were forced to take refuge in the Residency and its compound and Machhi Bhawan numbering about three thousand. Later on, the British were forced to leave Machhi Bhawan as it was destroyed by the revolutionaries. The British troops met a heavy loss of men and money.[32]

Now the revolutionaries fully occupied the city of Lucknow, and the siege of the Lucknow Residency commenced on 1st of July 1857. About 6000 revolutionaries fought during the siege of Residency, and they got trumped success when Henry Lawrence, the Chief Commissioner of Awadh was killed in the first few days of the siege, on 4th July 1857. The revolutionaries by shouting the war cry, "Ali, Ali" and "*Chalo Bahadur*" filled the passion of war among them and attacked upon the British sheltered in the Residency from all its sides.[33]

Like Delhi, the revolutionaries of Lucknow also set up a new Government by proclaiming the end of the East India Company's Government. They recognized the authority of Begum Hazrat

Mahal, the former wife, who remained their foremost leader throughout the duration of the siege. Begum Hazrat Mahal's minor son Birjis Qadr was declared as the ruler of Awadh.

On 5th July, 1857, representatives of the armed forces, Shahabuddin and Barkat Ahmad placed 13 or 14 years old Prince Birjis Qadr on the chair of ruler ship. A Military Council, based on Delhi Council of Administration, was also established in Lucknow to govern almost all state of affairs in the Government of Brijis Qadr. His mother Begum Hazrat Mahal played very important role in mobilizing the revolutionaries and controlling the administration.[34]

After the reoccupation of Delhi, it became the matter of 'do or die' for the British to re-conquer Lucknow, the second most important bastion of Indian revolutionaries. The recapture of Lucknow was a matter of urgency; without control over Lucknow, British rule could not be re-established in Awadh. On 25th September 1857, the British forces under Havelock and Outram tried to attack on Lucknow. General Havelock's force consisted of three thousand one hundred and seventy-nine men of all arms. All these combined forces managed to reach the Residency, but at last they were besieged with the loss of infamous General Neill.[35]

The problem with the British garrison was that the revolutionaries from all parts of India were daily crowding at Lucknow. Kaye and Malleson write that the strength of the revolutionaries at Lucknow was about 96,000. This count did not include artillerymen, whose number was unknown, and the armed followers of the talluqdars, estimated at 20,000. Altogether there could not have been less than 120,000 armed men in Lucknow at the end of January, 1858.[36]

However, the siege of the Residency continued and again in November, 1857 the British forces bit the dust by the hands of the revolutionaries. Colin Campbell's military action on this occasion was only having a partial success. Havelock and Inglis were killed during the siege. The city contained 30,000 revolted Sepoys, 50,000 volunteers or *Mujahideens* and armed retainers of chieftains. The British garrison was also reinforced with many British regiments, including ten thousand Gorkhas under Jang Bahadur, the Prime Minister of Nepal. A British siege-train also arrived from Agra.

Now the British garrison was totaling about 30,000 including 18,000 Europeans. Eventually, a massive offensive was launched in March, 1858. Campbell had set up his headquarters in the Dilkusha Palace located in the Dilkusha Gardens on the outskirts of the city. His contingents occupied Lucknow on 21st March, 1858 after capturing the Moosa Bagh.[37]

Jhansi was another centre of Uprising, which proved tough for the British. Its ruler Raja Gangadhar Rao left no child but on the day before he died, adopted child five years old, named Damodar Rao. However, unfortunately, this time the Governor-General Lord Dahousie didn't recognize the heir and pensioned off the widow Rani Luxmi Bai, 6,000 pounds a year.[38]

The Sepoys of 12th Bengal Infantry stationed at Jhansi, suddenly started firing on 5th of June. The mutiny commenced in Jhansi and the European by leaving their women and children in the Town Fort remained themselves in the cantonment. On 7th of June, the British held a council of war and decided to send three of the garrison to the Rani to ask her to use her influence to enable them to proceed unmolested to some place of refuge within British territory. Nevertheless, all the three were then dragged out of the palace. Mr. Andrews was killed before the very gate of the Rani's residence, and the other two were dispatched beyond the walls of the town."[39]

Rani also supplied the arms to the revolutionaries who were busy in the siege of the fort. When the revolutionaries of Jhansi were successful in crushing the walls of the Town Fort, they hatched a treachery. Malleson writes that Rani sent messengers to the fort under a flag of truce, demanding a parley. Captain Skene responded. The native messengers then declared that the Rani wanted only the fort; that if the Europeans laid down their arms and surrender the position they held they would be escorted to some other station. These terms were affirmed by the most solemn oaths. Captain Skene, on behalf of the garrison, acceded to them. They seemed indeed to offer the only chance of life. The members of the garrison then laid down their arms, and walked out of the fort in the evening of 8th June, but on the crossing of the Fort gate, they were forced to range in three lines, the first containing the adult males, the second the adult females, the third the children.

Then, suddenly, the head native official of the jail raised his sword and cut down Captain Skene. This was the signal. The captives numbering about 66 were pitilessly hewn down. Not a man, woman, or child, survived that afternoon's butchery.[40]

After cleaning the Jhansi from the Europeans Rani raised fresh troops; she strengthened her fortified places; she established a mint; and she sent delegates to Dhondu Pant, Nana Sahib, with whom she had previously been in communication.[41]

The Rani remained in power until April 1858, when by the advent of a British army and its operations against the doomed city the situation was again changed. Major-General Sir Hugh Rose launched an attack on Jhansi in March 1858, and got a tough resistance from the Rani and her forces. Rani was having a garrison of eleven thousand five hundred men, including fifteen hundred Sepoys who had been trained in the British army. The column of troops with General Rose was also equal in number. On the bravery of Rani, Hugh Rose describes her as, "The best and bravest military leader of the rebels".[42]

The battle was started on 25th of March with great enthusiasm among the forces of Rani. Even ladies and children provided their services according to their capability. The British force was seemed to be more powerful but as surprisingly, Tatya Tope joined the forces of Rani, their number increased vehemently about twenty-two thousand in total. However in a pitched battle, the revolutionary forces under Tatya Tope met a crushing defeat with a loss of fifteen hundred dead and wounded along with several guns. The remaining force of the revolutionaries under Tatya Tope fled towards Kalpi, the stronghold of Nana Sahib.[43]

At last, the fort was besieged by the British with loss of three hundred forty three dead and wounded of whom thirty six were officers. The total loss of the revolutionaries was about five thousand. Rani fled from Jhansi along with some of her soldiers numbering about five hundred and rode straight to Kalpi, which was about ninety five miles away. Both the armies of Rani and Tatya Tope joined at Kalpi, where Nana's nephew Rao Sahib was stationed with a number of revolutionaries.[44]

Nawab of Banda along with two thousand soldiers and personal followers joined the company of Rani and Rao Sahib at

Kalpi. Hugh Rose was also reinforced by the assistance send by the Commander-in-Chief Collin Campbell. On 22nd May, battle started and again the victory sided with the British. The revolutionaries fled towards Gwalior and stationed at Gopalpur town, forty six miles south-west of Gwalior. From that very station, the revolutionary tried to oust the ruler Jiyaji Rao Sindhia from Gwalior. A battle was fought between Sindhia and the revolutionaries on 1st of June in which Scindhia was defeated badly and fled away towards Agra. The revolutionaries formed their Government at Gwalior. Nana Sahib was declared as Peshwa, Rao Sahib as Governor of Gwalior, Rani Luxmi Bai was made commander of the forces outside of the city, and Tatya Tope was the commander of the forces inside of the city.[45]

On 17th June 1858, the final battle was held between British and the revolutionaries in which the British became victorious. By the 19th of June, Gwalior was captured by Lieutenants Rose and Waller. Tatya Tope was captured by Captain Richard Meade on 7th April, and executed at Sipri on the 18th of April, 1859. Rani fought gallantly but she too bound to flee after her defeat. However, her horse in crossing the canal near the cantonment stumbled and fell. Then a Cavalry soldier, ignorant of her sex and her rank, cut her down. That night her devoted followers burned her body, determined that the English should not boast that they had captured her though dead.[46]

Kanpur was another station of Uprising, which proved hard nut to the British. Here Nana Sahib took the command of the revolutionaries and the mutinous Sepoys. Nana Sahib was adopted son of last Peshwa Baji Rao II, who also deprived from title and pension after Peshwa's death. Nana also appealed to the Court of Directors in England through his vakil Azimullah. However, Azimullah Khan could not induce the Company to grant his master the pension. The non-acceptance of his appeal turned Nana Sahib's heart black with hatred against the British.[47]

In Kanpur, the Sepoys mutinied on 6th of June 1857, when the 2nd Cavalry broke out in the night. They first set fire to the riding-master's bungalow, and then fled, carrying off with them horses, arms, colours, and the regimental treasure-chest. An hour or two after the flight of the cavalry, the 1st Native Infantry also revolted, leaving their officers untouched by the parade ground. The 56th Native Infantry followed the next morning. The 53rd mutinied in the last. The mutineers made their way to Delhi. Mowbray Thomson narrates that when they reached Nawabgunj, the Nana came out to meet them, and at their head proceeded to the treasury, where he had all the Government elephants laden with the public money, and distributed a vast amount of it among the Sepoys, whose command he forthwith assumed.[48]

On the forenoon of the 7th June, Nana and his associates like skilful soldier, Tatya Tope, Azimullah Khan along with their forces opened their heaviest batteries on the rude parapets of the entrenchments. Hillersdon was killed by a round shot; his chief subordinate, McKillop, was shot as he was drawing water for the women from an unprotected well; Hillersdon's brother, wife, and two children perished in the fatal enceinte. The Europeans suffered a lot from thirst, especially the women and children. For three dreadful weeks, the wretched Europeans were sapped, bombarded, starved, and eventually lost the battle. The revolutionaries became successful to siege the Europeans of Kanpur cantonment on June 23, 1857, proposed to mark the centenary of Plassey by an assault. Nevertheless, the Europeans still not surrendered.[49]

After twenty-one days full fight, on 25th June Wheeler received an unsigned letter on the writing of Azimullah Khan. It was offered to the British that if they lay down their arms, they shall be allowed a safe passage to Allahabad. On this matter, Wheeler consented to evacuate the scene of horror. Wheeler and the remaining Europeans, about 450 in the number, evacuating the position, moved down on 27th of June, to the river at Satichaura Ghat where boats were ready to embark. Nana and his associates arranged 40 boats for the escape of the Europeans. However, when the Europeans reached in the mid-stream and sailed towards Allahabad, Nana's forces started firing. Most of them were killed and some of them surrendered and sent back as captives. Nevertheless, some of them still sailed their boats and faced the firings in the streams and were killed except for one boat's crew, of whom four only finally escaped, two, at least, of whom were alive until 1883. The surviving Europeans, who were in captivity, were separated from their women and children and killed in the evening of 1st July. Only 5 men and 206 women and children totaling 211 (Frazer records the number as 118 women and 92 children) were lodged in a small house named Bibighar. Here they were in very miserable position and severely suffered from cholera, diarrhea, and dysentery and about 26 women and children died. After Nana's defeat by General Havelock, the captives of Bibighar were massacred and their bodies were thrown into the nearby dry well.[50]

Nana continued to rule on Kanpur and the adjacent areas until 13th of July, when Havelock encountered the Nana's troops at Fatehpur, under Teeka Singh, a Risaldar of the 2nd Cavalry. The revolutionaries were totally routed out and returned to Kanpur. On the 15th of July, the revolutionaries again engaged with General Havelock at Pandu River but met the same defeat. In utter confusion on that day, the Nana put all his captives to death. On the 16th, another fight took place in which Nana and his ten thousand revolutionaries were defeated after a few hours battle. On the morning of the 17th, General Havelock along with his forces entered the city, and the native populace fled in every direction to the villages adjacent. After finishing his work at Kanpur, Havelock left the place which was occupied by Brigadier General Neill on 20th of July 1857. His infamous order, to clean the blood of the slayed Europeans by the tongues of the Indian captives, was carried on after his arrival.[51]

Nana fled towards Lucknow and after fall of Lucknow in mid- March 1858, Nana along with other revolutionaries fled towards Ruhelkand to join the Government of Maulvi Ahmadullah Shah at Mohammadi. Nevertheless, after fall of the Mohammadi Nana rode away to an unknown destination in Nepal in 1859 and probably died in the forest.[52]

Jagdishpur, the Jagir of Kunwar Singh, was another centre of Uprising, which was liquidated by the British. He led the revolutionaries of all parts of Bihar and also routed the eastern areas of UP. After the rebellion in Patna, the Sepoys of all the three regiments 7th, 8th, and 40th Native Infantry at Dinapur mutinied on 25th July 1857. There was only one British regiment 10th Foot to guard over there. Finding the right opportunity, Kunwar Singh also gathered a large number of followers, who included his brothers Amar Singh and Ritnarain Singh; his nephews Nishan Singh and Jai Krishna Singh; Thakur Dayal Singh and Bisheswar Singh. The revolutionaries of Dinapur, Chhotanagpur, Manbhum, Singhbhum, and Palamau wanted to carry on the struggle together under the common leadership of Kunwar Singh. Almost all Bihar was united under him.[53]

On 26th July 1857, the troops reached the district headquarter, Shahabad in order to plunder the treasury and kill the Europeans. They had also an intention to organize themselves under the leadership of Kunwar Singh, the Raja of Jagdishpur, who had already launched a movement against the British. Hearing the news of Sepoys' revolt, Kunwar Singh also marched along with his men. They all joined at Arrah and on the morning of 27th of July, they broke open the jail, looted the treasury of 70,000 rupees, and were joined by the jail guards, prisoners, and hundreds of revolutionaries from the neighbouring villages. They besieged the European officials and civilians of Arrah and Shahbad. George Trevelyan writes that Kunwar Singh brought with him a mighty following, and recruits poured in by hundreds and thousands daily. The Sepoy veterans, who were living on pensions in their native villages, came forward to share the fortunes of their ancient regiments in greater numbers. George Trevelyan quotes the Calcutta papers, "That old fool, Coer Sing,' have held a review of eight thousand armed men, besides the three regular battalions. There was one cry throughout the province — that now or never was the time to shake off the oppression of the stranger."[54]

The British sent an expedition from Patna under Captain Dunbar to defeat the Kunwar Singh. The force was consisting of nearly three hundred and fifty men of the 37th Queen's regiment, sixty Sikhs, and some young civilians who volunteered to accompany the party. Captain Dunbar was quite unfit for such a duty, his military experience having been gained in a paymaster's bureau. Due to weak command of Dunbar and strong revolutionary force under experienced Kunwar Singh, the British met the defeat with heavy losses in this battle near Arrah. Captain Dunbar and several officers were shot dead at the first discharge.[55]

About the battle James Halls writes, "Out of the 400 fine fellows that started for Arrah, nearly 200 were killed, and of the remainder, I do not think more than fifty to sixty were not wounded; out of seven volunteers, five were knocked over, four killed and one wounded. This has been the most disastrous affair that has happened out here."[56]

Hearing the news about the defeat of the British force under Dunbar, Major Vincent Eyre marched with his force consisted of hundred and fifty and four English bayonets, twelve mounted volunteers, and three field-pieces, with their complement of artillerymen. George Trevelyan writes that Kunwar Singh's whole forces; two thousand five hundred mutineers, and his own force, estimated at eight thousand men. The rebels, whom their recent success had inspired with unwonted confidence, did not wait to be attacked. The battle was started at Bibigunj on 3rd of August in which Kunwar Singh was defeated and fled to his stronghold Jagdishpur.[57]

After the victory of the British at Arrah, they started retribution and after completing the punishment of the revolutionaries and even innocents, Major Vincent Eyre decided to take an expedition to Jagdishpur, to track out the escaped Rajah and his army. He only waited until he was reinforced by the Her Majesty's 10th Foot, and by 100 of Rattray's Sikhs from Dinapur, and then he started from Arrah on 11th of August. Here at Jagdishpur, Kunwar Singh had in the field altogether about five thousand two hundred men, of whom twelve hundred were Sepoys. However, the fight was almost one sided; Eyre had taken Jagdishpur, the abode of the King, after only about two-and-a-half hours' fighting. The total loss in Kunwar Singh's army was about 200 or 300 men, whilst in the English camp, there was no loss of life, only six men wounded.[58]

For the British, the campaign terminated by the victory at Jagdishpur but this did not mark the end of Kunwar Singh's struggle. He shifted out of Bihar, moving to Mirzapur, Rewa, Banda, Kalpi, Lucknow, Azamgarh, Ghazipur, and Kanpur, along with his comrade-in-arms Nishan Singh. Passing through Mirzapur and Rewa, he arrived at Banda in September with a view to joining Tatya Tope. He was joined by the Gwalior forces at Kalpi, and fought at the battle of Kanpur in December 1857.[59]

Eventually, he decided to return to his home district and re-entered Jagdishpur on 23rd of April 1858. He was grievously injured during the retreat and lost his right hand but his determination to fight the English had not weakened. The next day a force under Captian Le Grand proceeded to attack the old, injured veteran, but it was repulsed. Three days later, Kunwar Singh died of injuries.[60]

It must not be misunderstood that after the fall of the important centres of the Uprising and martyrdom of the torch bearer revolutionaries of Uprising, the war came to an end. However, the diehard *Mijahideen,* Ulema and other Muslims continued the struggle in the Frontier or the Peshawar valley with the support of men and money of the north Indian Muslims. The struggle continued until the martyrdom of thousands of *Mujahideen* and brutal killing of Lord Mayo by Sher Ali Afridi.

REFERENCES

1. Malleson, George Bruce, *Indian Mutiny of 1857*, London, 1912, p. 23, see also Frazer, R. W., *British India*, New York 1896, pp. 274-275, Cunningham, Henry Stewart, *Earl Canning*, Oxford, 1891, p. 53, and Aitchison, Charles, *Rulers of India: Lord Lawrence*, Oxford, 1892, p. 73 (The proclamation pasted on the wall of great mosque at Delhi, which purported to be a manifesto from the Shah of Persia addressed to the people. "All the Faithful in India! The infidels had brought troops to the soil of a power of Islam. They desired to destroy the religions of Islam in Persia in like manner as the religion of the Muslims of India. It was incumbent on the Faithful to rise against them everywhere. Let them unite all differences, and remember that they had but one Quraan and one Qiblah, and extend the hand of brotherhood, remembering the words of the Prophet, 'Verily all true believers are brothers.' Let them all take part in the *Jihad*, or Holy War. Let the Faithful in Hindustan unite with him (the Shah) against this tribe of wanderers from the path of righteousness, and have no friendship with a tribe of whom the Prophet said, 'Verily they do not love you, and neither do you love them. Let all the Faithful in Hindustan consider it incumbent upon them to follow the precept, 'Slay, in the name of God, those who wish to slay you'; and let the old and the young, the small and the great, the wise and the ignorant, the ryot and the Sepoy, all without exception arise in the defence of the orthodox faith of the Prophet,

and, having girt up the waist of valour, adorn their persons with arms and weapons. And for the purpose of settling the quarrel, it is necessary that not only a small number of true believers should stand forth in defence of the faith, but that the whole should answer our call. And the victory should be with them, to make manifest the decree of God, 'Verily the Almighty will weigh the wicked in different scales from the pure." Forrest, Robert Edward, *Eight Days; A Tale of the Indian Mutiny*, London (ND), pp. 34-35).

2. Kofoid, Charles Alwood, *The Story of the Indian Mutiny, 1857-58,* Edinburgh, 1898, p. 20.
3. Khan, Syed Ahmad, *Asbab-e-Baghawat-e-Hind*, (Eng. Trans.), Patna, 1999, p. 3, (Hereafter cited as *Asbab-e-Baghawat-e-Hind*).
4. *New York Daily Tribune*, July 15, 1857.
5. Dodd, George, *The History of the Indian Revolt and of the Expeditions to Persia, China, and Japan, 1856-7-8,* London, 1859, p. 38, hereafter cited as Dodd, see also Forrest, G.W., *A History of the Indian Mutiny; Reviewed and Illustrated from Original Documents,* Vol. I, London 1904, p. 2, and *Defence Journal*, Vol. 3, No. 9, Islamabad, December, 1999.
6. Argyl, Campbell, George Douglas, Duke of, *India Under Dalhousie and Canning*, London, 1865, p. 77, see also Surridge, Victor, *Romance of Empire, India*, London, 1909, pp. 249-50.
7. *Ibid.*, pp. 78-79, see also Dodd, p. 2, *The Living Age,* Volume 0055, Issue 702, New York, November 7, 1857, pp. 325-326, Beveridge, Henry, *A Comprehensive History of India*, Vol. III, London, 1962, p. 556, 557-561, and *New York Daily Tribune*, July 15, 1857.
8. Forrest, G. W., *A History of the Indian Mutiny; Reviewed and Illustrated from Original Documents,* Vol. I, London 1904, pp. 11-12 and 18, see also Dodd, p. 40.
9. Edward, Gilliat, *Heroes of the Indian Mutiny; Stories of Heroic Deeds*, London 1914, p. 25, see also Kaye, John William, *A History of the Sepoy War in India, 1857-58,* Vol. I, London 1875, pp. 539-540, *The Living Age,* Volume 0055, Issue 702, New York, November 7, 1857, p. 326, Forrest, G. W., *A History of the Indian Mutiny; Reviewed and Illustrated from Original Documents,* Vol. I, London 1904, pp. 20-21, Wood, Evelyn, *The Revolt in Hindustan 1857-59*, London, 1908, p. 9, Norman, Henry Wylie, *Delhi - 1857; The Siege, Assault, and Capture as given in the Diary and Correspondence of the Late Colonel Keith Young*, London 1902, pp. 5-6, and Malleson, George Bruce, *Indian Mutiny of 1857*, London, 1912, pp. 53-56.
10. Nevill, H. R., *District Gazetteers of the United Provinces of Agra and Oudh*, Vol. IV, Allahabad, 1904, p. 163.
11. Kaye, John William, *A History of the Sepoy War in India, 1857-58,*

Vol. II, London 1874, pp. 48-51 see also *Defence Journal*, Vol. 3, No. 9, Islamabad, December,1999, *The Living Age,* Volume 0055, Issue 702, New York, November 7, 1857, p. 329, and Qasmi, Ataur Rahman, *Hindustan Ki Pahli Jang Azadi 1857 Me Musalmanon Ka Hissa*, New Delhi, 2008, p. 40.

12. Nevill, H. R., *District Gazetteers of the United Provinces of Agra and Oudh*, Vol. IV, Allahabad, 1904, p. 164 (It was really strange that the army (Native and European) stationed at Meerut was almost equal in number (2,028 Europeans against 2,057 Natives), yet the mutineers originally few hundred could not be controlled. The General Officer Commanding Major General William Henry Hewitt answered, when he once asked the reasons for his inaction at Meerut, "As soon as the alarm was given, the artillery, carabineers, and 60th Rifles were got under arms, but by the time we reached the native parade ground, it was too dark to act with efficiency in that direction; consequently the troops were retired to the north of the nullah." *Defence Journal*, Vol. 3, No. 9, Islamabad, December,1999).
13. *Ibid.*, see also Gilliat Edward, *Heroes of the Indian Mutiny; Stories of Heroic Deeds*, London 1914, p. 133.
14. Argyl, Campbell, George Douglas, Duke of, *India Under Dalhousie and Canning*, London, 1865, pp. 88-89, see also *The Guardian*, 10th May, 2007, Anderson, Clare, *The Indian Uprising of 1857-8: Prisons, Prisoners and Rebellion*, London, 2007, p. 3, and Tracy, Louis, *The Red Year; A Story of The Indian Mutiny*, New York 1907, p. 42.
15. Kaye, John William, *Kay's and Malleson's History of the Indian Mutiny of 1857-8,* Vol. II, London, 1910, pp. 81-82, see also Edward, Gilliat, *Heroes of the Indian Mutiny; Stories of Heroic Deeds*, London 1914, p.141.
16. Edward, Gilliat, *Heroes of the Indian Mutiny; Stories of Heroic Deeds*, London 1914, pp. 137-138, see also Wagnor, Kim A., *The Great Fear of 1857, Rumours, Conspiracies and the Making of the Indian Uprising*, Witney (UK), 2010, p. 201, and Fanshawe, H.C., *Delhi Past and Present*, London 1902, pp. 96-103.
17. Kaye, John William, *Kay's and Malleson's History of the Indian Mutiny of 1857-8,* Vol. II, London, 1910, pp. 74-75.
18. Metcalfe, Charles Theophilus, *Two Native Narratives of the Mutiny in Delhi,* (Eng. Trans. of *Roznamcha Mainudin Hasan Khan* and *Munshi Jeewan Lal*), London, 1898, pp. 83-86, (Hereafter cited as *Two Native Narratives*) see also Anderson, Clare, *The Indian Uprising of 1857-8: Prisons, Prisoners and Rebellion*, London, 2007, p. 3.
19. *Ibid.*, see also *The Guardian*, 10th May, 2007 (John Kaye says, "The

courtyards and the corridors of the Palace were swarming with the mutineers of the 3rd Cavalry and of the 38th, and soon the Meerut Infantry Regiments began to swell the dangerous crowd, whilst an excited Mohammadan rabble mingled with the Sipahis and the Palace Guards. The troopers stabled their horses in the courts of the Palace. The foot-men, weary with the long night march, turned the Hall of Audience into a barrack, and littered down on the floor. Guards were posted all about the Palace. And the wretched, helpless King found that his royal dwelling-house was in military occupation." Kaye, John William, *Kay's and Malleson's History of the Indian Mutiny of 1857-8,* Vol. II, London, 1910, p. 61).

20. *Defence Journal*, Vol. 3, No. 9, Islamabad, December,1999.
21. *People's Democracy,* (*The 1857 Revolt in India: Lessons for Us*-Jyoti Basu) Vol. XXXI, No. 10, March 11, 2007 see also *New York Daily Tribune,* July 15, 1857.
22. Malleson, George Bruce, *Indian Mutiny of 1857,* London, 1912, pp. 125-126, see also, Roberts, P.E., *A Historical Geography of the British Dependencies: India,* Vol. VII, London, 1914, p. 371, and Greathed, Harvey Harris, *Letters Written During the Siege of Delhi,* London, 1858, pp. 29-36 (Greathed quotes the letter written from Delhi, Alipur on June 7, "We had a tempestuous ride from Bagpat to this, last evening.... The force is in great spirits, and awaits anxiously the order for attack; and our next move must bring us under the walls of Delhi.... I am glad to find here a native named Rajab Ali, who was George Clerk's head munshi: he had been pensioned and had been living in retirement; but being sent for he came at once. He is a first-rate man. The camp is very large and well formed; and we have certainly a very perfect force and unusually strong in Artillery." Greathed, Harvey Harris, *Letters Written During the Siege of Delhi*, London, 1858, pp. 26-29).
23. *New York Daily Tribune*, August 4, 1857, see also, Edward, Gilliat, *Heroes of the Indian Mutiny; Stories of Heroic Deeds*, London 1914, p. 82, and Grant, Hope, *Incidents in the Sepoy War 1857-58*, Edinburgh, 1873, p. 74 (Greathed quotes the letter written from Delhi Camp on June 24, "I missed writing yesterday,—I had nothing very pleasant to say, and the continued roll of musketry and booming of cannon, from 6 a.m. to 5 p.m., distracted my attention from other matters. The enemy came out with the object of intercepting a convoy, and then attacking us in the rear, ...the mass then got into the Shabzi Mandi and gardens on our right, and made repeated attempts on the rear of Hindu Rao's house

and on the mound.... It was a tiresome action, knowing that nothing could be gained beyond driving them away.... It is said in the city 400 were killed and 300 wounded. We lost nearly 100 killed and wounded. Jackson of the Fusiliers was killed; Welchman and Captain Jones of the Rifles wounded. Our troops fought admirably, and showed an utter disregard not only of danger, but of fatigue, but it is a pity they had to endure so much to gain so little...." Greathed, Harvey Harris, *Letters Written During the Siege of Delhi*, London, 1858, pp. 68-69).

24. *Two Native Narratives*, p. 134-136, see also Spear, Percival, *Twilight of the Mughals: Studies in Late Mughal Delhi*, Cambridge, 1951, p. 206.
25. *Ibid.*
26. *Ibid.*, p. 205, see also Edward, Gilliat, *Heroes of the Indian Mutiny; Stories of Heroic Deeds*, London 1914, p. 153.
27. *New Statesman,* October, 16, 2006, see also Rotten, J.E.W., *Captains Narratives of the Siege of Delhi from the Outbreak at Meerut to the Capture of Delhi*, London, 1858, p. 316.
28. Griffiths, Charles John, *A Narrative of the Seige of Delhi with an Account of the Mutiny at Firozpur in 1857*, London, 1910, pp. 186-187, see also Kaye, John William, *A History of the Sepoy War in India, 1857-58,* Vol. III, London 1876, p. 630, Fanshawe, H.C., *Delhi Past and Present*, London 1902, p. 217, and Malleson, George Bruce, *Kay's and Malleson's History of the Indian Mutiny of 1857-8,* Vol. IV, London, 1911, pp. 58-59 (One thousand six hundred and seventy men and officers, killed and wounded, fell in the actual siege, from the 7th to the 20th of September, of which 1,170 fell on the great day of the assault. The total loss of the army, from June to September, was 8,637 men, killed, wounded, and missing,—besides very many more, who died of their wounds, or of disease and exposure, of whom I have no account,—out of a force never numbering 10,000 effectives. *Julius George Medley, A Years Campaigning in India from March 1857 to March 1858*, London 1858, pp. 117-118), (In another source Frazre states that from 30th of May to the 20th of September, having cost the lives of 2,151 Europeans and 1,686 natives, who fell fighting on the side of the Europeans. Frazer, R. W., *British India*, New York 1896, p. 303).
29. Hodson, George Herbert, *Hodson of Hodson's Horse or the Twelve Years of a Soldiers Life in India: Being Extracts from the Letters of the Late Major W. S. R. Hodson*, London, 1889, p. 224, see also Norman, Henry Wylie, *Delhi-1857; The Siege, Assault, and Capture as given in*

the Diary and Correspondence of the Late Colonel Keith Young, London 1902, p. 299.

30. Innes, McLeod, *The Sepoy Revolt: A Critical Narrative*, London, 1897, p. 99, see also Malleson, George Bruce, *History of the Indian Mutiny of 1857-58, Commencing from the Close of the Second Volume of Sir John Kaye's History of the Sepoy War*, Vol. III, (Contemporaneous with Sir John Kay's Third Volume), London, 1878, p. 12.
31. Wood, Evelyn, *The Revolt in Hindustan 1857-59*, London, 1908, pp. 129-131, see also *People's Democracy, (Lucknow In 1857-58: The Epic Siege*-Amar Farooqui), Vol. XXXI, No. 41, October 14, 2007, and Gubbins, Martin Richard, *An Account of the Mutinies of Oudh and of the Siege of the Lucknow Residency; With some Observation on the Condition of the Province of Oudh and of the Causes of the Mutiny of the Bengal Army*, London, 1858, pp. 120, 128 and131.
32. Gubbins, Martin Richard, *An Account of the Mutinies of Oudh and of the Siege of the Lucknow Residency; With some Observation on the Condition of the Province of Oudh and of the Causes of the Mutiny of the Bengal Army*, London, 1858, pp. 212-214 (John William Kaye quotes Brigadier Havelock, "This morning, we went out eight miles to meet the enemy, and we were defeated and lost five guns, through the misconduct chiefly of our Native artillerymen, many of whom have deserted. The enemy have followed us up, and we have now been besieged for four hours, and shall probably to night be surrounded. The enemy are very bold, and our Europeans are very low. I look upon our position as ten times as bad as it was yesterday. Indeed, it is now critical. We shall be obliged to concentrate, if we are able. We shall have to abandon much supply, and to blow up much powder. Unless we are relieved quickly, say in fifteen or twenty days, we shall hardly be able to maintain our position." Kaye, John William, *A History of the Sepoy War in India, 1857-58,* Vol. III, London 1876, p. 512).
33. *Ibid.*, pp. 227-228 and 244, see also *People's Democracy, (Lucknow In 1857-58: The Epic Siege*-Amar Farooqui), Vol. XXXI, No. 41, October 14, 2007.
34. *Naya Daur*, (*Brijis Qadr: The Last King of Awadh*- Mirza Qaukab Qadr) Awadh Number, a Monthly Urdu Journal published by the Information and Public Relations Department of the Government of Uttar Pradesh, Lucknow, February-March 1994, see also *People's Democracy, (Lucknow In 1857-58: The Epic Siege*-Amar Farooqui), Vol. XXXI, No. 41, October 14, 2007, and Dodd, p. 413.
35. Malleson, George Bruce, *History of the Indian Mutiny of 1857-58, Commencing from the Close of the Second Volume of Sir John Kaye's*

History of the Sepoy War, Vol. III, (Contemporaneous with Sir John Kay's Third Volume), London, 1878, pp. 526 and 545-546.

36. Malleson, George Bruce, *Kay's and Malleson's History of the Indian Mutiny of 1857-8,* Vol. IV, London, 1911, pp. 251 and 254.
37. Dodd, pp. 413 and 415, see also *People's Democracy, (Lucknow In 1857-58: The Epic Siege*-Amar Farooqui), Vol. XXXI, No. 41, October 14, 2007, and G. W. Forrest, *A History of the Indian Mutiny; Reviewed and Illustrated from Original Documents,* Vol. II, London 1904, p. 368.
38. Malleson, George Bruce, *History of the Indian Mutiny of 1857-58, Commencing from the Close of the Second Volume of Sir John Kaye's History of the Sepoy War*, Vol. III, (Contemporaneous with Sir John Kay's Third Volume), London, 1878, p. 182, see also, Forrest, G. W., *A History of the Indian Mutiny; Reviewed and Illustrated from Original Documents,* Vol. III, London 1904, p. 4 and Argyl, Campbell, George Douglas, Duke of, *India Under Dalhousie and Canning*, London, 1865, p. 33.
39. *Ibid.*, pp. 187-188, see also Forrest, G.W., *A History of the Indian Mutiny; Reviewed and Illustrated from Original Documents,* Vol. III, London 1904, pp. 6-9.
40. *Ibid.*, pp. 189-190 (Regiment Subedar wrote to Captain Skene to come out of the fort saying, 'we will not kill any of you, we will send you all to your own country'; so Captain Skene wrote to the Rani to tell the Sepoys to take their oath and to sign her name on the letter, all the Hindus took their oath: 'if any of us touch your people just as we eat beef; and those Muslims took their oath 'if any of us touch you just as we eat pork.' And the Rani signed her name on the top of the letter and it was given to Captain Skene. As soon as he read the note everyone was agreed to it. Forrest, G. W., *A History of the Indian Mutiny; Reviewed and Illustrated from Original Documents,* Vol. III, London 1904, pp. 9-12).
41. John William Kaye quotes the report of a most trusted authority that she, "endeavoured to keep terms with our Government, by writing to the Commissioner of Jabalpure and to others, lamenting the massacre of our countrymen; stating that she was in no way concerned in it; and declaring that she only held the Jhansi district till our Government could make arrangements to reoccupy it." (Kaye, John William, *A History of the Sepoy War in India, 1857-58,* Vol. III, London 1876, p. 370).
42. James F. Holcomb, and Helen H. Holcomb, *In the Heart of India: or, Beginnings of Missionary work in Bundela Land, with a short chapter on*

the Characteristics of Bundelkhand and its People, and Four Chapters of Jhansi History, Philadelphia 1905, pp. 53, 55 and 57.

43. *Ibid.*, pp. 62, 65 and 70.
44. *Ibid.*, pp. 72,76 and 78, see also Edward, Gilliat, *Heroes of the Indian Mutiny; Stories of Heroic Deeds*, London 1914, p. 343.
45. *Ibid.*, pp. 83-85 and 89-90.
46. Malleson, George Bruce, *Kay's and Malleson's History of the Indian Mutiny of 1857-8,* Vol. V, London, 1911, p. 154, see also James F. Holcomb, and Helen H. Holcomb, *In the Heart of India: or, Beginnings of Missionary work in Bundela Land, with a short chapter on the Characteristics of Bundelkhand and its People, and Four Chapters of Jhansi History*, Philadelphia 1905, p. 92.
47. Malleson, George Bruce, *Indian Mutiny of 1857*, London, 1912, p. 29, see also, Sherer, John Walter, *Havelock's March on Cawnpore, 1857*, London 1910, p. 168, and Sherer, John Walter, *Daily Life During the Indian Mutiny: Personal Experiences of 1857*, Allahabad, 1910, p. 86.
48. Thomson, Mowbray, *The Story of Cawnpore*, London 1859, pp. 38-41.
49. Keene, Henry George, *Fifty-Seven: Some Account of the Administration of Indian Districts during the Revolt of the Bengal Army*, London, 1883, p. 73, see also Wood, Evelyn, *The Revolt in Hindustan 1857-59*, London, 1908, pp. 21 and 61-62 and Edward, Gilliat, *Heroes of the Indian Mutiny; Stories of Heroic Deeds*, London 1914, p. 262.
50. *Ibid.*, pp. 73-74, see also Wood, Evelyn, *The Revolt in Hindustan 1857-59*, London, 1908, pp. 64-66, Frazer, R. W., *British India*, New York 1896, p. 298, and Forrest, G. W., *A History of the Indian Mutiny; Reviewed and Illustrated from Original Documents,* Vol. I, London 1904, p. 451 (George Dodd writes that their number was 900 and further says that it might be possible that the number who took their departure in this mournful procession from the entrenchment was four hundred and fifty, then one half of the original number of nine hundred must have fallen victims to three weeks of privation and suffering. Dodd, p. 137).
51. Thomson, Mowbray, *The Story of Cawnpore*, London 1859, pp. 213-214, see also Sherer, John Walter, *Havelock's March on Cawnpore, 1857*, London 1910, p. 172.
52. Forrest, G. W., *A History of the Indian Mutiny; Reviewed and Illustrated from Original Documents,* Vol. I, London 1904, pp. 502-5.
53. *People's Democracy*, (Ram Swaroop- *Some Aspects of the 1857 Rebellion in Bihar*), Vol. XXXI, No. 18, May 6, 2007.
54. Halls, John James, *Two Months in Arrah in 1857*, London, 1860,

p. 39, see also Trevelyan, George, *The Competition Wallah*, London, 1864, p. 92.

55. Trevelyan, George, *The Competition Wallah*, London, 1864, pp. 93-96, see also Malleson, George Bruce, *History of the Indian Mutiny of 1857-58, Commencing from the Close of the Second Volume of Sir John Kaye's History of the Sepoy War*, Vol. III, (Contemporaneous with Sir John Kay's Third Volume), London, 1878, p. 85.
56. Halls, John James, *Two Months in Arrah in 1857*, London, 1860, p. 94.
57. Trevelyan, George, *The Competition Wallah*, London, 1864, pp. 105-109, see also Malleson, George Bruce, *History of the Indian Mutiny of 1857-58, Commencing from the Close of the Second Volume of Sir John Kaye's History of the Sepoy War*, Vol. III, (Contemporaneous with Sir John Kay's Third Volume), London, 1878, p. 102.
58. Sieveking, Isabel Giberne, *A Turning Point in the Indian Mutiny*, London, 1910, pp. 110-112, see also Malleson, George Bruce, *History of the Indian Mutiny of 1857-58, Commencing from the Close of the Second Volume of Sir John Kaye's History of the Sepoy War*, Vol. III, (Contemporaneous with Sir John Kay's Third Volume), London, 1878, p. 129.
59. *People's Democracy*, (Ram Swaroop- *Some Aspects of the 1857 Rebellion in Bihar*), Vol. XXXI, No. 18, May 6, 2007.
60. *Ibid.*, see also John James Halls, *Two Months in Arrah in 1857*, London, 1860, p. 87.

CHAPTER 2

Holy War against the British

More than hundred and fifty years of the Indian Uprising have been passed, but the controversy regarding its nature and perspective still exists. Although there were a lot of factors, which were responsible for the Uprising but the religious factor or perspective dominates over all. Modern historians by thorough study of contemporary sources more firmly prove that it was the religion which had provoked most to the revolutionaries. Even the contemporary officers, who experienced a lot while crushing the Uprising, Sir James Outram and W. Taylor, has treated this incident as the combined conspiracy of Hindus and Muslims based on religion. Undoubtedly, by more emphasizing the incidents, the scholars have characterized the revolt as a conflict between the black and white; a religious war against Christianity; tug of war between civilization and barbarism and an elitist movement. However, the religious factor could not be ignored at all. The modern historian Dalrymple, on the basis of the original documents, proves the Uprising as war of religion.

Right from the beginning of the British rule in India, not only the Christian Missionaries but the British authorities of the Company also tried their level best to propagate Christianity through their policies. Both the major religions of India were on the stake. Macaulay's introduction on English as the medium of instruction in the educational institutions was perhaps one of the processes of Christianizing the Indian sub-continent. In 1836,

Macaulay, when schools in which English education was to be given were first opened in Bengal, had expressed a hope amounting almost to a conviction that, in thirty years, there would be no idol-worshiper left in Bengal. The chairman of the Directors of the East India Company, Mr. Mangles, said in the House of Commons, in 1857, "Providence has entrusted the extensive empire of Hindustan to England in order that the banner of Christ should wave triumphant from one end of India to the other. Everyone must exert all his strength that there may be no dilatoriness on any account in continuing in the country the grand work of making all India Christian."[1]

V.D. Savarkar quotes the words of Revered Kennedy, "let us not forget that our chief work is the propagation of Christianity in the land. Until Hindustan, from Cape Comorin to the Himalayas, embraces the religion of Christ and until it condemns the Hindu and the Muslim religions, our efforts must continue persistently. For this work, we must make all the efforts we can and use all the power and all the authority in our hands; and continuous and unceasing efforts must be kept on until India becomes a magnificent nation, the bulwark of Christianity in the East. If, with such uninterrupted perseverance, we continue our efforts, then I do not doubt that, by the grace of God, we shall be successful in the end."[2]

The Christian Missionaries in their street preaching at various places, used to say openly that India would soon be Christianized. The Government had already begun to pass one law after another to destroy the foundations of the Hindu and Muslim religions. However, it was very well known to the Indians about the intention of the British Government, officers, and Missionaries that they all are bending to reduce the Indian religion into Christianity. The Indians found the opportunity to uproot the British Empire in 1857 in order to save their religion and nation. All the Indians irrespective of their religion race and caste jumped into this war filled with the national and religious passion.

War of Religion

The Uprising of 1857 was undoubtedly a reaction of the British policies, but definitely it was the religious persecution of the British Government which resulted the loss of control of the Indian population, irrespective of class and creed. The contemporary scholars had much stressed on Company's Missionary operations and also told this factor as one of the chief factors of the Uprising.

Among the Hindus, the Brahmans were leading in the society. They suffered a lot from the British Government's policies. Formerly, they ruled all the social life of the Hindus. They got fees for marriages, births, and deaths; education, law, and religion, and every kind of business were in their hands. However, during the British rule the telegraphs, railways, European education, and worst of all, a Court of Appeal, were breaking down their privileges and power. They skillfully played on one supposed grievance, by spreading about reports that the Government intended to abolish caste and religion. These reports became, among the mass of Hindus and Muslims, the principal incitement to revolt. For any violation of the arbitrary rules of caste appeared to all to be a step towards forcible conversion to Christianity.[3]

The Muslim Ulema also suffered by the same above mentioned reasons. They thought that the introduction of English medium of instruction in the schools, changing of Court language, propagation of Christianity, were the direct attacks on their religion. In the schools run by the Christian Missionary or the British Government, the boys heard much about the Christian religion, of which the parents disapproved, but they were unable to withdraw their boys in the desire of Government jobs. Any measure of development started by the British was considered as a prelude to the conversion into Christianity.

In 1856, Lord Canning promulgated the law, legalizing the remarriage of Hindu widows, and of course this was an act of the purest benevolence from a British point of view. However, unfortunately, the publication of this law was coincident with increased Missionary activity, which added the proof of polluting the caste and forcible conversion.

The new research of the modern historians proved the religious factor as one of the strongest factors and became one of the natures of Uprising in the form of 'war of religion' or *Jihad*. The term *Jihad* is of course to be stated is a richly ambiguous one, that it varies according to context, and that the struggle referred to can take many forms. Primarily, the *Jihad* is a term to wage war against the infidels to save the religion and generally it was used by the Muslims but in 1857 during the Uprising this term was also used by the Hindu Sepoys. In the Mutiny Papers in Delhi, there are two of the Hindu Sepoy generals, Generals Sudhari and Hira Singh using the term of *Jihad* to describe their fight against the British.[4]

The modern historians prove this fact of religious perspective of the Uprising based on very authentic contemporary documents. Particularly, Dalrymple's research which emphasizes the religious factor based on Urdu documents in the National Archives. The words *Deen* and *Dharma* (the Muslim and Hindu words for religion) appear constantly in rebel proclamations, and were used as war cries by the combatants. These facts show the extent to which religious feelings drove the revolutionaries; it goes well beyond the question of greased cartridges.

The revolutionaries issued different proclamations to invite the general people against the British. Many of these proclamations were written by Mirza Mughal, who endeavoured to take charge and unite the chaotic rebel force in Delhi. Others were written by outlying mansabdars and supporters of the revolt who endeavoured to rally supplies and troops by invoking the authority and name of the Emperor. The famous Azamgarh Proclamation of August 1857, issued by the Feroz Shah, the grandson of Mughal Emperor, invites the both Hindus and Muslims to fight against the British.[5]

V.D. Savarkar has given much emphasis to this point and says that thousands of Fakirs, Pandits, and Sanyasis were sent out to preach among the people in an incredibly short time. They influenced and impressed the people better, and the Government also in many cases suspected them. Influential and noble Maulvis were appointed to preach the political *Jihad*, and they were rewarded with thousands of Rupees. Through towns and villages, these Maulvis and Pandits, these Fakirs and these Sanyasis began to travel, from one end of the country to the other, preaching secretly the war for political independence. Begging from door to door, they began to sow, in all directions, the principles of independence, patriotism, and love of Dharma—for the awakening of strength among the people. This work of *Jihad* was done so cautiously and secretly that not the slightest inkling of what was going on could reach even such cunning people as the English, until the explosion actually took place.[6]

Savarkar further narrates that these Fakirs and Pandits used to walk around and more particularly, in the military cantonments. From Barrackpore to Meerut, Ambala, and Peshawar, the Maulvis started secret societies and, more than that, practically surrounded every military cantonment. The Hindu and Muslim Sepoys in the army being very devoted to their religious teachers, the British Government, though they might suspect them, could hardly proceed against them. For instance, they feared that the Sepoys would find in it another grievance against the Government. These political Sanyasis sowed the seeds of the Revolutionary War not only in the cantonment but in the very houses of the Sepoys of a neighbouring village.[7]

The Sepoys from Meerut mutinied and shouted the religious slogans like Muslims as Ali! Ali! And Hindus and Sikhs as Jai! Jai! On reaching at Delhi, they told Mughal Emperor Bahadur Shah Zafar on 11th May 1857, "We have joined hands to protect our religion and our faith." Later, they stood in the Chandni Chowk, the main street of Delhi, and asked people: "Brothers: are you with those of the faith?" When the Uprising started, the British men who had converted to Islam, were not hurt but Indians who had converted to Christianity were cut down immediately.[8]

Bahadur Shah Zafar's eldest surviving legitimate son Mirza Mughal was most likely behind a circular letter sent out in Zafar's name to all the Princes and Rajahs of India, asking for them to join the Uprising and appealing for their loyalty on the grounds that all faiths were under attack by the British. The letter refers specifically to the laws banning sati and allowing converts to inherit, and Company's facilitation of Missionary activity and the alleged conversion of prisoner's locked in British jails:[9]

> "The English are people who overthrow all religions," it states. "You should understand well their object of destroying the religions of Hindustan… It is now my firm

> convictions that if the English continue in Hindustan they will...utterly overthrow our religions. As the English are the common enemy of both (Hindus and Muslims), we should unite in considering their slaughter...for by this alone will the lives and faiths of both be saved."

Even Mughal Emperor Bahadur Shah Zafar himself articulated the Uprising as a religious war. As late as the 6th September, 1857 at the very end of the siege when calling the people of Delhi to rally against the coming assault by the British, a proclamation issued by the name of Bahadur Shah Zafar spelled out very plainly as follows:[10]

> "This is a religious war, and is being prosecuted on account of the faith, and it behoves all Hindus and Musalman residents of the imperial city or of the villages in the country... to continue true to their faith and creeds."

In Kanpur, the Sepoys mutinied on 5th of June 1857, when the 2nd Native Cavalry broke out in the morning. On the second day of the siege, they adopted more energetic measures; the Islamic green flag was raised in the city; all true Muslims were directed to join, and those who demurred were threatened, insulted, or fined. The Nana's force was soon augmented by large numbers, and reinforced daily.[11]

The Hindu and Muslim equality was such an extent that the Hindus willingly accepted the Islamic green flag and forced others to array under it. On the 8th of July 1857, a rebellious proclamation was issued, and green Islamic flag was hoisted, and it was made an appeal to all to under this sacred flag. George W. Forrest writes, "As I had not joined with the men of the *Jhunda* (flag), two troopers were sent by the Nana to fetch me, saying that they have waited long for me, how it was that I did not join the *Jhunda*, it appears that I was not a Mohammadan but a Christian, I had better soon attend the Nana's Court, or they have orders to take my head to the Nana: so saying, they took me along with them before the Nana, where Teeka Sing, Subadar-Major Bahadur of the 2nd Light Cavalry, heaped abuses on me, and threatened to have me tied to a tree and there mangled, as I appeared to be averse to the *Jhunda*."[12]

The State Papers printed by the order of Nana Sahib, dated 8th Hijri, 1275 found at Bithoor, narrates that, "...previously to the distribution of the cartridges for the purpose of taking away the religion and caste of the people of Hindustan, a council was held, at which it was resolved that, as this was a matter of religion, it would be necessary to employ 7,000 or 8,000 Europeans, and to kill 60,000 Hindustanis, and then all Hindustan would be converted to Christianity.... A petition to this effect was sent to Queen Victoria and the opinion of the council was adopted. ...When this petition was perused in England, 35,000 European troops were embarked in ships with the utmost rapidity and dispatched to India. Intelligence of their dispatch was received in Calcutta, and the gentlemen of Calcutta issued orders for the distribution of cartridges. Their real object was to make Christians of the army under the idea that when this was done there would be no delay in Christianizing the people generally. In the cartridges the fat of swine and cows was used...the Ambassador of the Sultan of Constantinople at the Court of London sent information to the Sultan that 35,000 English troops were to be dispatched to India to make Christians of that country. The Sultan sent a Farman to the Pasha of Egypt...if the English succeeded in making Christians of the people of Hindustan, they would attempt the same in his country. On the receipt of this farman of the Sultan, the Pasha (of Egypt), before the arrival of the English troops, made his arrangements and collected his troops at Alexandria... and on the arrival of the English army the troops of the Pasha of Egypt began firing on them with cannon from all sides, and destroyed and sank the ships so that not a single Englishman of them remained. ...God, by the exercise of His Almighty power, settled their business there...."[13]

Another letter of Nana bears the same religious feelings, "As, by the kindness of God and the *ikbal* of good fortune of the Emperor, all the Christians who were at Delhi, Poona, Satarah, and other places, and even those 5,000 European soldiers who went in disguise into the former city and were discovered, are destroyed and sent to hell by the pious and sagacious troops, who are firm to their religion; ...that it is the incumbent duty of all the ryots and landed proprietors of every district to rejoice at the thought that the Christians have been sent to hell, and both the Hindu and Mohammadan religions have been confirmed...."[14]

When the news of Uprising at Kanpur reached at Delhi, a letter or rather proclamation was issued in the month of June 1857. That was a religious proclamation addressed to all the Hindus and Muslims, citizens and servants of India, from the officers of the army now at Delhi and Meerut, was sent as greetings. The proclamation was as follows:[15]

> "It is well known that in these days all the English have entertained these evil designs; first to destroy the religion of the whole Hindustani army, and then to make the people Christians by compulsion. Therefore we, solely on account of our religion, have combined with the people, and have not spared alive one infidel, and have re-established the Delhi dynasty on these terms, and thus act in obedience to orders and receive double pay. Hundreds of guns and a large amount of treasure have fallen into our hands; therefore it is fitting that whoever of the soldiers and people dislike turning Christians should unite with one heart and act courageously, not leaving the seed of these infidels remaining. For any quantity of supplies delivered to the army the owners are to take the receipts of the officers; and they will receive double payment from the Imperial Government. Whoever shall in these times exhibit cowardice, or credulously believe the promises of those impostors the English, shall very shortly be put to shame for such a deed; and, rubbing the hands of sorrow, shall receive for their fidelity the reward the ruler of Lucknow got. It is further necessary that all Hindus and Musalmans unite in this struggle, and, following the instructions of some respectable people, keep themselves secure, so that good order may be maintained, the poorer classes kept contented, and they themselves be exalted to rank and dignity; also, that all, so far as it is possible, copy this proclamation, and dispatch

> it everywhere, so that all true Hindus and Musalmans may be alive and watchful, and fix in some conspicuous place (but prudently to avoid detection), and strike a blow with a sword before giving circulation to it. The first pay of the soldiers of Delhi will be 30 rupees per month for a trooper, and rupees 10 for a foot-man. Nearly 100,000 men are ready, and there are 13 flags of the English regiments and about 14 standards from different parts now raised aloft for our religion, for God, and the conqueror, and it is the intention of Kanpur to root out the seed of the Devil. This is what we of the army here wish."

By all the proclamations, letters and handbills, it becomes clear that it was the religion which goaded the people against the British. Right from the beginning of the Company rule there was a constant attack on the religion of both Hindus and Muslims. The religious matter affected the Indian people on two sides. The first was the civil side in which the rules and regulations of the British Government which was considered as promotion of Christianity were affected to the civil population of Hindus and Muslims of India. The other was the military side in which the rules and orders of the Government affected the religions of Hindus and Muslim Sepoys employed in the British army. On the civil side Dalhousie as a governor general encouraged Christian missionaries and societies to provide missions to care for the needy and low caste Indians. The passing of Act XXI of 1850 further intensified the doubt of the conversion. According to this Act, to such men, however, as became Christians it offered great advantages. Hence this act was said not only to interfere with people's religion but to hold out strong inducements to conversion. Act 15 of 1856 relating to Hindu widows was also an attack upon Hindu religion.[16]

On the military side, the promotion of Christianity was too dangerous. As the Christian Missionaries promoted and encouraged the conversion into Christianity, it was rapidly spreading among the British army officers. They readout the verses of Bible before the Sepoys while the daily parade. There was also the demolition of mosques and temples on the petty pretext. The

Government financial aid was also stopped to the *Madarsas* and *Pathshalas* (Muslim and Hindu schools) which were being received since long back. The Mughal Emperor's helplessness and powerlessness further enraged the Indian population. It is evident that the Mughal Emperor was still considered as their national symbol by both Hindus and Muslims.[17]

The British Government's step to cancel the Persian as the Government official language and adopting the English in that place also infuriated the Muslims. Fortunately, the period when the war broke out was the month of *Ramadhan,* and every Muslim was filled with religious zeal. The Uprising provided the chance to the people, particularly the Muslims to get the maximum religious benefits by waging war against the *Kafirs* (infidels). Muslim clerics declared that their religion was in danger, and everyone should wage war against the British to save the religion. That's why band after band of *Jihadis* (freelance religious revolutionaries) joined the Sepoys against the British.[18]

Sir Syed Ahmad, although denying it as war of religion, declared the religious factor as one of the important causes of the Uprising. All the people of India irrespective of their caste, religion, and social status were in firm conviction that the English Government was bent on interfering with their religion and with their old established customs and intended to force the Christian religion and foreign customs upon both the Hindus and Muslims. The people thought that the Government would change their religion through indirect steps, such as doing away with the study of Arabic and Sanskrit, and reducing the people to ignorance and poverty. It became general perception that by depriving the Indians from the knowledge of their faith and religion the Government would compel them to turn to books of the Christian creed and also to the employment in its services on the conditions of abjuring their faith.[19]

Regarding Christian Missionaries, Indian masses were also having a lot of objections. Sir Syed Ahmad Khan wrote, "The Missionaries, moreover introduced a new system of preaching. They took to printing and circulating controversial tracts, in the shape of questions and answers. Men of a different faith were spoken of in a most offensive and irritating way....In violent and unmeasured language they attacked the followers and the holy places of other creeds: annoying, and insulting beyond expression, the feelings of those who listened to them." He continues, "In the Missionary schools, the principles of the Christian faith were taught.... Examinations were held in books, which taught the tenets of the Christian religion. Lads who attended the schools used to be asked such questions as the following: "Who is your God?" "Who is your Redeemer?" and these questions they were obliged to answer agreeably to the Christian belief; prizes being given accordingly."[20]

In 1855, a letter written by Mr. Edmond was circulated publicly from Calcutta to all the principal officials and other Government employees. This letter further strengthened the doubt of conversion. The people presumed it a direct message of conversion from the Government. It was to the effect that all Hindustan was now under one rule, that the telegraph had so connected all parts of the country that they were as one, that the railroad had brought them so near that all towns were as one, the time had clearly come when there should be but one faith; it was right therefore, that everyone should become the Christians.[21] Although the British Government tried to subsidize the matter in fear of religious Uprising, but this dissatisfaction was delayed rather than controlled.[22]

In the House of Commons in England, a debate was held regarding the Uprising in India in which Mr. Vernon Smith, President of the Board of Control, in opposing the some petition of the Missionaries in Bengal told the House, "It could not be disguised that considerable disaffection prevailed among the troops, in consequence, of a prevalent notion that a compulsory conversion of the natives was intended."[23]

The British policies and orders that affected the religious sentiments of the Sepoys were more serious than the policies which affected the civilian population. William Dalrymple along with Mahmood Farooqi used the 20,000 rebel documents in Urdu and Persian, which survive from the Sepoy camp and palace in Delhi, all of which were found in the National Archives. In the rebel's own papers, they refer over and again to their Uprising being a war of religion. There was no doubt a multitude of private grievances, but it is now unambiguously clear that the rebels saw themselves as fighting a war to preserve their religion. The words *Deen* and *Dharma* (the Muslim and Hindu words for religion) appear constantly in rebel proclamations, and were used as war cries by the combatants.

Besides the Missionary attack on Hinduism and Islam, the rumours of the bone-dust factor along with greased cartridges were the additional strike. In a letter of Mrs. Keith Young to her sister in London, she writes, "I hear that there is a general feeling among the Natives that our Government is trying to make Christians of them by these unclean cartridges, and by mixing with their *Atta* (flour) beef and pig's bones finely ground. Some months ago I was sending some whole wheat to a little mill on a stream a short distance from Simla to be ground and it makes such nice brown bread. We had often found our bread gritty with dust. My Aya, when she heard that I was sending this wheat, asked me to send some for her also, as there was a report in the bazaar that all the flour was mixed with the bones, finely ground, of cows and pigs. I laughed at her, and said, Aya, what nonsense! Who says so? 'She replied, 'It is quite true; all the bazaar people say so.' I thought it meant merely that the baniyas (merchants) did it to increase the weight of their flour."[24]

In the areas of Awadh, as Gubbins stated, bone dust and cartridge factor aroused the sentiments of both the Sepoys and common people. Although the rumour of bone-dust was baseless, but as it was fanned by the followers of ex-Nawab of Awadh, and it became most burning factor for common peoples' resentment. It was said that the British Government at Lucknow had sent up cart-loads and boat-loads of bone-dust, which was to be mixed with the flour and sweetmeats sold in the bazaar, whereby the whole population would lose their caste. The public mind became greatly excited. On one day, at Sultanpur, it was spread over the station that a boat had reached a certain Ghat on the river Gomati laden with bone-dust. A few days later, at the station of Salone, two camels, laden with ammunition, arrived at the house of Captain Thompson, the commandant. It was rumoured that the packages contained bone-dust, and a panic spread through the station. Not only, the Sepoys in their lines, but the domestic servants about the officers' bungalows, and the villagers and zemindars attending court, hastily flung away, untested, the food which they had cooked, and fasted for the day. The Sepoys of Kanpur refused to accept the Government flour, which they alleged had been mingled with the dust of cow bones so that the caste of the Hindus might be destroyed. At Lucknow, the rumours which were whispered about were perpetual, and the public mind was never allowed to rest. If it was at one shop, the next day in another bazaar, that dispatches of bone-dust had, it was asserted, been received.[25]

In the real sense all the Indian masses irrespective of their caste, and creed were maligned with the British policies and the rumours of greased cartridges and bone dust flour. Even the economic class, Baniya, or trader was unsatisfied with the Europeans. It was also rumoured that besides the bone dust flour, the British were also mixing bone dust into the salt and polluting the well by throwing flesh into them. All the above rumours affected a lot both the Hindu and Muslim communities.[26]

Besides Sepoys and civilians, there was another front of revolutionaries. This third front was of the Muslim fanatics, generally called by the British as *Ghazis* or *Jihadis* or *Mujahideen,* who were unpaid, bind with religious ties, rose in open rebellion following the Sepoys and civilians. They were led by Muslim Ulema. A number of sources prove that along with the '*Poorbeas*' (rebel Sepoys of Awadh Province) who entered Delhi after fleeing their cantonments, were large numbers of 'freelance' and 'untrained' Muslims or *Mujahideen.* A noted *Mujahid* Maulvi Ahmadullah Shah was one of them. He was radicalised by the preaching of Sayyad Ahmad Shaheed of Rae Bareli whilst performing the Haj on his way back to India. Ahmadullah Shah's ideas for a *Jihad* against the British were ridiculed by the Ulema in Delhi, and he was soon after captured and imprisoned by the British. However, when the Sepoys released him from jail in Faizabad, he had immediately cleaved to the side of the rebels in Lucknow and became an influential adviser to the Begum Hazrat Mahal.[27]

There are sufficient proofs of active participation of Ulema in the Uprising, but some scholars give a slight different theory and stressed that their participation was not for relieving the country from the British. Marina Carter and Crispin Bates in their article 'Religion and retribution in the Indian rebellion of 1857' says that most of the Ulema sided the Sepoys on the decree of *Jihad* either to save the Muslims from British oppression or to quell the excesses of rebel troops. Maulana Mohammad Qasim Nanautawi and Maulana Rashid Ahmad Gangohi, the famous scholar of the Deoband Islamic seminary, were initially hostile to the revolt, only took up the rebel's cause after being persuaded of the injustice of the English in their campaign of repression. Mirza Firoz Shah, the Mughal Emperor's grandson, who for some time commanded the rebel forces in Delhi, invoked the concept of *Jihad* in order to curb and quell the excesses of Sepoys, who had indulged in plundering and looting and had failed to protect women, children, and the innocent.[28]

No doubt the main aim of the revolutionaries of both Hindus and Muslims was to save their religion and country from the British oppressions. For that very cause, they adopted different methods, which were perhaps misunderstood by a few European scholars but majority believes in the religious motives of the revolutionaries.

Theory of Jihad or Holy War

There are a lot of controversies regarding the Uprising of 1857 that whether it was a *Jihad* or Holy War waged by the Muslim cleric along with the *Ghazis, Mujahideen,* or *Jihadi* forces. If it was so, then what the role played by Nana Sahib, Rani Luxmi Bai, and Tatya Tope? Shesh Rao More in his book "*The 1857 Jihad*" claims that the Uprising was a *Jihad* waged by Muslims to regain control over India which they have lost from the time of Aurangzeb. He strengthens his argument that loss of Muslim power was the primary cause in the Uprising. The issue of fat-smeared cartridges, in fact, he dismisses as "absurd".[29] More also asserts that Nana Sahib, Luxmi Bai and Mangal Pandey, who is credited as being the 'first freedom fighter', had all been enticed, coerced, beguiled or befuddled into the fray. More claims that Luxmi Bai was essentially a British loyalist and had been appointed by them to rule Jhansi on their behalf for a full ten months from July 2, 1857, even after the Uprising had broken out in that principality. They would hardly have done so if they had even a faint suspicion about her loyalty. Her ultimate undoing was due to a conspiracy engineered by Nathhe Khan of nearby Orchha, who waylaid every conciliatory or explanatory communication sent by her to the British, thus precipitating the fatal confrontation between them.[30]

More also says that Mangal Pandey too was the victim of machinations of his trusted friend Naki Khan.[31] Ha also proves that Nana Sahib, in fact, was threatened with death by rebel Sepoys if he declined to lead them.[32]

By quoting different religious decrees of the Muslim theologians and their active participation in various battles in the Uprising, Shesh Rao More confirms that Nana Sahib and Luxmi Bai were actually drafted by Muslim clerics. They passed off in the names of influential persons like Nana Sahib and Luxmi Bai, who had no choice but to sanction them. Whatever were the circumstances but it might be concluded that the Indian people, including civilian, Sepoys, and Muslim fanatics in the Uprising joined their hands in order to save their religion and nation. At that time when there was no question of one nation or nationalism or any common political factor, it was the religion alone which played important role during the Uprising. Although there were multiple factors but the religion filled them such an enthusiasm, which lasted until the last blood in their body. The Muslim Ulema were the main target in the suppression of the Uprising as they were considered the mastermind of the entire insurrection in 1857. It is estimated that over half million of Muslim Ulema alone were killed in their war of *Jihad*.

In comparison to the other peoples of India, the Muslims were more sufferers in the British rule. McLeod Innes narrates that among the hosts of malcontents the most powerful and dangerous were the Muslims. The entire Muslim population was, as a body, rebels at heart, and resented the Christian supremacy, if only on religious grounds and from fanatical pride. And the Mughals of the Upper Provinces had, in addition, a natural longing to revive their old predominance, and restore their historic Empire.[33]

Cunningham has rightly mentioned in his book *Earl Canning*, "He (Muslim) was feeling the dull pain of humiliated authority and tarnished prestige. In the days of the great Mughal Emperors the Mohammadan rule had stretched far and wide. Eastward and southward, across the rich delta of Bengal, the rice fields of Dacca, the fat homesteads of Arcot, Mohammadan rulers had exercised sway, and Mohammadan soldiers and officials had enjoyed the pleasant privileges of victorious rule. Those halcyon days had passed. The Mohammadan had now to compete on equal terms with the race which he had conquered and despised. His temperament, his creed, his education, disabled him from contending successfully with the subtle and quick-witted Hindu. The present was distressful. He brooded gloomily over the past. His lawful Sovereign sat with his sham Court at Delhi, more prisoner than prince, a pale shade of his former greatness."[34]

Almost all the policies of the British Government in India were anti-Muslim. The Muslims were considered in doubtful position. The battle of Plassey and Mysore were the examples of Muslim enmity before the British. On the religious side, the Muslims were more rigid than the others and were never ready to compromise at any cost. British considered the Muslims as the only danger and adopted the anti-Muslim policies and reduced them to poverty and starvation. At that time, the Muslim population in India was fifty millions and almost suffered the same oppressive policies of the British. The Muslim Ulema in their retaliation hatched a conspiracy to oust the foreigners from India and live with previous honour and independence. The anti-Muslim policies of Lord Ellen Burough and Lord Dalhousie further prepared an atmosphere against the British Government in India.

In a function of installing the gates of Somnath Temple, Lord Ellen Burough spoke that today after eight hundred years the revenge of dishonour has been taken. He again said that the Muslim's minds could be set. Lord Dalhousie also once said that king of Awadh is seems to be mental otherwise it would have become very difficult to digest the state before his departure. He further said that the old King of Delhi was almost dead, and he must have ended the dynastic rule of Taimur if the Court of Directors had not obstructed in this regard.[35]

Before reaching on any conclusion, there is earnest need to go through the religious policy of the East India Company. British East India Company, which came out to the East to trade, snatched a country from its Muslim rulers. The growing power of the British in the late eighteenth century gave a stimulus to the preaching of Christianity. The initial success of the Christian Missionaries with a section of community of the Hindus emboldened them to work for the conversion of the entire populace. Christian Missionary was financed by the Government of the East India Company. Missionary organisations like the Church Mission Society, the Bible Society, the Mission Fund, Mission hospitals, schools, and colleges were established throughout the country. A campaign was launched with the help of books, newspapers, magazines, and pamphlets to undermine the religious beliefs of the people and to convert them to Christianity. The Company officials regarded it as their bounden duty to aid and assist, and extend their patronage to the Missionary groups.

The Christian Missionary movement had gained much ground in 1857 when the question of establishing a bishopric at Delhi arose. There was also a rumour that the Company Government had the proposal to convert the Jama Masjid at Delhi into a church. This state of affairs infuriated the Muslims who already hated the British for having robbed them of their political power. As the Christian Missionaries, with the assistance of the entire apparatus of Government, were becoming strong and aggressive, the need was felt for a vigorous defence of the frontiers of the Islamic faith. The Missionaries, who had bagged large numbers of lower caste Hindus, had misjudged the fibre of the Muslims. The Muslim scholars and religious leaders could not sit quietly in the face of this conspiracy against Islam. Although some Muslims who were not satisfied with their progress fell into their clutches in search of something big and spectacular.

Jihad against the British

The Ulema like Maulana Al-e-Hasan, Maulana Rahmatullah and Dr. Maulana Wazir Khan, recognised the growing danger against Islam. They wrote several books in affirmation of Islam and the rebuttal of Christian doctrines. They also held open debates with Christian scholars. Maulana Rahmatullah's religious debate of 1854 at Agra with Padre Fonder and Padre French was successful, and the clergymen defeated in their goal. About one hundred Muslim scholars were present to assist Maulana Rahmatullah. Their number doubled on the following day. Maulana Rahmatullah organised this movement and included a large number of extreme revolutionary Musalmans, who were the followers of Maulana Ismail Shaheed. These Ulema along with the other revolutionaries waged the war against the British when the Uprising broke out in May 1857.

The day when Delhi was occupied by the revolutionaries, there was an intense anxiety in the city. Everybody was yelling to fight against the English for the sake of the religion. John William Kaye writes that everywhere it had been noised about from early morning that the King was on the side of the mutineers, and that to fight against the English was to fight for the King, to fight for the restoration of the Mughal throne, to fight for the religion of the Prophet. Kaye also states that the movement against the British authority appeared to be mainly a Musalman movement. At all events, at the great centre of Delhi, it took the shape of a Mohammadan revolution, culminating in the restoration of the Mughal Empire. It was not likely that the Hindu States would sympathize with this movement. Lieutenant-Governor reported on 15th of May, "Sindhia and Bharatpur will be heartily with us against the new dynasty of the House of Taimur." Both Princes responded readily to the call, and, for good or for evil, sent in their military aid to the British.[36]

Although most of the rebellious Sepoys in Delhi were Hindus, the flag of *Jihad* was raised on Jama Masjid Delhi. The revolutionaries appealed to the people, "the English are people who overthrow all religions... As the English are the common enemy of both Hindus and Muslims, we should unite in their slaughter... By this alone will the lives and faiths of both be saved." The proportion of *Ghazis* grew to be about a quarter of the local fighting force by the end of the siege, and included a regiment of suicide *Ghazis* from Gwalior who had vowed never to eat again and to fight until they met certain death at the hands of British troops. As the Uprising spread and progressed, the Sepoys were joined by large numbers of freelance *Ghazis*, while in Delhi, the failure to provide pay or food for the troops meant that the number of Sepoys gradually diminished as August progressed and much returned home, hungry and disillusioned. By the end of the siege of Delhi, several observers estimated that the *Jihadis or Ghazis* made up at least half of the remaining resistance, and it was they who put up the stoutest resistance when the British finally assaulted the city on 14th of September.[37]

After the occupation of Delhi by the revolutionaries, the combined forces of the revolutionaries raised the religious slogan, "*Kafir Murdabad, Nasrani Murdabad*" (Down with Infidel and Christians) rather than "*Angrez Murdabad, Firangi Murdabad*" (Down with English and Foreigners). In Delhi, Maulvi Baqar through his newspaper *Dehli Urdu Akhbar* and Maulvi Sarfaraz Ali through his impressive speeches in Shahjahanpur propagated that Islam is in danger and Muslims are bent upon to the unholy infidels.[38]

On 19th May, the standard of the Holy War was raised by the Muslims under Maulvi Mohammad Sayeed in the Jama Masjid. The people of Dharampur and the low characters of the city were concerned in this act. The Emperor Bahadur Shah Zafar was angry, and remonstrated, because such a display of fanaticism would only tend to exasperate the Hindus. A deputation of Hindu officers arrived to complain of the war against Hindus being preached. Emperor Bahadur Shah Zafar replied: "The Holy War is against the English; I have forbidden it against the Hindus." The Emperor Bahadur Shah Zafar dismayed the people who wanted to convert this war against the European infidels into civil war.[39]

On the arrival of General Bakht Khan in Delhi, he forged an idea to publish a religious decree of holy war (*Fatwa of Jihad*) against the British. The decree of *Jihad* was planned by General Bakht Khan to capture religious passions and step up recruitment for the cause of Uprising. It is said that on his request Maulana Fazle Haque Khairabadi prepared that decree which was signed and sealed by many reputed theologians of that time. Maulana Fazle Haque Khairabadi was formerly chief judge in Lucknow.

Although accused of supporting a *Jihad* against the British, there was no documentary evidence of this, and his correspondence reveals instead detailed theological and practical criticisms of Hazrat Mahal and other leaders of the revolt. On this decree of *Jihad*, 35 Ulema including Chief Qazi signed and sealed. In this decree, there was, firstly, a question and later there was the answer by the clerics who signed the decree. The decree is as follows:[40]

Question: What the Muslim Ulema says when the Englishmen are about to attack on Delhi and having an intention to destroy the followers of Islam and their wealth? In these situations, the *Jihad* is the duty (*Farz*) to the inhabitants of this city or not? In case of being it the duty, then whether it is compulsory duty (*Farz-ul-Ain*) or not? Whether the *Jihad* is the duty to those who are inhabitants of other cities and places or not?

Answer: In the current situations, the *Jihad* is the compulsory duty, and the submission (to the Almighty) is necessary for the inhabitants of this city. For this cause of the duty, the inhabitants of this city should have power to encounter and fight. In the presence of such a huge force and armament, the *Jihad* is no doubt compulsory for the inhabitants of this city and also to the people of the far-flung areas. If the inhabitants of this city keep themselves away from encounter or show laziness, then the *Jihad* would be their compulsory duty. The *Jihad* would be also the compulsory duty by Islamic law to all the inhabitants of the earth on the same pattern. The places which are under the threat of murder and plunder, the *Jihad* would be the duty to the inhabitants on the condition of having the power and strength.

Khan Bahadur Khan the rebellious ruler of Bareilly also declared his rule on Islamic principles under Bahadur Shah Zafar and demanded donations by the name of Islam to carry on the fight against the British. John William Kaye mentions about his proclamations, which need to be quoted as such, "He, who will willingly give a pice in this cause will get from God on the day of judgment seven hundred pice. And he who will spend a rupee in this cause, and will use his sword also against the infidels, will get from God seven thousand rupees."[41]

No doubt the Ulema and *Mujahideen* fought the war to save both the religion and country as the later was converted into *Darul Harab* (abode of infidel) after the occupation of the British. Men of the *Jihadi* mentality were mostly followers of the renowned Ulema of that time and considered the British as their utmost enemy. Most probably these Ulema utilised the Hindu Sepoys and masses and their leaders like Nana Sahib, Luxmi Bai and Tatya Tope. This was all due to the annexation of the Muslim States, imposition of Christian laws, education, and religious practices, uprooting the oriental philosophy, introduction of greased cartridges and propagating Christianity among the Indian masses. The Uprising was consistently articulated as a defensive action against the inroads' Missionaries, and their ideas were making in India, combined with a generalised fight for freedom from western occupation. During the Uprising they formed an unpaid *Jihadi* force and fought shoulder to shoulder with their counterparts until their death. They considered it their religious obligation to fight the British, and the Uprising provided them the opportunity. In Delhi and other parts of India, this group consisting of thousands of fighters who fought with the British soldiers.

Irfan Habib has defined the *Mujahideen,* and the *Ghazis* were the armed Muslim groups that arrived at Delhi, made up of a ragtag assortment of Wahhabi Maulvis, militant Naqshandis and, most numerous of all, pious Muslim civilians; especially weavers, artisans and other wage earners, who believed it was their duty to free what they regarded as the *Darul Islam* from the rule of the *Kafirs* (infidels), and some of whom are explicit in their wish to seek martyrdom.[42]

William Dalrymple argues that although the great majorities of the Sepoys were Hindus, a flag of *Jihad* was raised in the principal mosque of Delhi, and many of the resistance fighters described themselves as *Mujahideen* or *Jihadis.* There was even a regiment of "suicide *Ghazis*" who vowed to fight until they met death. It was the religious extremism that the Sepoys hunted down and killed all the Christian converts they could find on the day they first took Delhi. In Delhi, there were at least three major cases of Dr. Chimman Lal, who was in the British medical service and attended upon the Emperor too, Master Ram Chandra, a mathematician, who was a highly respected and popular teacher at Delhi College and Maulavi Imaduddin, who came to be known as Padri Imaduddin and was later a most active Christian polemicist. The Sepoys not even touched the Europeans who embraced Islam. These were Abdullah Beg and Sergeant Major Gordan. The two British new Muslims led the rebels in many important fronts of the Uprising.[43]

According to William Dalrymple, the fighters of the underground *Mujahideen* network were survived on the trading route linking Peshawar, Tonk, Delhi and Patna since the time of Sayyad Ahmad Barelvi, a brotherhood, bound to fight the *Jihad* by oaths of allegiance (*bayat)* to a leader (*Ameer*). These now cast off their veil of secrecy and began to mass in Delhi, ready for the holy war they had so long prepared for. In the first week of the Uprising, four hundred *Mujahideen* and *Ghazis* marched to Delhi from nearby Gurgaon, Hansi, and Hissar, but much the largest contingent over 4,000 strong *Mujahideen* came from the small Muslim principality of Tonk in Rajasthan, an underground centre of the *Mujahideen* movement since the time Sayyad Ahmad of Rai Bareilly. In this manner fully five thousand men from various quarters poured into Delhi as *Ghazis*, the majority armed with *gundasahs* (battle axes) and dressed in blue tunics and green turbans.[44]

Many Muslim clerics entered the Sepoy army and preached the glory of *Jihad* during the regular parade and invoked the Muslim soldiers. While in Delhi, the failure to provide pay or food for the troops meant that the number of Sepoys gradually diminished as August progressed and much returned home, hungry and disillusioned. By the end of the siege of Delhi, several observers estimated that the *Jihadis* made up at least half of the remaining resistance, and it was they who put up the stoutest resistance when the British finally assaulted the city on 14th September 1857. Even after 14th September, until the occupation of Red Fort on 20th September, 1857, the *Jihadis* were most active in street fighting. They thought the Uprising as the only and last military attempt to overthrow the British.[45]

It has also been seen that sometimes there was non-cooperation between the *Mujahideen* and the Sepoys due to some confusion and misunderstanding. There is a complaint to the Emperor Bahadur Shah Zafar by Principal Risaldar of Tonk *Mujahideen* in which he said that his *Mujahideen* had been deserted by the Sepoys during an assault and left to take on the *Kafir* infidels all by themselves. The complaint was as follows:[46]

> "We joined in the attack yesterday, and 18 infidels were dispatched to Hell by your slave's own hands, and five of his followers were killed and five wounded. Your Majesty, the rest of the army gave us no help, whilst we were engaged in combat with the infidels. Had they even made a show of support, as was to have been expected, with the help of Providence a complete victory yesterday would have been achieved... I trust that now some arms, together with some trifling funds, may be bestowed on my followers, so that they might have the strength to fight and slay the infidels, and so realise their desires."

The entire walled city of Delhi was full of the *Jihadis,* who has as much gallantry and enthusiasm, as the Sepoys. Even the British officers were more fearful of the *Jihadis* than the Sepoys. Hope Grant writes that in the last of July, the mutineer's force amounted to 40,000 men, exclusive of the male adult population, principally Muslims, who must have numbered 70,000 or 80,000 men, armed to the teeth, and capable of fighting even more desperately than the Sepoys. He further writes, "It was manifest that, until we were reinforced, we were in extreme jeopardy, and Brigadier-General Wilson recognised the imperative necessity for caution."[47]

On 14th September, 1857, when British forces attacked the besieged city, they proceeded to massacre not only the rebel Sepoys and *Jihadis,* but also the ordinary citizens of Delhi. The area of Kucha Chelan of Delhi witnesses the most heinous barbarism of the so called most civilized race of the world. 1,400 unarmed citizens of Kucha Chelan were mercilessly shot dead and thrown their deadbodies into the river Jumna. The ladies in order to save their honour jumped into the well along with the children in their lap. Zaheer Dehlavi in his "*Dastane Ghadar*" writes that every well of Kucha Chelan is filling of the dead bodies. Even a Christian Professor Ram Chander and a Hindu Brahman who engaged in this area in charitable work were not spared by the Europeans.[48]

It was estimated that the numbers of Sepoys in Delhi had fallen significantly as a result of desertion, and the number of *Mujahideen* rose vehemently. According to an estimate, the number of *Ghazis* crossed over 25,000 in Delhi in August 1857. Other accounts suggest that the British forces were assaulted outside Delhi by 'a mass of *Ghazis* from the Bareilly and Nimach who hastened to the swords and hurled themselves upon the British. Charles Griffiths provided this account as follows:[49]

> "The city was entirely in our possession by noon of September 20, 1857, I threaded my way through the streets and interminable narrow lanes, which were all blocked up with heaps of broken furniture and rubbish that had been thrown out of the houses by our troops, and formed in places an almost impassable barrier. Not a soul was to be seen; all was still as death.... I started in the afternoon with two of our officers to view a portion of the city. We made our way first in the direction of the Palace.... From the first we learnt particulars of the easy capture of the Palace that morning, and were shown the bodies of the fanatics who had disputed the entrance and had been killed in the enclosure. None of them were Sepoys, but belonged to that class of men called "*Ghazis*," or champions of the faith...fierce madmen, devotees to death in the cause of religion."

Even after the fall of Delhi the *Ghazis* never stopped themselves and continued their fight in various cities of northern India. William Russell describes the *Ghazis* at the time of Battle of Bareilly that, "The *Ghazis* were fine fellows, grizzly-bearded elderly men for the most part, with green turbans and cummerbunds, and every one of them had a silver signet-ring, a long text of the Koran engraved on it. They came on with their heads down below their shields, and their tulwars flashing as they whirled them over their heads shouting '*Deen! Deen!*' and dancing like madmen."[50]

Forbes and Mitchell of the 93rd Highlanders writes as an eye witness at the Battle of Bareilly on 5th May 1858, as follows:[51]

> "The Sikhs and our light company advanced in skirmishing order, when some seven to eight hundred matchlock-men opened fire on them, and all at once a most furious charge was made by a body of about 360 Rohilla *Ghazis*, who rushed out, shouting '*Bismillah! Allah! Allah! Deen! Deen!*'. Sir Colin Campbell was close by, and called out '*Ghazis, Ghazis*! Close up the ranks! Bayonet them as they come on. However, they inclined to our left, and only a few came on to the Ninety-Third, and these were mostly bayoneted by the light company which was extended in front of the line. The main body rushed on the centre of the Forty-Second; but as soon as he saw them change their direction Sir Colin galloped on, shouting out, 'Close up, Forty-Second! Bayonet them as they come on.' But that was not so easily done; the *Ghazis* charged in blind fury, with their round shields on their left arms, their bodies bent low, waving their tulwars (swords) over their heads, throwing themselves under the bayonets, and cutting at the men's legs. The struggle was short, but every one of the *Ghazis* was killed. None attempted to escape; they had evidently come on to kill or be killed, and a hundred and thirty three lay in one circle right in front of the colours of the Forty-Second....One of the *Ghazis* is described as 'enveloped in a thick quilted tunic of green silk, through which the blunt Enfield bayonet would not pass'. He looked to be getting the better of the Highlander's bayonet until a Sikh officer of the Fourth Punjabis took the *Ghazis'* head clean off with one sweep of his keen tulwar (Sword)."

The native troops controlled the areas deserted by the British, but it was also the fact that their resistance could not last longer and the leadership as well as the military switched over to the Muslim *Ghazis* and general public. The Sepoys, in the lack of resources and regular monthly salary, started deserting their duties and returned to their villages. That's why the unpaid *Mujahideen,* and along with the common people with the common national goal remained to fight until the last moment.

The next station after Bareilly was Mohammadi (a tehsil of Lakhimpur Khiri) near Shahjahanpur where a pitched battle was fought between *Ghazis* and the British on 18th May 1858. Here Maulvi Ahmadullah Shah and Prince Firoz Shah were fought near Mohammadi along with the *Ghazis* and 5,000 irregular cavalry, and a body of infantry, with eight or nine guns. However, they lost the battle with fifty or sixty men killed and wounded.[52]

There were many other Muslim dominated districts, which particularly rose against the British in the name *Jihad* even after the fall of Delhi. Robertson gives the example of a Muslim dominated district, Saharanpur, where he was stationed. He narrates that early in the disturbances, it being evident that the outbreak had assumed a religious character; the Missionaries at Saharanpur had been requested to proceed to the hills. Immediately, after the fall of Delhi, a junior member of this mission returned and announced his intention of preaching in public in the city. The natives still disbelieved in the fall of Delhi, and on his attempt to preach, they killed him. So by this folly of the young Missionary preachers the Muslims of Saharanpur were provoked for ultimate rising.[53]

This war as has been mentioned above witnessed the pivotal role of the Muslim religious people, but this is not sufficient to prove that the Uprising was a *Jihad* or War of Religion against the infidels or the Christians. Undoubtedly, it was having a unique character that Hindus blindly followed the Muslims, and Muslims had full faith in Hindus. It was the first time when both the communities hoisted the flags and chanted each other's slogans. Nana Sahib's ishtihar not only published in Urdu, and bears a *Hijri* date, but its main theme was that the Sultan of Turkey had intervened on behalf of the Indians. As for the Rani of Jhansi, some of her most determined fighters were Muslim gunners and Pathan guards. On the Muslim side, the standard of *Jihad* was removed from the Jama Masjid in May 1857 at Delhi, as it was being directed against all the non-Muslims, and all cows and buffalo-slaughter were banned at the Idul Azha festival. At Bareilly,

Bahadur Khan, the principal rebel leader, printed an appeal to Hindu chiefs to join the struggle against the British and requested the Muslims to utterly abjure cow-slaughter and the eating of beef.[54]

If it was *Jihad* or Holy War, then it was not against the entire non-Muslims community but the Christians and Christians alone. There are many instances when even the Hindus used the word *Jihad*. This *Jihad* was only an instrument which united the Hindus and Muslims to fight against the Christians or Europeans. According to Prof. Irfan Habib, Hindu contingents would elect Muslims as their representatives; Muslim contingents would accept a Hindu Subedar major as their head. In the *Risala Fath-i Islam* (Tract on the Victory of Islam) composed under Maulvi Ahmadullah Shah, the appeal was repeatedly made to both Hindus and Muslims to fight jointly to defend their respective faiths against their English oppressors. Among the Muslims who voluntarily joined the Uprising, under the impulse of joining a righteous war, or *Jihad* and so were called *Mujahideen* or *Jihadis.* There was the same acceptance of the need for Hindus and Muslims coming together to fight for a common cause: the target was only the British.[55]

By investigating the events of the Uprising and the root cause of dissatisfaction among the Indian population, the only theory of Holy War or *Jihad* does not fully suit. Although the *Mujahideen* or *Jihadis'* role could not be any way neglected then their counter religionist Hindus belonging to various classes of aristocracy, Sepoys, and peasants also could not be bypassed. The fact is undeniable that Uprising did show itself first to the Hindus, and though the Muslims joined the conspiracy, they were not the first to begin it. Actually, the Muslims took advantage and had turned it to their own ends. Murmurs of discontent among the Sepoy regiments stationed in Bengal were first heard in January, and gradually swelled into the uproar of open mutiny. In these regiments, the Hindus exceeded the Muslims in the proportion of five to one. After the outbreak of the Uprising, the British Government at Lucknow trusted the most on the Irregular Cavalry, in which Muslims prevailed.

According to Gubbins, "The most powerful Mohammadan chief in India, the Nizam of Hyderabad, has remained firm, and his contingent, comprising an elite Mohammadan cavalry, has not deserted us. To the north and west, the Mohammadan chiefs of Kabul, Qandhar, and Bulochistan have nowise molested our frontier. And even the fanatic Muslim bigots who inhabit the hills around Peshawar, far from joining any general conspiracy against us, have enlisted in our service, and have remained faithful. The city of Patna, supposed to be the hotbed of Musalman intrigue, has been little moved, even though the Sepoy brigade in the neighbouring cantonment of Dinapur succeeded in their tardy mutiny." By arguing that the participation of the people in the Uprising as region specific not the religion specific, Gubbin says, "While the Hindustani, both Hindu and Musalman, has equally proved faithless in the ranks of our Bengal army, the Punjabi of both denominations has maintained his fidelity. The marked difference in the conduct of the two is not, therefore, one of religion. The Mohammadan in the Punjab has been as faithful as the Hindu Sikh. The Hindu "*Poorbea*" has been as faithless as the Mohammadan Hindustani. Islamism has been faithless in the ranks of our Bengal army, and faithful in that of the Punjab."[56]

Gubbins further denies the conspiracy of the Muslims in regard to the Uprising of 1857 and advocates their loyalty to the British. He says that, although, at Dhaka, Murshidabad and in the eastern districts of Bengal, there was a large Muslim population, which has been in several quarters noted for bigotry and fanaticism, but there was neither any trace of the supposed widespread conspiracy nor any proof of having the league in a conspiracy against the British. The Madras Army, which took credit of fidelity during the Uprising equal to that of the Punjab; the Muslims found in its ranks were proportionately far more numerous than in the Bengal army and nearly one-half the Madras Sepoys were Muslims. They remained faithful like the soldiers of the Punjab and marched without the murmur beyond the limits of their own country, into North- Western India to quell their revolted co-religionists. Not a single Muslim prince of Southern India attempted to excite rebellion against the British.[57]

Muslims were the *Ghazis* and *Mujahideen* against the British in most parts of northern India, but they were loyal and faithful for the British Government during the Uprising in many parts of India. In most of the debates in England, it was resolved that it was the religious policy of the Government which had aroused the sentiments of Indian people. Martin quotes the comment of *The Times,* "We have made a great mistake in India. The religious policy pursued by the Government of that country, has made us, as one of its own servants declared, 'cowards in the eyes of men, and traitors in the eyes of God."[58]

Martin again quoted an Indian, Shiv Prashad, "It is absurd to think that the English are hated by the Hindus on account of their religion. It is not religion, but the want of religion, which has brought so much evil to this country. The people know that the Government is a Christian one. Let it act openly as a true Christian: the people will never feel themselves disappointed; they will only admire it....Who can detest 'religion?' It is the order of their own Shastras that every man is to revere his own religion. You may have a thousand Missionaries to preach, ...but take care that you do not interfere with their caste, you do not force them to eat the food cooked by another in the gaols, or thrust grease down their throats with the cartridges made by Europeans. Difference of caste must vanish, with many other offsprings of folly and ignorance, when its proper time comes. To try to exterminate it now must end in bloodshed."[59]

All the peoples of India, irrespective of their caste and religion filled with national enthusiasm rallied against the Colonial oppressive rule and fought according to their own way. The propagator of the imperialist historiography who brands the Uprising as mere mutiny, have just started their research with military dissatisfaction to the desertion of the Sepoys from the revolt. They perhaps intentionally in order to defend the Company rule tried to wash out the facts which were very widely covered in the eye-witness accounts of the British officers of that time. By concluding the topic it must be expressed that this war was a combined effort to defend the religious faiths of Indian people, war against an oppressive rule of the British Government, war to get sovereignty of their respective dominions or in nut shell war of independence against the British supremacy.

REFERENCES

1. Savarkar, V.D., *The Indian War of Independence of 1857*, London, 1909, p. 46, (Hereafter cited as Savarkar).
2. *Ibid.*, p. 47.
3. Wood, Evelyn, *The Revolt in Hindustan 1857-59*, London, 1908, pp. 4-5.
4. *Biblio*, Vol. XII, No. 3 and 4, March-April 2007, p.7.
5. *Ibid.*, p.6 ("It is well known to all, that in this age the people of Hindustan, both Hindus and Muslims, are being ruined under the tyranny and oppression of the treacherous and infidel and treacherous English. It is therefore the bounden duty of all the wealthy people of India, especially of those who have any sort of connection with any of the Muslim royal families, and are considered the pastors and masters of their people, to stake their lives and property for the well-being of the public. With the view of effecting this general good, several princes belonging to the royal family of Delhi, have dispersed themselves in the different parts of India, Iran, Turan, and Afghanistan, and have been long since taking measures to compass their favourite end; and it is to accomplish this charitable object that one of the aforesaid princes has, at the head of an army of Afghanistan, etc., made his appearance in India-and I, who am the grandson of Abul Muzuffer Sirajuddin Bahadur Shah Ghazi, king of India, having in the course of circuit come here to extirpate the infidels residing in the eastern part of the country, and to liberate and protect the poor helpless people now groaning under their iron rule, have, by the aid of the *Mujahideens*, or religious fanatics, erected—the standard of Mohammad, and persuaded the orthodox Hindus who had been subject to my ancestors, and have been and are still accessories in the destruction of the English, to raise the standard of Mahavir.
   Several of the Hindu and Muslim chiefs who have been trying their best to root out the English in India, have presented themselves to me, and taken part in the reigning Indian crusade, and it is more than probable that I shall very shortly receive succours from the west. Therefore, for the information of the public, the present *Ishtahar*, consisting of several sections, is put in circulation, and it is the imperative duty of all to take it into their careful consideration and abide by it. Parties anxious to participate in this common cause, but having no means to provide for themselves, shall receive their daily subsistence from me; and be it known to all, that the ancient works both of the Hindus and the Muslims, the writings of the

miracle-workers, and the calculations of the astrologers, pundits and rammals, all agree asserting that the English will no longer have any footing in India or elsewhere. Therefore it is incumbent on all to give up the hope of the continuation of the British sway, side with me, and deserve the consideration of the Badshahi, or imperial Government by their individual exertion in promoting the common good and thus attain their respective ends...." Jafri, Saiyid Zaheer Husain, *The Great Uprising of 1857*, Delhi, 2009, pp. 141-142).

6. Savarkar, pp. 67-68.
7. *Ibid.*, p. 68.
8. Tracy, Louis, *The Red Year; A Story of The Indian Mutiny*, New York 1907, p. 22, see also *Biblio*, Vol. XII, No. 3 and 4, March-April 2007, p.6.
9. *Biblio*, Vol. XII, No. 3 and 4, March-April 2007, p.7 taken from Salimuddin Quraishi, *Cry for Freedom: Proclamations of Muslim Revolutionaries of 1857*. Lahore 1997.
10. *Ibid.*
11. Forrest, George W., *Selections from the Letters Despatches and other State Papers Preserved in the Military Department of the Government of India 1857-58*, Volume III, Calcutta, 1902, p. Appendix-V.
12. *Ibid.*, p. Appendix-XI.
13. Thomson, Mowbray, *The Story of Cawnpore*, London 1859, pp. 144-146.
14. *Ibid.*, pp. 146-147.
15. *Ibid.*, pp. 143-144.
16. The suspicion arose that this act was intended to free widows from all restraint, and to give them the power of doing whatever they might think proper, even the married women were also recognized to the Criminal Courts as competent. (*Asbab-e-Baghawat-e-Hind*, pp. 24-25).
17. *Secular Qayadat*, Delhi, 21 August, 2007.
18. *Ibid.*
19. *Asbab-e-Baghawat-e-Hind*, pp. 16-17.
20. *Ibid.*, pp. 18-19.
21. *Ibid.*, p. 22, (**Extract of E. Edmond's Letter**—"The time appears to have come when earnest consideration should be given to the subject, whether or not all men should embrace the same system of religion. Railways, steam vessels and the electric telegraph are rapidly uniting all the nations of the earth: the more they are brought together, the more certain does the conclusion become that all have the same wants, the same anxieties, the same hopes,

the same fears, and therefore, the same nature and the same origin. It is also very certain that death universally closes the scene..... Now Christianity is a system which professes to have come by direct revelation from God Himself, as the only system by which happiness can be secured in this world or in that other world which it reveals. It has this peculiarity to distinguish it from every other system of religion in the world that it appeals to the reason as well as to the heart of man, and it is the only system in the world which has spread by the mere force of argument. ....we are anxious that others should be induced to receive them, and therefore, this solemn and earnest appeal is made to you to examine this important subject for yourself.... We urge you, therefore, as you value your own happiness forever, to examine this great subject, and to ask God himself to enable you, by His Holy Spirit's teaching to do so aright. ...be courageous and embrace it publicly: for He said Himself "whosoever shall be ashamed of me and of my words, in this adulterous and sinful generation, of him also shall the Son of Man be ashamed when He cometh in the Glory of His Father with the Holy Angels." .... Why not in this generation? Would it not be an infinite improvement upon the foolish, degrading, and wicked idolatry, which now defiles the land? "We speak as to wise men, judge ye what we say." *Asbab-e-Baghawat-e-Hind*, pp. 55-59).

22. **Extract of Eng, Trans. of a Persian notice, issued by the Lieutenant Governor of Bengal:** "His Honour the Lieutenant Governor of Bengal, having heard that the people of the country are unnecessarily apprehensive and uneasy on account of certain unreasonable and unfounded stories, fabricated and spread by people equally unreasonable and prejudiced, with regards to the religious rites and ceremonies of the Hindus and Mohammadans, hereby notifies that Government has no intention of interfering in the matters of religion, rites and ceremonies of the country, nor can it ever have such an intention. His Honour is sorry to find that the people of this country are unnecessarily alarmed at stories invented by seditious persons.... The principal objection of the Government is and ever shall be to protect the life, honour and property of its subjects, to respect their laws and customs and to do what it can to promote their welfare. Some of the Calcutta Missionaries have, as is their wont, but without the sanction of the Government, published religious discourses and circulated them amongst the natives who have wrongly understood them to have come indirectly from the Government. The Government has, however, had no hand in the affair. No attempt was ever made on

behalf of Government to persuade the natives to embrace the faith professed by the Government.... His Honour has been further given to understand that the inhabitants of this country regard the establishment of schools and colleges for the education of the natives in arts and sciences and in the English language as a means to mislead them from their faith, and that for this reason they are disinclined to send their children to school. This is undoubtedly a great mistake of theirs. The step has been misunderstood by the people.... It is a matter of great regret that the people have misunderstood the policy and the good intentions of Government in matters of education. His Honour, however, believes that the origin of all these evils is a misapprehension on the part of the natives, and that they do not proceed from prejudices or ill feelings. Be it known that by the spread of English education Government is simply desirous of opening to the people of India a path to all arts and sciences, and not to mislead them from their religion and time-honoured customs and habits. It must however be well borne in mind that works relating to all arts and sciences at present exist only in English language, and new discoveries and inventions are every day being brought to light. Moreover, English being the language of the rulers of the country, it is one of the duties of the subjects to learn it along with Urdu or Bengali, so that they may rise in honour and live in greater ease and comfort...(*Asbab-e-Bafhawat-e-Hind*, pp. 60-63).

23. *The Living Age*, Volume 0055, Issue 702, New York, November 7, 1857, p. 321.
24. Norman, Henry Wylie, *Delhi - 1857; The Siege, Assault, and Capture as given in the Diary and Correspondence of the Late Colonel Keith Young*, London 1902, pp. 17-18.
25. Gubbins, Martin Richard, *An Account of the Mutinies of Oudh and of the Siege of the Lucknow Residency; With some Observation on the Condition of the Province of Oudh and of the Causes of the Mutiny of the Bengal Army*, London, 1858, pp. 97-98 see also Frazer, R.W., *British India*, New York 1896, p. 280.
26. Forrest, Robert Edward, *Eight Days; A Tale of the Indian Mutiny*, London (ND), p. 93.
27. *Leidschrift*, Leiden, Netherlands, No. 24, December 3, 2009, p. 53
28. *Ibid.*
29. More, Sheshrao, *The 1857 Jihad*, (Eng. Trans. Bhalchandrarao C. Patwardhan), Delhi 2009, p. 103.
30. *Ibid.*, p. 306.
31. *Ibid.*, pp. 174-176.

32. *Ibid.*, pp. 237-238.
33. Innes, McLeod, *Lucknow and Oude in the Mutiny: A Narrative and a Study*, London, 1895, pp. 2-3.
34. Cunningham, Henry Stewart, *Earl Canning*, Oxford, 1891, p. 65.
35. *Jaam-e-Noor*, Delhi, August, 2007, pp. 5-6.
36. Kaye, John William, *A History of the Sepoy War in India, 1857-58*, Vol. II, London 1874, p. 93, see also Kaye, John William, *A History of the Sepoy War in India, 1857-58,* Vol. III, London 1876, pp. 208-209.
37. *The Guardian*, 10th May, 2007.
38. *Secular Qayadat*, Delhi, 21 August, 2007. Iit is highly significant that the Urdu sources from Delhi repeatedly refer to the British not as "*angrez*" (the English) or as *goras* (whites) or even *firangis* (foreigners, Franks), but instead almost always as *kafirs* (infidels) and *nasrani* (Christians).
39. *Two Native Narratives*, p. 98.
40. On the famous decree of *Jihad*, 35 Ulemas including Chief Qazi signed and sealed. The Ulemas were as follows: 1-Maulana Noor Jamal, 2-Maulana Mohammad Abdul Karim, 3-Maulana Sikander Ali, 4-Maulana sayyed Mohammad Nazir Hussain, 5-Maulana Rahmatullah, 6-Mufti Mohammad Sadruddin, 7-Mufti Ikramuddin urf Sayyed Rahmat Ali, 8-Maulana Ziauddin, 9- Maulana Ahmad Sayeed Ahmadi, 10- Maulana Meer Khan, 11-Maulana Mustafa Khan, 12-Maulana Abdul Qadir, 13-Maulana Karimullah, 14-Maulana Abdul Ghani, 15-Maulana Mohammad Ali, 16-Maulana Fariduddin, 17-Maulana Mohammad sarfaraz Ali, 18-Maulana Sayyed Mahboob Ali Jafari, 19-Mohammad Hamiuddin, 20-Mohammad Abu Ahmad, 21-Maulana Sayyed Ahmad Ali, 22-Maulana Mohammad Ilahi Baksh, 23-Maulana Mohammad Ansar Ali, 24-Maulana Saaduddin, 25-Name illegible, 26-Maulana Mufti Mohammad Rahmat Ali, 27-Maulana Haider Ali, 28-Maulana Hafizullzh Khan, 29-Maulana Nurul Haque Chishti, 30-Maulana Saifur Rahman, 31-Maulana Mohammad Hashim, 32-Maulana Abdul Majeed, 33-Maulana Sayyed Mohammad, 34-Maulana Mohammad Imdad Ali, 35-Maulana Mohammad Ali Hussain. (*Secular Qayadat*, Delhi, 21 August, 2007).
41. Kaye, John William, *A History of the Sepoy War in India, 1857-58,* Vol. III, London 1876, p. 291.
42. *Social Scientist*, Vol-26, No. 1-4, January-April 1998, p. 12.
43. *The Guardian*, 10th May, 2007, see also *Secular Qayadat*, Delhi, 21 August, 2007.

44. *Biblio*, Vol, XII, No. 3 and 4, March-April 2007, pp. 7-8.
45. *The Guardian*, 10th May, 2007, see also *Secular Qayadat*, Delhi, 21 August, 2007 and *Leidschrift*, Leiden, Netherlands, No. 24, December 3, 2009, p. 54.
46. *Biblio*, Vol, XII, No. 3 and 4, March-April 2007, p. 8.
47. Grant, Hope, *Incidents in the Sepoy War 1857-58*, Edinburgh, 1873, pp. 86-87.
48. *Secular Qayadat*, Delhi, 21 August, 2007.
49. Griffiths, Charles John, *A Narrative of the Siege of Delhi with an Account of the Mutiny at Ferozepore in 1857,* London 1910. pp. 192-193.
50. Russell, William Howard, *My Diary in India in the Year 1858-9*, Vol. II, London,1860, p. 14.
51. Forbes-Mitchell, *Reminiscences of the Great Mutiny, 1857-59,* London 1894, pp. 254-255, see also Edward, Gilliat, *Heroes of the Indian Mutiny; Stories of Heroic Deeds*, London 1914, p. 121.
52. Russell, William Howard, *My Diary in India in the Year 1858-9*, Vol. II, London, 1860, pp. 24-26
53. Robertson, Henry Dundas, *District Duties during the Revolt in the North-West Provinces of India in 1857: With Remarks on Subsequent Investigations during 1858-59*, London 1859, p. 172.
54. *Dawn*, Karachi, 26 January, 2008.
55. *Peoples Democracy*, (*Remembering 1857* - Irfan Habib), Vol. XXXI, No. 04, January 28, 2007.
56. Gubbins, Martin Richard, *An Account of the Mutinies of Oudh and of the Siege of the Lucknow Residency; With some Observation on the Condition of the Province of Oudh and of the Causes of the Mutiny of the Bengal Army*, London, 1858, pp. 51-52.
57. *Ibid.*, pp. 52-53.
58. Martin, R. Montgomery, *The Indian Empire,* Vol. II, London, 1858, p. 14.
59. *Ibid.*, p. 15.

CHAPTER 3

Wahabi or Waliullahi Movement

The Wahabi movement was basically a revivalist movement started in Arabia against the Ottoman rule. The term Wahabi is derived from the revivalist cleric Mohammad Ibn Abdul Wahab Najdi[1] (1704-1792) of Najd (middle part of the Arabic Peninsula). The followers of this movement follow the teachings of its cherished leader Mohammad Ibn Abdul Wahab. In Arabia, this movement was espoused by the local chieftain Mohammad ibn Saud (Al-Saud). The British Viceroy in India provided money and arms to the Wahabi followers such as Al-Saud rulers of Najd and other Gulf Shaikhdoms to brew this rebellion against the rulers of Ottoman Empire. The Arab resistance or Wahabi activity against Ottoman occupation of Arabia was politico-religious based. They targeted the Turkish Ottomans, who, as believed by the Wahabis, were responsible for polluting the fundamentalist Islam of Arabia with the traditionalist rituals of Ajam (non-Arabs). They wanted to revive the path of Islam based on only Hadith and Quraan by rejecting all the innovations from the religion.[2]

William Tayler who was Commissioner of Patna at the time of Uprising writes that Wahabis were very active in 1857. He describes them as, "The Wahabis are a set of Mohammadans, taking their name from Abdul Wahab…. The tenets originally professed by the Wahabis, have been described as a 'Mohammadan Puritanism,'……The unity of God, is the fundamental principle of their faith. They regard the Prophet, as a man, though gifted with a divine mission, reject the fables and false glosses of the Koran, but recognise and adopt the traditions of the Sunnis. They hold that all men are equal in the sight of God, and therefore, condemn the custom of invoking departed saints, or paying honour to their remains. They affect great purity of morals, abstain, or, at least, profess to abstain, from spirituous liquors, and all sensual indulgences. With the Sunnis, the Wahabis are on terms of tolerable agreement, though differing in certain points.... The sect in Bihar is daily increasing in numbers, and although the converts are principally obtained from the lowest classes, and are contemptible as a body, if openly opposed to the Government, they are dangerous in consequence of their union, their subservience to their leaders, and their extended communications. Without writing a line, a Wahabi Maulvi, or leader, could, it is said, convey a confidential message from Patna to Lahore, in an incredibly short space of time, and an order, however difficult to execute, would probably meet with unquestioning acquiescence."[3]

In India the term Wahabi, generally used by the scholars is a misnomer, and basically, it was a movement of an Indian origin started by Shah Waliullah Dehlavi[4] and followed by his disciples and the students of Madarsa Rahimiya. It is co-incident that at the same time there was also a similar movement in Arabia under Abdul Wahab Najdi. Surprisingly, the Muslim revivalist leader Shah Waliullah Dehlavi and Mohammad Ibn Abdul Wahab Najdi were contemporary scholars and studied at Madina. So, there is the intriguing possibility that the two greatest Sunni reformers of their age not only sat at the feet of the same teachers but may even have sat in the same classes. Apart from being the classmate, both the leaders were having different ideology. The one, after all, was a follower of the tolerant, inclusive Hanafi School of jurisprudence and a Naqshbandi Sufi initiate, while the other belonged to the intolerant, exclusive Hainbali School, was of viciously anti-Sufi and anti-Shia ideology.[5]

Shah Waliullah Dehlavi's eldest son and successor Shah Abdul Aziz[6] had initially followed the tolerant and non-violent basic teachings of his father's movement. However, when the British occupied the Mughal capital of Delhi in 1803 and humiliated the Emperor to the status of a pensioner, he issued a Fatwa that Hindustan to be a *Dar-ul-Harb* or "Country of the Enemy" and that it was now incumbent on all Muslims to strive to restore India to Islam. Hunter exactly quotes the Fatwa of Shah Abdul Aziz as, "When Infidels get hold of a Mohammadan country, and it becomes impossible for the Musalmans of the country, and of the people of the neighbouring districts, to drive them away, or to retain reasonable hope of ever doing so; and the power of the Infidels increases to such an extent, that they can abolish or retain the ordinances of Islam according to their pleasure; and no one is strong enough to seize on the revenues of the country without the permission of the Infidels; and the (Musalman) inhabitants do no longer live so secure as before; such a country is politically a Country of the Enemy (*Dar-ul-Harb*)." Based on the above statements, it rightly may be concluded that the Fatwa of Shah Abdul Aziz against the British was no more than a gesture.[7]

As the British were closely associated to Arabian Wahabis, they began to call the followers of Shah Waliullah in India 'Wahabi', while it was actually a Waliullahi movement, not the Wahabi. It was by chance that the religious puritan ideology of Mohammad Ibn Abdul Wahab Najdi was, to some extent, similar to that of Shah Waliullah. In India, the Wahabis, or the champion of Islam, were very firm with their belief and mission. To sacrifice the life for the Holy cause of Islam was the nobler achievement of a Wahabi. They knew no fear for themselves. Their path in life was clear, and neither warnings nor punishments could turn them to the right hand or the left. Due to their participation in the war of independence even after the surrender of the Sepoys and other Hindu revolutionaries, they must be called as Indian revolutionaries rather than Wahabis. They were undoubtedly the real hero of Indian independence and true patriot of the Indian nation.

Sayyad Ahmad Barelvi

Sayyad Ahmad was born on 24th October, 1786, in a famous Sayyad family of Rai Bareli, well known for its learning and saintliness. He had little inclination towards education during his childhood and was fond of manly exercises and passed his time in learning and practicing the use of arms. When fully grown up, Sayyad Ahmad, along with six companions, proceeded to Lucknow in search of employment. However, he did not stay there for long and set out on foot to Delhi in the quest of knowledge. In Delhi, he studied Quraan and Tradition under Shah Abdul Qadir, the brother of Shah Abdul Aziz. His spiritual guide Shah Abdul Aziz initiated him into the Chistiya, Qadariya, and Naqshbandiya orders of Sufism. After two years' stay at Delhi, he returned his home, Rai Bareli. After two years stay at home at the age of 24, he set out for Tonk to enter the service of Ameer Khan. Then followed several years of hazardous life and his participation in several campaigns fought by the Ameer, prepared him for his ultimate struggle for the faith which he was destined to lead. When Ameer Khan became subservient to the British by accepting the state of Tonk, Sayyad Ahmad left for Delhi in 1815. The two outstanding luminaries of Shah Abdul Aziz's family, Shah Ismail, his nephew, and Maulana Abdul Hai, his son-in-law, accepted Sayyad Ahmad as their spiritual guide.[8]

His proclaimed objective was to restore Islam to its pristine purity and to cleanse it from all types of innovation. In order to propagate his mission all over India, Sayyad Ahmad nominated four Khalifs or spiritual Viceregents, and a high priest, Maulvi Wilayat Ali, Maulvi Inayat Ali, Maulvi Marhamat, Maulvi Farhat Hussain; besides Shah Mohammad Hussain as chief priest.[9]

Sayyad Ahmad's puritan ideologies were based basically on two principles: The first consists in disbelieving that angels, spirits, spiritual guides, disciples, teachers, students, saints, etc. remove one's difficulties. It was to be denied that any of them has the power of granting favour or removing evils; in considering them as helpless and ignorant as one's self in respect to the power of God. It denied of making any offering to any prophet, saint, holy man, or angel for the obtaining of any object, but merely to consider them as the friends of God. With regard to the second point, true and undefiled religion consists in strongly adhering to all the devotions and practices in the affairs of life, which were observed in the time of the Prophet. In avoiding all such innovations as marriage ceremonies, mourning ceremonies, adorning of tombs, erection of large edifices over graves, lavish expenditure on the anniversaries of the dead, street processions and the like, and in endeavouring as far as may be practicable to put a stop to these practices.[10]

Sayyad Ahmad visited a number of places in Northern India, including Saharanpur, Muzaffarnagar, Deoband, Rampur, Bareilly, and Shahjahanpur. The reform movement was in full swing and Sayyad Ahmad now headed a country-wide organization. During his stay in Rampur, Sayyad Ahmad came into contact with certain Afghans coming from Kabul, who narrated to him the stories of Sikh atrocities committed on Muslims of North-Western India. Enraged at the brutalities of Sikhs, he resolved to wage *Jihad* against them after his return from the holy pilgrimage to Mecca; whither he proceeded in 1821, accompanied by a large party. His stay on the Holy land lasted for more than one and half years. During this period, he came into contact with many renowned Muslim scholars and learnt about many reformatory and revivalist movements throughout the world of Islam, including Wahabism.[11]

It is generally believed that Sayyad Ahmad Barelvi had imported Wahabism into India when he returned from the pilgrimage in Mecca in 1824. Nevertheless, the reality was totally different. He already accepted the basic principles of Waliullahi Movement and radical as well as aggressive ideology of the Wahahis of Arabia. However, it would be more suitable to say that it was Sayyad Ahmad who had radicalized the Waliullahi Movement based on of his experiences of his services under Ameer Khan of Tonk and his own personal interests in military actions. His ideology was radical long before sailing to Arabia, as a student of the Madarsa Rahimiya in Delhi and as a pupil of its leader, Shah Abdul Aziz, son of the reformer Shah Waliullah of Delhi.

Although it was a Waliullahi ideology, but the term Wahabi has been deliberately used here in order to provide clear understanding of the subject to the readers and also due to the similarity of the objectives. The Wahabis under Sayyad Ahmad Barelvi condemned all accretions to and innovations in Islam and advocated a return to the pure Islam and society of Arabia of the Prophet's times. Many Sunnis now saw him as the inheritor of the mantle of the Shah Waliullah and hundreds flocked to join his cause.

Sayyad Ahmad Barelvi was a devout student of Shah Abdul Aziz and carried on the mission of Waliullahi or the so-called Wahabi movement in the far-off places in India. In 1820, when Sayyad Ahmad started his mission of teaching basic tenets of Islam, particularly unity of God and equality of manhood, and acquired much name and fame, he was about thirty-four years old, a little above the middle height, and with a long beard falling on his chest. One day, he saw in his dream that the beloved daughter of Mohammad and her husband (his lineal ancestors) visited him, saluted him as their son, bathed him in sweet essences, and arrayed him in royal apparel. Until his pilgrimage to Mecca, however, he does not appear to have reduced his doctrines to any formulated system. His idea of a reformation of religion was a purely practical one. He told his hearers, that if they were to escape divine wrath, they must live better lives.[12]

After his return from Arabia, along with the teachings of Islam, he encouraged the Holy War or *Jihad* against the British oppressors. This movement was a part of the freedom movement in India, which mobilized the Muslim masses against the British, but as it was based on the religious tenets of Islam, it could not find support of their co-religionists. Later on, Sayyad Ahmad Barelvi gave the movement a military turn on situational ground. Sayyad Ahmad Barelvi appealed the Hindus for support and tried to prove that the political motive of the movement was India's freedom from British domination. In this regard, a letter of Sayyad Ahmad Barelvi written to a Maratha Chief Raja Hindu Rai needs to be quoted here:[13]

> "It is apparent to you that unfriendly foreigners of a distant land have become the masters of the country, that traders have assumed the dignity of the 'Sultanate' and destroyer of the rule of great rulers and chieftainship of high placed chiefs by depriving them of their respect and honour."

> "Since the rulers and statesmen have sought refuge and privacy, a band of poor and helpless persons have girded up their loins. This weak band does not aspire to any worldly gains. They are inspired by the spirit of service to God without the least desire for wealth and power."
>
> "The moment India is cleared of the foreigners and the arrow of efforts reached its target, the offices and rulership shall remain intact for those who want it and their dignity and power shall be strengthened. This weak band wants only this much from the great rulers and high dignitaries that while they occupy the '*Masnad*' of rulership, service to Islam with heart and soul should be done."
>
> "Although this poor band has not got this ample means, yet by the desire of the Lord, it is glad and cheerful and detests the desire for power of pelf and keeps it's off from wealth and riches which they do not want to enjoy either now or in future."
>
> "Anyone of the rulers of old states that may come forward to help, will only be strengthening the foundation of his own state. The purport of this affectionate letter will truly be explained to you in details by Haji Bahadur Shah who is an old associate of mine"

This movement offered the most serious and well-planned challenge to British supremacy right from 1830s to 1860s. The idea of *Jihad* against Raja Ranjit Singh of Punjab was a circumstantial addition when the Raja started to torture and oppression of his Muslim subjects.

When Sayyad Ahmad Barelvi came to know the atrocities committed by Raja Ranjit Singh to his Muslim subjects and the neighbouring areas, he intended to settle the matter of Punjabi and Frontier Muslims. As the circumstantial measure, he adopted a policy to wage war or *Jihad* against Ranjit Singh and opened recruitment centres for military warriors in Punjab, Rajasthan Awadh, Agra, Bengal and Bihar. British officers had the knowledge of this recruitment, and they let it happen because the target of this recruitment was not the British but the Sikh empire of Ranjit Singh. Sayyad Ahmad was successful in conquering

Peshawar and its surrounding areas up to Mansehra and Balakot. This local war gained much importance and became a proxy war between the British and the French as the Sikhs were officered by the French generals to support Maharaja Ranjeet against the British expansion. The Wahabis were enjoying tacit support of the British and the French helped the Sikh armies.[14]

On his return from the holy pilgrimage, he appealed to the people to wage Holy War against the Sikh ruler of Punjab Maharaja Ranjit Singh. Finally, on 16th January 1826, he left home on an arduous journey, never to return. He was accompanied by five to six thousand companions; all prepared to die for delivering their brethren from the tyrannical Sikh rule. Sayyad Ahmad and his party arrived at their destination at Naushehra and made it his headquarters in December, 1826. Despite the overwhelming superiority of the Sikh army which was disciplined and led by experienced foreign soldiers and was equipped with the latest weapons of war, the *Mujahideen* inflicted on them defeats in several encounters. At one stage Ranjit Singh even sued for peace, but his terms were not acceptable to Sayyad Ahmad. He, therefore, sowed dissensions among the Pathan supporters of the Sayyad through bribery and intrigue, including Yar Mohammad, the Chief of Peshawar. The fateful battle at Saidu Sharif fought in March 1827, in which Yar Mohammad, along with his men, deserted the Muslim ranks at the very crucial stage. Their victory turned into a rout in which several thousand Muslims lost their lives.[15]

In the skirmishes between *Mujahideen* and Pathans, Yar Mohammad Khan, the Chief of Peshawar, and Khadi Khan, the Chief of Hund, were killed. The *Mujahideen* occupied Peshawar in 1830. However, instead of removing Sultan Khan, brother of the treacherous Yar Mohanmad Khan, the Sayyad retained him as the Governor of the city. Sayyad Ahmad declared himself Emperor and imposed strict Wahhabi rules on Peshawar and the surrounding country. The imposition of basic tenets of Islam was an attack on the traditions and rituals of the Pathans and just after two months of Wahabi rule, the local population rebelled and arrayed under Sultan Khan. Sultan Khan, in order to avenge the death of his brother, secretly killed the *Mujahideen* when they were offering the prayer. Sayyad Ahmad and his remaining followers being greatly disappointed arrived at Balakot, a small town in the Kaghan valley, surrounded on three sides by high mountains, he set up his Headquarters there, considering it safe for the *Mujahideen*. Here, too, the local Muslims spied for the Sikhs and in a decisive battle on 8th May 1831, more than six thousand Muslims killed in the battlefield. The leader of the movement, Sayyad Ahmad, along with his chief lieutenant, Shah Ismail, died fighting until the end.[16]

After this shock, the movement stopped its military operations but its religious preaching continued. After the overthrow of the Sikh ruler and incorporation of the Punjab into the East India Company's dominion in 1849, the sole target of the Wahabi's attack became the English dominion in India.

Maulvi Wilayat Ali

Maulvi Wilayat Ali was the eldest son of Fateh Ali of Patna who was a great disciple of Sayyad Ahmad Barelvi. His younger brother Maulvi Inayat Ali had also accompanied him in the movement to which he was associated. They were themselves the disciples of the same *Imam* and preacher of the movement. While Wilayat Ali possessed better political wisdom and experience, Inayat Ali was brave and valiant soldier and a forceful preacher and organizer. They actively lead the revivalist movement (so-called Wahabi Movement) in Bengal, Bihar, United Provinces, and Frontier Provinces and as far as Deccan.

In the life time of Sayyad Ahmad Barelvi, there was a Council of six members and four out of them died along with him on the frontier. The fifth Fateh Ali died of the natural causes leaving the sixth Shah Mohammad Hussain of Sadiqpur as the head of the Wahabis in India. The five vacant posts of the Council were now filled with younger generation with title of Maulvi. They were Fateh Ali's three sons Maulvi Wilayat Ali, Maulvi Inayat Ali and Maulvi Farhat Husain; two eldest sons of Ilahi Baksh, Maulvi Ahmadullah and Maulvi Yahya Ali. After reformation of the Council, the five members of the younger generation re-started the Holy War but now the Europeans were the target not the Sikhs.

Maulvi Wilayat Ali was the senior among the new-generation Wahabis who lead the mission. He served as Shah Mohammad Hussain's *Wazir* (Chief Councillor) before succeeding him as *Imam* (Chief) of the Wahabis in India. Inayat Ali was acted as Minister of War, Ahmadullah the new Councilor of the Chief Wilayat Ali, Yahya Ali as treasurer and bursar and Farhat Husain as recruiter and religious ideologue of the Wahabi Movement.[17]

All the new post-holders were great warriors and brilliant propagandists. After assuming leadership, Maulvi Wilayat Ali made his first public announcement that their beloved master is indeed alive and well, but God had withdrawn him from the sight of men because He was displeased by the faint-hearted response of Indian Muslims to His *Imam's* call to arms. He also said that their Imam was even now hidden in the caves in the Buner Mountains, waited on by his true faithful disciples. When his followers had proven their faith by uniting once more to renew the *Jihad,* only then their lost leader would reappear. He would then manifest himself as ruler and lead them to victory against the unbelievers. Wilayat Ali sent his brother Inayat Ali to Sitana to look after the affairs of the Wahabis in 1839. In 1844, Maulvi Wilayat Ali, himself left for the frontiers along with 80 followers, including Maulvi Faiyaz Ali, Maulvi Yahya Ali, Maulvi Akbar Ali, and some other members of his family. Sitana was made permanent base of the *Jihadis* and Patna became the fund collecting area for *Jihad.* However, due to the British resistance they surrendered at Haripur in 1847, and Sir Henry Lawrence sent them to their homes at Patna, as dangerous characters, where security was taken from them for their future good conduct.[18]

In 1851, Maulvi Wilayat Ali, notwithstanding that bound by bond and security to remain at his home at Patna, again marched towards Sitana along with 250 followers, including Maulvi Yahaya Ali and Maulvi Faiyaz Ali. In 1852, they established a regular organisation for passing up men and arms from Bengal to the rebel camp at Sitana. Maulvi Wilayat Ali began to preach in the area and also held military parades of his followers every day.[19]

In January 1853, the Commissioner of Peshawar, Frederick Mackeson, launched a raid on the Hindustani camp at Sitana, driving its inhabitants further into the mountains. In September of the same year the Commissioner was knifed to death in his bungalow by a tribesman from Swat. But that could not stop the British hunting expedition, and the British troops' continuous raids forced the Hindustanis to put off their *Jihad*. The unfortunate death of Maulvi Wilayat Ali in 1854 due to the short illness further gave a setback to the mission of the Wahabis.[20]

Maulvi Inayat Ali

After the death of Maulvi Wilayat Ali, his brother Maulvi Inayat Ali assumed the leadership of the movement and laboured hard to induce the Pathans of the frontier to support him for the sacred cause. He also became successful to win the support of Akhund of Swat and Sayyads of Sitana. Maulvi Inayat Ali made several attacks on the British but was forced to retreat several times. On many occasions, he became successful and distributed war booty among the villagers, whom he wanted to win over to his side.[21]

Maulvi Inayat Ali was successful in most of his campaigns against the British, but due to the outbreak of the Uprising of 1857, communications and sources of supply from the Patna centre were cut off. In the lack of resources and supply he could not wage any successful war during the Uprising. He moved to Swat where he died after a short illness in 1858.[22]

After the death of Maulvi Inayat Ali, Maulvi Maqsood Ali took the charge of Wahabi leadership and lastly Maulvi Abdullah the son of Wilayat Ali assumed the leadership. This movement offered the most serious and well-planned challenge to the British supremacy in India until the failure of the Uprising.

According to Hunter, "Throughout the whole period the fanatics kept the border tribes in a state of chronic hostility to the British Power. A single fact will speak volumes. Between 1850 and 1857, the Frontier disorders forced us to send out sixteen distinct expeditions, aggregating 33,000 Regular Troops; and between 1850 and 1863, the number rose to twenty separate expeditions, aggregating 60,000 Regular Troops, besides Irregular Auxiliaries and Police. During this time, the Sitana Colony, although stirring up a perpetual spirit of fanaticism along the Frontier, had wisely avoided direct collision with our troops. They might secretly help the tribes whom they had incited against us, but they did not darc to wage war on their own account. But in 1857 they openly formed a coalition against us."[23]

When the Uprising started from Meerut and spread over Delhi and the whole northern India, the followers of Sayyad Ahmad Barelvi or Wahabis played a vital role in spreading anti- British sentiments and to crush the British in different fronts. In the final assault on Delhi by the British forces, it were these unpaid *Ghazis* or *Jihadis* or *Mujahideen* bound by religious ties who arrived from different areas of India, fought to the death while a bulk of the Sepoys slipped away. They were led by Muslim Ulema. A number of sources proven that along with the '*Poorbeas*' (rebel Sepoys of Awadh Province) who entered Delhi after fleeing their cantonments, there were large numbers of 'freelance' Muslims or *Mujahideen*.

Even after failure of the Uprising, these *Mujahideen* or Wahabis continued their open fight from their stronghold in the Frontier area in the west of the Indus, amid the fastnesses of the outlying spurs of the Hindu Kush. Here the Wahabis had formed a colony, whence they had spread seditious exhortations to all true Muslims to aid with money, arms, and prayers in an unrelenting war against the British. Sitana, Jadun, and Malka in the Mahaban, or Mountains of the Great Forest, were the centres of the Wahabis where mutinous Sepoys from the lowlands, wild Pathans and fierce Afridis flocked in numbers for the sake of the religion of Islam. In April 1858, the British military commander in Peshawar, General Sir Sidney Cotton, entered the hills with an Army of 5000 men led an assault to wipe out the Indian fanatics. The British raided and burnt to the ground their abiding-place at Sitana. Inayat Ali, the leader of the Wahabis died of fever, and they were surrounded and wiped out, yet somehow Wilayat Ali's eldest son, Abdullah Ali, escaped to fight another day. The survivors moved to an abandoned settlement named Malka, where they were entirely dependent on the charity of their neighbours.[24]

Maulana Mohammad Jafar Thanesari

Maulana Mohammad Jafar Thanesari was born in 1838 in Thanesar of District Ambala, Punjab. In his childhood, his father

Miyan Jeewan died. He got his education in patronage of his mother. At that time the religious activities of the followers of Sayyad Ahmad Shaheed were at peak under the aegis of the movement of Shah Waliullah. Under the influence of the philosophy of Sayyad Ahmad Shaheed (so-called Wahabi Movement), he jumped in *Jihad* against the British power.

His role in the Uprising of 1857 is not much known, but the Deoband Ulema claims that Maulana Jafar Thanesari gave tough resistance to the British from the Ambala side. At that time, he was a young revolutionary of merely 19 years old and was not much popular as *Ghazi* or *Mujahid.* He might have fought under the command of some other revolutionary cleric. That's why the British brutality could not reach to his neck when the torture was carried on by the British throughout the northern India. William Wilson Hunter also gives the account as follows:[25]

> "When the mutiny of 1857 broke out, Jafar chose twelve of his most trustworthy disciples, and repaired to the Rebel Camp. Even in the unwonted work of fighting his force of character made him conspicuous, and he gained the reputation of being a man fit to be trusted with treasonable secrets. Upon the downfall of the rebel hopes at Delhi, he returned to his attorney's business at Thaneswar, brooding over the inscrutable decree of Providence which had given victory to the Unbelievers, and more than ever discontented with what he calls 'this exceedingly dirty business of Petition-writing.' Open force had failed, and it remained to be seen what could be effected by secret conspiracy. Jafar soon became a member of the widespread Wahabi confederacy. His secret duties threw a religious halo even over his detested profession; for 'be it known,' he writes at this period, 'I do this by order of a Certain Person, and for a Hidden Object.' This Certain Person was Maulvi Yahya Ali of Patna, Spiritual Director of the Wahabi sect in India. The Hidden Object was the forwarding of recruits and munitions of war to the Wahabi colony on the Mahaban, then in open hostilities against the British Crown."

Although torture was inflicted upon the Indian Ulema, they carried on Holy War against the British even after the suppression of the Uprising. The Ulema, along with the tribes of the North-West Frontier area, continued their *Jihad* against the British. Towards the end of 1863, a great war started in the Yaghistan territory, at the western frontier of India. General Chamberlain was in command of the British troops, which suffered many casualties in the Ambeyla Pass area. Mulla Abdul Ghafur and Akhund of Swat, accompanied by many of his disciples, rushed to the front to fight the invaders. A large number of Afghans and local Pathans, in their own defence, also joined the battle against the English army. The *Mujahideen* fought valiantly in their passion for martyrdom, and the masses also rose up against the British to guard their liberty. In this fierce battle which lasted about two or three months, General Chamberlain himself was gravely wounded and the casualties soared to about seven thousand.[26]

Maulana Jafar Thanesari was most active in the later phase of this war of independence and in connection of supplying money and men to the Frontier *Mujahideen*, he was arrested. Hunter says that Munshi Jafar of Thaneswar, whom men call Khalifa, was the great man who passed up the Bengalis and their carbines and rifles for the Frontier War against the British. Maulana Thanesari himself writes in his account titled, 'Counsels of Jafar' that Police Superintendent searched his house and found a letter which was addressed to the leader of the *Mujahideen* and contained a coded message about the dispatch of a few thousand guineas. Although there was a proof of his involvement in the Frontier War, the Police only arrested two of his companions. The police took Munshi Abdul Ghafoor a resident of the district of Gaya in the Bihar province who was working as a clerk in his office, as well as Abbas a Bengali boy who used to sleep in his sitting suite. Maulana Thanesari was left alone at his house and find chance to escape. He decided to go to Delhi and left his wife and children at Panipat in the way. In Delhi, he stayed at Miyan Nasiruddin's residence where he gave the guineas to Miyan Husaini of Thanesar instructing him to carry this sacred consignment as expeditiously as possible to the caravan of the *Mujahideen*. Maulana Thanesari himself writes about him, "I was about twenty-five years old then and brimming with religious zeal. I paid no attention to the ups and downs of what took place in the world and had complete faith that God would take care of all matters concerning me since it was His Cause that I was pursuing."[27]

He left Delhi for Ambala *via* Aligarh. He wanted to know about his case and find out the identity of the informer. In Thanesar, Police again marched and in order to arrest him they searched hundreds of houses and apprehended scores of men and women. His old mother, twelve or thirteen-year old brother Mohammad Sayeed, and his wife were all arrested and excessively beaten and tortured. Even purdah-observing housewives were subjected to heartrending cruelty and dishonour. Posters advertising a Rs. 10,000 award for his arrest were distributed. Police reached Delhi and after finding that he had departed to Aligarh, an order of his arrest was telegraphed to Aligarh. On reaching Aligarh, he was immediately arrested and put in tight custody. Maulana Thanesari says, "the guards on duty at the Aligarh jail asked me what kind of crime I had committed that required the stationing of three men to guard my cell, when usually a single watchman is sufficient even for criminals condemned to death. I replied, 'I shirked from the duty that my Master had assigned to me. That is why He is angry with me and had me captured en route while I was fleeing'."[28]

Maulana Thanesari was taken to Ambala *via* Delhi and Karnal. He suffered enough torture and beating in the police custody. During April 1864, the case was presented for trial to the Magistrate's Court and later to the Session Court of Ambala. After completing its proper hearing, the Court, on 2nd May 1864, gave its decision as follows:[29]

> "You are a clever and knowledgeable person. You know the law. You are also a nobleman and the *Nambardar* of your city. But you used all your knowledge of the law and your intelligence to combat the Government. You undertook to supply men and money to the enemies of the Government. Except when trying to refute the argument in the trial, you never uttered a word of loyalty to the Government, and never helped anyone prove that

you meant well. You will therefore be hanged, and all your assets will be confiscated by the Government. Even your dead corpse will not be given to your heirs, but will be buried with ignominy in the jail graveyard" He finally added, "It will give me great pleasure to see you hanged." Maulana Thanesari responded to the last sentence and said, "I said, it is up to God, not up to you, to decide who lives and who dies. God Almighty has the power to end your life before mine"

In response to the decision of the Court, Maulana expressed the happiness, but the audience started crying. Some policemen under the orders of Captain Parsons, the Superintendent of Police, approached him and said, "You have been sentenced to be hanged. You should be crying. Why are you so cheerful" Maulana answered them, "Because we are hopeful that we will attain martyrdom, which is the greatest blessing. Nevertheless, you cannot comprehend that."[30]

The two defence attorneys, having received some extra fees, went to the Chief Court, but again, the case was postponed for a few days for further consultation. Maulana Thanesari was from among the eleven Muslims whose fate was decided. During the trial, they were defended by English Counsel; six of their countrymen sat as Assessors with the Judge on the bench; and the trial ended in the condemnation of eight of them to transportation for life, and of the remaining three to the last penalty of the law. On 6th of September, the Deputy Commissioner of Ambala read to him the Chief Court's Order that since they rejoiced at their sentence of hanging, regarding it as martyrdom, the Government, which had no desire to give them their coveted punishment, had commuted their death sentence to lifetime imprisonment overseas. He was then shifted to the regular jail. According to Maulana Jafar, "Following the jail regulations, our beards, mustaches, and hair were clipped short with scissors, making us look like fleeced sheep." He along with his companion Maulvi Yahya Ali and remaining others journeyed to Black Water on 8th December 1865, from Bombay on the boat and reached Port Blair of Andaman on 11th January 1866, after thirty four days of sailing. Maulana Jafar Thanesari writes, "From that day to the date when we were set free, we never had to suffer living in jail cells, wearing prisoner garbs, or eating in the mess with other prisoners. So, for all practical purposes, we became free persons on that day, even though we stayed confined to Black Water for another eighteen years."[31] After a week of landing him on the Island, Maulana Thanesari was appointed as Deputy Head Clerk in the Court attached to the offices of the Superintendent and the Chief Commissioner. He moved into a comfortable house, and not the barracks in which convicts usually lived in the initial phase of their stay in the Andamans. The Maulana was given full freedom within the confines of the penal colony, and, to make life even easier; he was assigned a servant, whose wages were paid by the settlement authorities. At the age of 27, he was married to a Kashmiri girl but when she died in 1868, he got married to another girl, Brahmin by caste, from Almora. Maulana Jafar says, "I applied once again for my wife to be allowed to move from Panipat to join me, but this time she herself seemed hesitant to relocate. Later, she showed some willingness, but the authorities rejected my application..... I organized a big feast during which she embraced Islam. After she had thoroughly learned the Pillars of Islam and the prayer rituals, etc., I reported our intention to wed to the authorities and married her on 15th April 1870. Hundreds of people attended the ceremony. The marriage was solemnized by Maulana A?madullah. A splendid reception took place the next day."[32]

When Maulana Jafar Thanesari freed in 1885, after twenty years on that island, and returned in India with his wife and many children, he found that all his possessions, including houses, lands, and farms, had been seized by the Government and auctioned off.[33]

Maulvi Yahya Ali

Maulvi Yahya Ali and Maulvi Ahmadullah were the two eldest sons of Ilahi Bux of Patna. They were high priests of Patna and not only fully influenced with the ideology of Sayyad Ahmad Barelvi but actively engaged in Wahabi activities from Patna to Sitana in the Frontier area. They provided men and money to the Wahabi *Mujahideen* fighting on the Frontiers against the British. They were also involved in preaching of *Jihadi* philosophy among the Muslims of Patna and other areas of Northern India.

Maulvi Yahya Ali was leading Wahabi at Patna. William Wilson Hunter describes about Maulvi Yahya Ali, "The Chief Priest, Yahya Ali, had many duties. He corresponded with all the itinerant preachers as Spiritual Director of the sect in India. He organised and personally worked a complicated system of drafts in a secret language, by which he safely transmitted large sums from the centre of the Empire to the Rebel Camp beyond the Frontier. He conducted the public ministrations in the mosque. He examined and passed the rifles for the Fanatic Host, delivered a course of divinity lectures to the students, and by private study acquired an intimate acquaintance with the Arabic Fathers. But the most delicate operation of the conspirators was the transmission of recruits from the Patna Propaganda, or Little Warehouse, as it was called in their secret language, to the Great Warehouse or Rebel Camp beyond the Frontier..... He organised a system of Wahabi hospices along the route, and placed each under the charge of a proven disciple...."[34]

At the time of Uprising, Patna was under the influence of Maulvis of Wahabi mentality, which created a drastic trouble for Mr. Tayler who was controlling the city. Private information also satisfied Mr. Tayler that the chiefs of the disaffected natives were the Wahabi Maulvis. These men were the leaders of the most bigoted Muslims, and as such commanded implicit obedience from the mass of Patna Muslims and held in their hands the strings of the contemplated movement. Prominent among these Maulvis were Yahya Ali, Shah Mohammad Hasan, Maulvi Ahmadullah, and Waiz-ul-Haqq. To avoid the revolt by directly arresting these people, Tayler, therefore, requested their presence, and the presence of others, to consult on the state of affairs. When the conference was over, he allowed the others to depart, but detained the three men, Shah Mohammad Hasan, Maulvi Ahmadullah, and Waiz-ul-Haqq, informing them that in the then-existing state of affairs, it was necessary that they should remain under supervision. They were conducted to a comfortable house near the Sikh encampment where suitable accommodation was provided for them.[35]

The arrest of the above Maulvis infuriated the people of Patna and consequently, Sir William Macnaghten was assassinated by Maulvi Mohammad Akbar Khan. It led to the arrest of Maulvi Mehdi. Tayler also ordered citizens of Patna to deliver up their arms, within twenty-four hours, and some were ordered to leave their homes after 9 o'clock at night on 20th of June 1857. In following days Maulvi Waris Ali was arrested at his own station, in Tirhut, under most suspicious circumstances. Upon his person was found a bundle of letters implicating him in the rebellious movement. Another one Maulvi Ali Karim, residing nine miles from Patna was also raided but escaped.[36]

Maulvi Yahya Ali was behind the scenes and away from the reach of the British. Kaye quotes the words of Sir Robert Edwardes, "The arch-offender was one Yahya Ali, high priest of Patna. It is proved against the prisoner that he has been the mainspring of the great treason which this trial has laid bare. He has been the religious preacher, spreading from his mosque at Patna, under the most solemn sanctity, the hateful principles of the Crescentade. He has enlisted subordinate agents to collect money and preach the Muslim *Jihad.* He has deluded hundreds and thousands of his countrymen into treason and rebellion. He has plunged the Government of British India, by his intrigues, into a frontier war, which has cost hundreds of lives. He is a highly-educated man, who can plead no excuse of ignorance. What he has done, he has done with forethought, resolution, and the bitterest treason."[37]

Maulvi Yahya Ali was found guilty of the charges framed upon him and was sentenced to death by Ambala Session Court in 1864. Hunter quotes the words about him, "that he was the mainspring of the great treason which this trial has laid bare. He has been the religious preacher, spreading from his mosque at Patna, under the most solemn sanctions, the hateful principles of the Crescentade. He has enlisted subordinate Agents to collect money and preach the Muslim *Jihad* (War against the Infidel). He has deluded hundreds and thousands of his countrymen into treason and rebellion. He has plunged the Government of British India, by his intrigues, into a Frontier War, which has cost hundreds of lives. He is a highly educated man, who can plead no excuse of ignorance. What he has done, he has done with forethought, resolution, and the bitterest treason. He belongs to a hereditarily disloyal and fanatical family. He aspires to the merit of a religious reformer; but instead of appealing to reason and to conscience, like his Hindu fellowcountrymen in Bengal, of the Brahma Samaj, he seeks his end in political revolution, and madly plots against the Government, which probably saved the Mohammadans of India from extinction, and certainly brought in religious freedom."[38]

However, in the Chief Court, his death sentence was changed to the punishment of transportation for life and confiscation of his property. He was transported to the Andamans accordingly and reached on the Island on 11th January 1866 along with Maulana Jafar Thanesari. His brother Maulvi Ahmadullah was eagerly waiting upon him on the port and received him very cordially. Maulvi Yahya Ali passed away at Ross Island during his imprisonment on 20th February 1868.[39]

Maulvi Ahmadullah

Maulvi Ahmadullah, the brother of Maulvi Yahya Ali was also of the same mentality and suffered the retribution of the British Government. Mr. Tayler, the Patna Commissioner arrested him in June 1857. However, after some time, Maulvi Ahmadullah was fondled by the Government officials of Bengal. Kay narrates that he might have been seen shaking hands at Belvedere with the Lieutenant Governor, in the presence of the Viceroy. It was said that the inoffensive Wahabi gentleman, whom Tayler had arrested, was a harmless "book-man".[40]

In 1864, Maulvi Ahmadullah, the official pluralist, high in honour, drawing the money of the State, could not save himself from the eyes of Captain Parsons. The good fortune, which had compassed him for so many years and enabled him to laugh at his enemies, would much longer sustain him in prosperity. Captain Parsons hunted down the Wahabis and found him guilty of making war against the British Government. Maulvi Ahmadullah was tried at Patna, before Mr. Ainslie, the Sessions Judge, and convicted mainly upon the evidence of one of his fellows, who had been tried and sentenced at Ambala. The Sessions Judge awarded the punishment of death; but the High Court commuted it to transportation for life and confiscation of property. So the honoured guest and favoured friend of the Patna Commissioner, and the Lieutenant Governor of Bengal was sent to the Andaman Islands on 15th June 1865 after one-year punishment in Patna.[41]

Maulvi Peer Ali Khan

Maulvi Peer Ali was born in 1820 in a village Mohammadpur in Azamgarh District of UP. His father's name was Mehar Ali Khan. As his economic position was not so good, Peer Ali left his house in the quest of knowledge or in disgust at the age of seven and reached Patna city. His biographer Khan Mohammad Sadiq Khan very beautifully mentions his migration that while going to Patna, he was tired and took the rest beneath a banyan tree and slept. He was suddenly woken up on hearing some noise. He saw that some armed men, and a palki (litter) were heading towards the tree where he was resting, he became fearful and climbed the tree. It was actually the Nawab Mir Abdullah, a zamindar and a very resourceful person of Azeemabad (Patna), along with his servants. Peer Ali observed the activities of the people very closely and after some time he saw that the servants of the Nawab were very nervous as he eagerly waited for *huqqah* and they were unable to serve it, because a broken part of a shrub stick was blocked in its pipe, and they had failed to remove it. Breaking his silence, Peer Ali offered his services for solving the problem on the condition that he would not be harmed. On getting assurance of Mir Abdullah for his safety, he came down the tree and after cutting a part at the edge of the pipe, he pulled the stick by teeth. Nawab Sahib was quite impressed by the intelligence of the boy. After inquiring about his background and reason of his presence in that secluded place, he took him to Patna and made necessary arrangement for his education along with his son Lutf Ali Khan under his care. In this way, he became educated in Urdu, Arabic, and Persian.[42]

Patna was the centre of Muslim clerics and the so-called Wahabi leaders. They were always subject to the alarm for the British administration. William Tayler, the Commissioner of Patna shows his suspicion regarding the Muslims of that area. He says, "The quarters from which as it appeared to me, immediate danger was to be apprehended, were three. Firstly, from the Wahabis of the city and the neighbourhood. Secondly, from the Lucknow immigrants and partisans, either permanently residing, or sojourning for a time in the city. Thirdly, from the thieves and scoundrels of the city, known by the term '*Budmashes*'." Maulvi Mohammad Hussain, Maulvi Waizul Haq, and Maulvi Ahmadullah were from the first category while Maulvi Peer Ali and Maulvi Lutf Ali Khan were belonged to the second.[43]

After completing his education, Maulvi Peer Ali opened a book shop in Patna with the support of his patron Mir Abdullah. He had imbibed the ideas of independence by reading the books which he used to sell. The conditions of dependence and slavery became unbearable to him. He placed himself in communication with the revolutionaries at Delhi and Lucknow. He imparted to others his passionate patriotism. Although, he belonged to a poor family and worked simply as a book-seller, he amazingly became the chief coordinator of the anti-British activities in Patna. Working from the same shop, his close associates carried on the regular campaign against the British Government and generated much heat among the local people against them. He collected together a large number of armed men with the help of the wealthy members of the secret society, and they were all sworn to rise against the British power at a given signal. His shop was actually a meeting place of the local revolutionaries who were planning against the British and channel of communication with the freedom fighters of other places and the Indian Sepoys working in the British army.[44]

Maulvi Peer Ali had, a close link with the Sepoys of Dinapur cantonment and collected arms from the aid of Maulvi Mehdi and other various sources and distributed among his followers. According to Khan Mohammad Sadiq Khan, he prepared a flag of white and blue colour for his followers, which was similar to the flag of Tipu Sultan, who had hoisted it at Sri Rangapatam fighting against the British. His close associates were Maulvi Karim, a rich zamindar of Dausi, Waris Ali, a British army officer of Tirhut, Maulvi Mehdi, a patrolling magistrate of Patna, Maulvi Yahya Ali, Imamuddin, Shaikh Ghulam Abbas, Budhan Jan, Ghasita Khalifa, Nandu Kahar, Ausaf Husain, and a number of Sepoys of the Dinapur cantonment. Besides, he was in regular touch with Maulana Masihuzzaman and Maulana Ahmadullah Shah Madrasi, the famous freedom fighters of the Awadh region and Maulvi Liaqat Ali of Allahabad.[45]

William Tayler mentions in his book that from the letters discovered in his house shows clearly that he was in correspondence with different parties, principally with Maulana Masihuzzaman of Lucknow and deliberately discussed and matured seditious plans against the British Government. He frequently called the public to fight for their '*Deen* (religion) and the Emperor of Delhi.' William Tayler writes that the letters found in Peer Ali's house shows the following important intentions:[46]

> "Firstly, that an anti-Christian crusade or *Futeh Ooper Nasara* (Victory over the Europeans). Secondly, that for the accomplishment of this object, it was understood and enjoined that all sects and classes, Hindus, Wahabis and even Faraizees, were to combine with the orthodox Mohammadans. Thirdly, that the arguments employed to excite the conspirators to action, are all based on the assumption, whether sincere or pretended, that the covert purpose of the British Government has been, for some years past, secretly to undermine and destroy the religion of the natives, whether Mohammadan or Hindu, and thus, many of the late orders, rules and regulations, the abolition of oaths, the new rules regarding the prisoners' food, the shaving of their beards, each and all of these

> matters were taken advantage of, and employed by the instigators of the insurrection, to exasperate the people, and seduce the army from its allegiance."

When the English smelt the suspicion of treason, the commissioner of Patna, Mr. Tayler, began a campaign of torture and oppression. Peer Ali's hot nature could not keep quiet. He could not bear to see the tortures of his countrymen, and therefore, he rose prematurely. In the evening of 3rd July 1857, Maulvi Peer Ali along with his close associates and around 200 followers, by shouting slogans marched towards Gulzar Bagh, the headquarters of the state administration. It was expected that help would come from Dinapur Sepoys but unfortunately, they could not revolt on that day and when their turn came on 25th of July, the brave leader Peer Ali was not there to command. In the way to Gulzar Bagh, the Peer Ali and his party came into confrontation with Dr. Lyell, the Deputy Opium Agent of the Patna Opium Agency, and a band of nine Sikh soldiers. On being attacked by the latter, the agitators got provoked and in the counter attack Dr. Lyell was killed. When Commissioner of Patna William Tayler came to know about this sudden happening of showing open defiance of the Government, he ordered a Sikh battalion of 150 men under Captain Rattray to rush to the troubled spot and crush turbulence. Subsequently, the British forces indiscriminately fired into the crowd, and this resulted in killing and injuring of a large number of people. Besides, the army unleashed terror in the city of Patna.[47]

Next day on 4th of July 1857, and the day following, the city was searched for the ringleaders of the outbreak. A lot of people were arrested including Maulvi Peer Ali, the actual leader, and Shaikh Ghasita, the confidential servant of Lutf Ali Khan, the richest banker in the city. Maulvi Peer Ali and Shaikh Ghasita were sentenced to death but remanded for three days for further examination. V.D. Savarkar describes that Peer Ali stood before the scaffold, with a heroic smile on his face, defying the death that was awaiting him. There was only a slight sob when he took the name of his beloved son. Immediately, the English officer, to take advantage of his emotion, addressed him these words: "Peer Ali, you might even now save your life by disclosing the names of the other leaders." Turning calmly to the Firangi, he replied in bold and noble words, "There are some occasions in life when it is desirable to save one's life—but there are some others when it is more desirable to sacrifice it. This moment is one of the latter kind, when to embrace death at once is the means of eternal life!" Then, describing in plain language the numerous acts of injustice and oppression committed by the English, the martyr dying for his people said, "You might hang me, you might hang other men like me; but, you cannot hang our ideal. If 1 die, thousands of heroes will rise out of my blood and will destroy your kingdom."[48]

After three days of remands and examination, Maulvi Peer Ali was hanged. Apart from Ali, sixteen more revolutionaries were hanged for their participation in the Patna Uprising another seventeen were imprisoned with hard labour, and two were transported to penal settlements.[49]

Maulvi Peer Ali was charged for promoting crusade against the English and also engaged in paying the numerous men who should be ready, when called upon, to fight for their religion and the nation. For those patriotic engagements to the nation, he was hanged but still alive in the hearts of millions of Indians. In this connection, the banker Lutf Ali was also arrested and charged for harbouring the mutinous Sepoys. Lutf Ali, however, acquitted by the judge on the ground of insufficient evidence, who promptly released, and shortly afterwards was welcomed and honoured as a martyr by the successor of Mr. Tayler. Thus, the outbreak was suppressed as it was premature. Malleson mentions that Maulvi Peer Ali had admitted that the strong measures of Mr. Tayler had compelled him to strike against the British Government. However, for those strong measures, the conspiracy would have been silently hatched until the outbreak at Dinapur should have given it the signal for explosion.[50]

John William Kaye, while describing Peer Ali, as brave and unscrupulous man who hated the English, charged him for plotting against the English since long and communicating with the seditious leaders of Delhi and Lucknow. Kaye quotes one of his letters of treasonable correspondence found while searching the house of Maulvi Peer Ali, "The state of affairs at Patna is as follows. Some respectable persons of the city are in prison, and the subjects are all weary and disgusted with the tyranny and oppression exercised by Government, whom they all curse. May God hear the prayers of the oppressed very soon!"[51]

Maulvi Peer Ali was charged with killing of Dr. Lyell with his own hands and waging war against the Crown. He was tried and sentenced to death. William Tayler himself narrates, "After capital sentence had been pronounced upon him, I sent for him (as I generally did with such criminals) and questioned him in my private room, in hopes of eliciting some further information regarding the plot. Heavily fettered, his soiled garments stained deeply with blood from a wound in his side, confronted with myself and several other English gentlemen, the last hope of life departed, not for a moment did he betray agitation, despondency, or fear. On being asked whether he could do anything to make it worthwhile to spare his life, he answered with supreme coolness and some contempt: 'There are some cases in which it is good to save life, others in which it is better to lose it.' He then taunted me with the oppression I had exercised, and concluded his speech by saying, 'You may hang me, or such as me, every day, but thousands will rise in my place, and your object will never be gained'."[52]

William Tayler continues in writing, "After this defiance, he joined his manacled hands, and said, with the utmost politeness, as if he was on the best of terms with himself, the world, and me, 'I have something to ask.' 'Well, what is it? Speak,' 'My house?' 'It will be razed to the ground,' 'My property?' 'It will be confiscated.' 'My children,' and here for the first time, his voice faltered and his tone betrayed emotion. On my asking him where his children were, he said they were in Awadh, and all I could tell him was, that, under the circumstances of that country, it was impossible to make either guess or promise in regard to them. He then salaamed, respectfully rose, on the order being given, and walked out unmoved, and, to all appearances, unconcerned." He was hanged in Patna on 7th July 1857. His house was razed to the ground, and his property was confiscated.[53]

William Tayler, distinguished for his sadistic brutality, describes him, "Peer Ali himself was a model of the desperate and determined fanatic; repulsive in appearance, with a brutal and sullen countenance, he was calm, self-possessed, and almost dignified, in language and demeanour."[54]

William Tayler, writing of Peer Ali's valiant conduct on the eve of his execution, was forced to remark: "...he is the type of a class with many of whom we have, in this country to deal, men whose unconquerable fanaticism renders them dangerous enemies and whose stern resolution entitles them in some measure to admiration and respect"![55]

Sher Ali Afridi

Sher Ali Afridi belonged to Tirah Valley in Khaiber Agency. He had served as a cavalry trooper at Peshawar and later on mounted as orderly for Reynell Taylor, who had rewarded him with 'a horse, a pistol and a certificate'. He was sentenced for life in the Penal Colony in connection with the murder of a man named Haider a resident of Kadam, near Peshawar, in broad daylight. By nature, Sher Ali was a kind man, but a family feud had brought him to this situation. Sher Ali was a man who gave great respect to everybody. His overall nature was well cultured even after receiving the death penalty. His death penalty was switched to deportation to Kala Pani, when he made an appeal. In 1869, he reached the Andaman Islands to serve his sentence. Here in Penal Colony he was in constant touch of Wahabi activist and Ulema like Maulana Jafar Thanesari, Maulvi Yahya Ali and Maulvi Ahmadullah of Patna. It is said that he was greatly influenced with the Wahabi ideology.[56]

During his stay in Andaman jail, the money that he earned while serving in the jail he always gave away to other poor prisoners as charity. Moreover, every second or third month, he provided some food for the orphaned prisoners as well. The officers never strictly monitored his activities because of his charitable nature. In the Andaman, he was appointed as a barber for the labourers in the Islands.

Lord Mayo, the Viceroy of India was very cautious about the Wahabi activity in the Frontiers and other parts of India. At the time of his Viceroyalty, the *Mujahideen* of Frontier Province were continuously fighting against the British Government. During the same time, Mr. Norman, the Chief Justice of Bengal, was also assassinated by the Wahabis. So Lord Mayo was very harsh to the Wahabis and committed to eliminate the Wahabis from India. It was also notable that the Wahabi group in Andaman Islands was deadly against the Viceroy Lord Mayo in connection with his policies against them. It was also certain that the Wahabis as a whole were anti-British due to their oppressive policy against Muslims who participated in the Uprising of 1857. Conversion of Delhi into a ghost city, entirely cleansed by the Muslims by the end of September 1857, was another reason of grave enmity. Due to all the above reasons, a Wahabi *Mujahideen* Sher Ali Afridi, imprisoned in the Andaman Islands, intended to kill any high-ranking British official but destiny fixed the name of Lord Mayo.

It was reported to Lord Mayo that the prisoners of the Andaman Islands are in very miserable condition. In this connection Lord Mayo had ordered some reformations in the harshness and treatment meted out by the prisoners. He lightened the hard labour and improved the habitation of the prisoners of the Islands. For the personal inspection of his reformations in the prison colony of Islands, Lard Mayo fixed his Viceregal visit to Port Blair[57] on 8th February 1872 where he was assassinated by that valiant Pathan, Sher Ali Afridi.[58]

The caravan of Lord Mayo departed from Calcutta on 24th January 1872, by two ships, "Glasgow" and "Dhaka." The Viceroy was lodged in "Glasgow". He first reached Burma at the end of January and on hearing the satisfactory position at the Frontiers, he ordered to sail for Andaman Islands and reached the sea port of the Hope Town at Port Blair on the morning of 8th Februáry, 1872. Lord Mayo started his inspection in tight security. He read the applications of the prisoners and assured justice for them. He also passed some orders related to the prisoners. He was not in favour of tight security and thought that the time of death of everybody is fixed and at that appointed time, no security can change the happening. There was the example of Mr. Norman, the Chief Justice of Bengal, who was killed in tight security a few weeks ago. At the evening, he enjoyed the scenic beauty of the sun set, and commented that he had never seen such a beautiful scene until today. After sun set he turned towards the port and in order to reach the "Glasgow", he embarked on the board ship "Rule Brittania." The moment the Viceroy stepped on the board ship, Sher Ali attacked him with a sharp knife and wounded his shoulder. The Viceroy left the world after a few minutes, and the security embarked the dead Viceroy Lord Mayo from "Rule Brittania" to the "Glasgow" where his wife was eagerly waiting.[59]

Sher Ali was again tried for murder and was given the death penalty once again. At his trial when asked if he had anything to say in his defence, Sher Ali replied that he had nothing to say further than that the judge had heard the evidence and might decide as he wished, and that when the account was made in the next world, the judge would then know. He added that he did not care to beg for his life or words to that effect, but that on the day when he was going to be hanged, he gave the statement that he had waited for almost all day near the small ship which the Viceroy was about to board. By asking about who had hired him to do this job. He simply replied that, "I killed him by the Order of Allah!" He said that he had no associate in his crime, but that God was his partner. During his trial, Sher Ali admitted that part of his motivation arose from the act of his brother (religious brother not real) Ábdullah, who had assassinated Mr. Norman, the Chief Justice of Bengal.[60]

It is said that on the 11th March 1873, when he was brought to the gallows, there was a look of satisfaction in his eyes. He kissed the rope from which he would be hanged and addressed the Muslims, who had come to watch the penalty being enforced, "Brothers, I have killed your enemy. You witness that I am a Muslim." With this, he recited the Kalma *Shahadah*. Twice he was able to complete it. The third time, he was not able to do so because of suffocation.[61]

British Action against the Frontier Tribes

Even after the big assault of 1858, and death of their cherished leader Maulvi Wilayat Ali and Inayat Ali, the Wahabis did not lose their heart, and continued their struggle under the newly appointed leaders. They continued to recruit their fighters from the Muslim cities in the Punjab, Bihar, and Bengal. The Wahabis of plains supplied them men and money to carry on *Jihad* against the British. After the death of Maulvi Maqsood Ali in 1861, Maulvi Abdullah continued the fight and in 1863, they boldly occupied Sitana. The British tried a lot to suppress the Wahabis with thousands of reinforcement, but their attacks were thwarted successfully. On 16th of December, British forces cunningly won over the Bonair tribe which proved serious blow to the Wahabi forces. Some other tribes of the area also followed the same. On the guidance of the Bonair tribe, the British forces completely routed their centre Malka. The remaining forces of the Wahabis under Maulvi Abdullah rushed into the mountains of Afghanistan in order to prepare for another war. The British attempt to attack on Malka and series of arrests in the plains, achieved nothing beyond uniting the Pathan tribes against the British and raising the Wahabis' prestige as champions of Islam.[62]

The Wahabis still held hold at Ambeyla Pass, a mountainous region of frontier, and had support of a lot of tribes of the area. The Afghan tribes under the influence of Wahabis were bitterly against the British. However, it was the prestige issue for the mighty British Government to suppress these Afghan tribes. On the 18th October 1863, a British Army of 7000 men, under General Sir Neville Chamberlain, moved out to the Ambeyla Pass. The fighting men against the British were around 53,500, including the men among the tribes, Husainzai, 2000; Akazai, 1000; Chigazai, 6000; Madakhail, 4000; Amaz, 1500; Jaduns, 4000; Khuddkhail, 2000; Bonaire, 12,000; Bajaure, 3000; Ranizai, 2000; Dher Clan, 6000; Swat tribes, 10,000. Keeping in view of the strength of the tribals, the British were further reinforced with around 2000 men but could not dare to advance the fanatic colony Malka; although, they repulsed the small skirmishes and night attacks. Nevertheless, they could not sustain in the daily attack and met the heavy loss. It was the 25th December, perhaps due to the tricks; the British were able to turn back most of the tribes, and finding the situation in their favour; they advanced and burned the Ambeyla village.[63]

About this campaign, Hunter writes, "The coalition dissolved like a mountain mist, and the Bonair tribes, on whom the Rebel Settlement had chiefly depended, entered into an engagement with us to burn the Fanatics in their den. In less than a week a strong British brigade, reinforced and guided by the Bonairs, advanced in perfect safety through the mountains to the Fanatical Settlement at Malka, and reduced it to ashes. The force returned to the ill-fated Ambeyla Pass on the 23rd December, and on the 25th, the whole Army once more reached the plains, not a shot being fired on its homeward march. Meanwhile we had left the fatal Defile thickly planted with the graves of British soldiers. Our loss amounted to no less than 847 men killed and wounded, or close on one-tenth of the total strength of the Army when it was eventually raised to 9000 Regular Troops."[64]

After the victory in the mountains, the British started a suppressive measure in the plains of India during 1860s and 1870s. A number of leaders were condemned to death, subsequently commuted to transportation for life on the Andaman Islands, and others sentenced to various terms of imprisonment. This suppressive measure did not stop the Wahabi activity, and they renewed their fight with a new strategy. Regarding the Wahabi persecution, two famous trials were held, first at Ambala in 1864 and other at Patna in 1865. The first was presided over by Sir Herbert Edwardes, before whom eleven prisoners were brought charged with attempting to wage war and abetting the waging of war against the Queen. Five of these prisoners were the residents of Patna.

On 20th September 1871, the British Acting Chief Justice, John Norman, on his way into court to preside over a Wahabi trial in Calcutta, was stabbed to death by a Wahabi follower Pathan named Abdullah, who went to the gallows without giving a coherent account of his motives. It was an alarm for the British that there is the possibility of the expected disaster recurring, especially since the trials in India of leading Wahabis found to be preaching *Jihad* and violent overthrow of the colonial Government had only recently been concluded.[65]

After the assassination of Lord Mayo, the Viceroy by a Wahabi convict Sher Ali at Port Blair, vigorous measures were taken by the British to eliminate the Wahabi elements. The ruler of Swat, in accordance with his understanding with British, also expelled the Indian fanatics from his territories. By 1883, the

Wahabi Movement had been thoroughly suppressed and after 1884, little was heard of it.

REFERENCES

1. Mohammad ibn Abdul Wahab Najdi, belonging to Banu Sinan, a branch of Tamim, was born in 1703 at Uyaina, a place now in ruins. He studied at Madina under Sulaiman al-Kurdi and Mohammad Hayat al-Sindi. Later, he spent many years in travels, four years in Basra and five years in Baghdad, one year in Kurdistan, two years in Hamdan and four years in Isfahan, where he studied the Mystic and Ishrakiya philosophy. Returning to Uyaina, he spent about a year in speculation. Thereafter, he publicly preached his doctrines as set forth in his Kitab al-Tauhid. Due to the opposition from his own relatives he left along with his family his ancestral place and was received at Dariya, where the Chieftain Mohammad bin Saud accepted his doctrine and undertook its propagation. In 1765, Ibn Saud died and was succeeded by his son, Abdul Aziz, who retained Mohammad ibn Abdul Wahab Najdi as his spiritual guide. The Wahabi Theology is mainly based on the teachings of Ibn Taimiya and its jurisprudence on the Hambali Fiqh. They called themselves as Mowahideen and criticized the cult of saints and condemned the visits to tombs. The aim of Mohammad ibn Abdul Wahab Najdi was to do away with all the innovations. They believe that all the objects of worship other than that of Allah are false. According to them, it is polytheism to seek intercession from any person except Allah. They destroyed tombs and graves, even at Jannat-ul Baqi, lest these may be worshipped by the non-orthodox and ignorant Muslims. He died in 1787, and the Saud family conquered the whole Saudi Arabia till 1804 including the Holy cities of Mecca and Medina. But it was checked by Mehmet Ali of Egypt and in 1813-1830, no Wahabi was dared to walk freely in the streets of Holy cities. (Ahmad, K.J., *100 Hundred Great Muslims*, San Francisco, 1987, pp. 305-306 and Hunter, William Wilson, *The Indian Musalmans*, London, 1876, pp. 55-59 & 108, hereafter cited as *The Indian Musalmans*).
2. Tariq, Shamim, *Ghalib, Bahadur Shah Zafar aur 1857*, New Delhi, 2008, pp. 22-23.
3. Tayler, William, *The Patna Crisis; or, Three months at Patna, during the Insurrection of 1857*, London 1858, pp. 45-47, hereafter cited as *The Patna Crisis*, (Wahabism, as Sir Syed Ahmad Khan describes,

is a system which reduces the religion of Mohammad to a pure theism, i.e., to what Islam was in the days of Mohammad, before it was encrusted with its present forms and ceremonies by medieval and modern Muslims. As Graham quotes Sir Sayed, "In the second century of the Hijra it was divided into four Churches; Hanafi, Shafai, Malki, and Humbali; and it was for some time after optional for Mohammadans to follow any doctrine of any of these four Churches. The kings Bani Umaiya and Bani Abboo, however, issued an edict that all Mohammadans were to embrace the whole doctrines of any one Church of the above four; and by this unjust order, free opinion was summarily suppressed, and religious intolerance gained supremacy. A few, however, clung to the former, the true faith, and they were called Ahal-i-Hadis, i.e., believers in the sayings of the Prophet. They were hated and held up to the execration of the faithful, and this continued till the beginning of the seventeenth century AD; Abdul Wahab of Najd then ascended a throne of his own making, and spread the doctrine of the Shah-i-Hadis. His successor being denied leave to perform the pilgrimage to Mecca, marched on and conquered both Mecca and Medina, abolished all the forms and ceremonies with which pure Mohammadanism had become encumbered, and destroyed the tombs of saints which were worshipped as idols. He was defeated by the Turks, and compelled to retire; and the Mohammadan world being deeply grieved at the—in their opinion—sacrileges perpetrated by the Ahal-i-Hadis, a bitter enmity sprang up between the Turks and them, and they were then called Wahabis. In India, Wahabis could only worship and preach with great danger to themselves; but on the advent of the English rule they came to the front and preached openly and fearlessly. The Indian Mohammadans, however, hated them as cordially as the Turks did, and also called them Wahabis." Graham, G.F.I., *The Life and Work of Sayed Ahmed Khan*, Edinburgh, 1885, pp. 211-212).

4. Shah Waliullah was born in 1703 A.D. His father Shah Abdur Rahim was a great Sufi saint and his grandfather Shaikh Wajihuddin was the Mughal courtier. Shah Waliullah received his early education from his illustrious father, who was his teacher as well as his spiritual guide. He committed the Holy Quraan to memory at an early age of 7 and started teaching in his fathers' Madarsa Rahimiya at the age of 17. Shah Waliullah came to Mecca on Hajj in 1730, when he was 27, and then spent 14 months studying in Medina. First among his teachers was Shaikh Abu Tahir Mohammad ibn Ibrahim al-Kurani al-Madani, a renowned teacher

of Hadith. During his stay at Mecca, Shah Waliullah had a dream in which the Holy Prophet commanded him to work for the organisation and emancipation of the Muslim community in the subcontinent. He, therefore, returned to Delhi on July 9, 1732 and started his work in real earnest. His was an uphill task in a period when Muslim India was passing through the most critical phase of its history and its entire social, political, economic, and spiritual fabric was torn to pieces. On his arrival in Delhi, he started training pupils in diverse branches of Islamic learning and entrusted them with the Missionary work of enlightening people with the true nature of Islam. Shah Waliullah, a great intellectual reformer, whose teachings paved the way for the renaissance of Islam in India, both in religious and political spheres. Shah Waliullah very first time translated the Holy Quraan into Persian. He embarked upon the task of producing standard works on Islamic learning and, before his death in 1762, completed a large number of outstanding works on Islam. Shah Waliullah was followed in his noble mission by his son Shah Abdul Aziz of Delhi and his disciple Sayyad Ahmad Barelvi, assisted by his associates. (Ahmad, K.J., *100 Hundred Great Muslims*, San Francisco, 1987, pp. 297-298 & 307).

5. *World Policy Journal*, (*The Hidden Roots of Wahhabism in British India*- Charles Allen), Vol. 22, No. 2, Massachusetts, USA, Summer 2005, p. 88.
6. Shah Abdul Aziz, the eldest son of Shah Waliullah was born in 1746 in Delhi. He was only 17 years old when Shah Waliullah died and he took over as the teacher of Hadith in place of his father. At that time he became an expert in the sciences of tafsir, hadith, fiqh, Usul al Fiqh, Aqaid, mantiq, kalam, maths, history, geography etc. He later on became famous as the Muhaddith of Delhi and one of India's greatest Islamic scholars. Shah Abdul Aziz was the most learned Islamic theologian in India, and his views on Muslim law were accepted by all parties among the Sunnis. Unlike most Muslims during this period, he recognized the value of learning English, and displayed no bitterness toward the British. In his later years he adopted the anti-British attitude and in 1803 he declared India as *Darul Harab* (abode of infidel). Shah Abdul Aziz planted the seeds of antagonism agaist the British. He was the first Alim in India who passed the Fatwa on the validity of *Jihad* against the British and their supporters in India. Unlike his father he preached ideas among the common people and youths. He created a group of youths including Shah Mohammad Ismail, Shah Abdul Hai, Shah Mohammad Ishaq, Maulana Mohammad Yaqub, and his

own brothers Shah Rafiuddin, Shah Abdul Qadir, Shah Abdul Ghani. (Tariq, Shamim, *Ghalib, Bahadur Shah Zafar aur 1857*, New Delhi, 2008, p. 21, and *Ulema of Deoband*, Abdul Hamid Ishaq, Madarsa Arabia Islamia, Azaadville, South Africa, 2011, p. 8).

7. *World Policy Journal*, (*The Hidden Roots of Wahhabism in British India*- Charles Allen), Vol. 22, No. 2, Massachusetts, USA, Summer 2005, p. 88, see also, *Indian Musalmans*, p. 142.
8. Ahmad, K.J., *100 Hundred Great Muslims*, San Francisco, 1987, pp. 307-308.
9. *Indian Musalmans,* p. 13.
10. *Ibid.*, pp. 54-55.
11. Ahmad, K.J., *100 Hundred Great Muslims*, San Francisco, 1987, p. 308.
12. *Indian Musalmans,* p. 53.
13. Bakshi, S.R. & Chaturvedi, Ritu, *Bihar Through the Ages*, Vol. 3, New Delhi 2007, p. 296.
14. *Dawn*, Karachi, 26 January, 2008.
15. Ahmad, K.J., *100 Hundred Great Muslims*, San Francisco, 1987, pp. 309-310, see also, *Indian Musalmans,* pp. 15-17.
16. *Ibid.*, pp. 310-311, see also, *World Policy Journal,* (*The Hidden Roots of Wahhabism in British India*- Charles Allen), Vol. 22, No. 2, Massachusetts, USA, Summer 2005, p. 91.
17. Allen, Charles, *God's Terrorists: The Wahabi Cult and the Hidden Roots of Modern Jihad,* Massachusetts, USA 2006 p. 97.
18. Bakshi, S.R. & Chaturvedi, Ritu, *Bihar Through the Ages*, Vol.3, New Delhi 2007, pp. 300-301, see also Malleson, George Bruce, *History of the Indian Mutiny of 1857-58, Commencing from the Close of the Second Volume of Sir John Kaye's History of the Sepoy War*, Vol. III, (Contemporaneous with Sir John Kay's Third Volume), London, 1878, p. 647.
19. *Ibid.*, pp. 301 & 303, see also Malleson, George Bruce, *History of the Indian Mutiny of 1857-58, Commencing from the Close of the Second Volume of Sir John Kaye's History of the Sepoy War*, Vol. III, (Contemporaneous with Sir John Kay's Third Volume), London, 1878, p. 647.
20. *World Policy Journal,* (*The Hidden Roots of Wahhabism in British India*- Charles Allen), Vol. 22, No. 2, Massachusetts, USA, Summer 2005, p. 91 see also Allen, Charles, *God's Terrorists: The Wahabi Cult and the Hidden Roots of Modern Jihad,* Massachusetts, USA 2006 p. 98 (On 10 September 1853, Colonel Frederick Mackeson, Commissioner of Peshawar and thus the most senior official on the NWFP in the Punjab, had been stabbed by a tribesman whilst

working on his papers on the veranda of his bungalow. The man had approached him with a petition, and when Mackeson took it to read, the assassin stabbed him in the breast with a dagger. Colonel Mackeson died four days later. At his interrogation and trial, the assassin was said to come from a village in Swat, then outside British control. The assassin said that the deed was done to prevent invasion of his land; he was identified in the official report of the incident as a 'religious fanatic' intent on martyrdom. He was tried and hanged as a common criminal; his ashes were thrown into the river in an attempt by the authorities to prevent the aura of martyrdom accruing to him the perception of him as a martyr. *The International Journal of Asia Pacific Studies*, (*The Assassination of Lord Mayo: The 'First' Jihad*- Helen James), Vol. 5, No. 2, 1–19, 2009, Penang, Malaysia, p. 12).

21. Bakshi, S.R. & Chaturvedi, Ritu, *Bihar Through the Ages*, Vol.3, New Delhi 2007, p. 305.
22. *Ibid.*, p. 306.
23. *Indian Musalmans,* p. 24.
24. Frazer, R. W., *British India*, New York 1896, pp. 318-319, see also *World Policy Journal,* (*The Hidden Roots of Wahhabism in British India*- Charles Allen), Vol. 22, No. 2, Massachusetts, USA, Summer 2005, p. 92, and *Indian Musalmans,* pp. 24-26.
25. *Indian Musalmans,* p. 90.
26. *The Annual of Urdu Studies,* (*Kaala Paani: Twarikh-e Ajib*, Mohammad Jafar Thanesari, Eng. Tr. S. Kamal Abdali), Vol. 26, Madison, USA, 2011, p. 172.
27. *Ibid.*, pp. 173-176, see also, *Indian Musalmans*, p. 87.
28. *Ibid.*, pp. 176-178.
29. *Ibid.*, p. 184 (The Judge, Sir Herbert Edwardes, died from pneumonia three and a half years later and the sentence of death of Maulana Thanesari was converted into life imprisonment and later on released.).
30. *Ibid.*, p. 185.
31. *Ibid.,* pp. 188 and 190-192, see also *Indian Musalmans*, pp. 84-85.
32. *Ibid.*, pp. 200-204.
33. *Ibid.*, p. 213.
34. *Indian Musalmans*, p. 92.
35. Malleson, George Bruce, *History of the Indian Mutiny of 1857-58, Commencing from the Close of the Second Volume of Sir John Kaye's History of the Sepoy War*, Vol. III, (Contemporaneous with Sir John Kay's Third Volume), London, 1878, p. 52.
36. *Ibid.*, pp. 53-54.

37. Kaye, John William, *A History of the Sepoy War in India, 1857-58,* Vol. III, London 1876, pp. 166-167.
38. *Indian Musalmans*, pp. 93-94.
39. *The Annual of Urdu Studies,* (*Kaala Paani: Twarikh-e Ajib*, Mohammad Jafar Thanesari, Eng. Tr. S. Kamal Abdali), Vol. 26, Madison, USA, 2011, pp. 191 and 202.
40. Kaye, John William, *A History of the Sepoy War in India, 1857-58,* Vol. III, London 1876, p. 167.
41. *Ibid.*, pp. 167-169 see also *The Annual of Urdu Studies,* (*Kaala Paani: Twarikh-e Ajib*, Mohammad Jafar Thanesari, Eng. Tr. S. Kamal Abdali), Vol. 26, Madison, USA, 2011, p. 191.
42. Khan Mohammad Sadiq Khan, *Excavation of Truth- Unsung Heroes of 1857 War of Independence*, New Delhi, 2007, p. 20.
43. *The Patna Crisis*, pp. 44, 45 and 49.
44. Savarkar, p. 261.
45. Khan Mohammad Sadiq Khan, *Excavation of Truth- Unsung Heroes of 1857 War of Independence*, New Delhi, 2007, pp. 11 and 106, see also *Islam and Muslim Societies- A Social Science Journal*, (Zafarul Islam- Book Review, *Excavation of Truth- Unsung Heroes of 1857 War of Independence* by Khan Mohammad Sadiq Khan) Vol. 4, No. 1, New Delhi, 2011.
46. *The Patna Crisis*, pp. 68-69.
47. Malleson, George Bruce, *History of the Indian Mutiny of 1857-58, Commencing from the Close of the Second Volume of Sir John Kaye's History of the Sepoy War*, Vol. III, (Contemporaneous with Sir John Kay's Third Volume), London, 1878, pp. 55-56, see also Martin, R. Montgomery, *The Indian Empire,* Vol. II, London, 1858, p. 399.
48. Savarkar, p. 261.
49. *People's Democracy*, (Ram swaroop- *Some Aspects of the 1857 Rebellion in Bihar*), Vol. XXXI, No. 18, May 6, 2007 (Mohammad Sadiq Khan writes that under the order of the Commissioner, twenty one were hanged and twenty three were imprisoned. Peer Ali's shop and house were broken open thoroughly searched and arms, bundle of letters along with English fencing mask were found and seized. For three days, he was interrogated and tortured to obtain information about conspiracy and details of his close associates, especially but Maulvi Peer Ali Khan did not open his mouth even on the allurement by Tayler to spare his life if he gives full details of his associates. Khan Mohammad Sadiq Khan, *Excavation of Truth- Unsung Heroes of 1857 War of Independence*, New Delhi, 2007, p. 110. Another historian Martin writes that thirty men, said to be concerned in the outbreak, were arrested and tried by the

commissioner and the magistrate, Mr. Lowis (who was subsequently removed from office by Mr. Tayler, for not seconding with sufficient energy his anti-native proceedings). Fourteen of the prisoners, including Peer Ali, (who is said to have shot Dr. Lyell), were condemned to death, and executed the same day; the remaining sixteen were sentenced to ten years' imprisonment. Martin, R. Montgomery, *The Indian Empire,* Vol. II, London, 1858, p. 399).

50. Malleson, George Bruce, *History of the Indian Mutiny of 1857-58, Commencing from the Close of the Second Volume of Sir John Kaye's History of the Sepoy War*, Vol. III, (Contemporaneous with Sir John Kay's Third Volume), London, 1878, pp. 57-58.
51. Kaye, John William, *A History of the Sepoy War in India, 1857-58,* Vol. III, London 1876, p. 85.
52. *Ibid.*, p. 86, see also *The Patna Crisis*, p. 66.
53. *Ibid.*, see also *The Patna Crisis*, p. 67.
54. *The Patna Crisis*, p. 66.
55. *People's Democracy*, (Ram swaroop- *Some Aspects of the 1857 Rebellion in Bihar*), Vol. XXXI, No. 18, May 6, 2007.
56. *The International Journal of Asia Pacific Studies*, (*The Assassination of Lord Mayo: The 'First' Jihad-* Helen James), Vol. 5, No. 2, 1–19, 2009, Penang, Malaysia, p. 10.
57. Port Blair was situated on the east coast of South Andaman Islands, was one of many fine harbours in the Andaman and Nicobar Islands, a fact that attracted the British to it in the late 18th century when they were establishing a global chain of strategic outposts from which to thwart French pretensions to naval supremacy. First selected in the memorable year of 1789 by Lieutenant Blair as the place for a settlement, it was deserted in 1796 because of malaria and the hostility of the indigenous people and remained unoccupied until 1858, when the fallout from the Indian Mutiny the previous year meant that the British authorities in India decided Port Blair would be an ideal location to send mutineers. The first batch of 200 prisoners arrived at Port Blair in January 1858. The convicts were divided into 6 classes, according to circumstances and character, and were distributed in the various islands and localities of the harbour. The worst characters were kept at Viper and Ross Islands. At the time of the ill-fated visit by Lord Mayo on 8th February 1872, there was a population of just over 8,000 residents at the penal colony, 7,000 of whom were convicts, around 900 females. A detachment of British Infantry, a wing of Native Infantry, and a body of 200 Police were also stationed at the

Settlement. (*The International Journal of Asia Pacific Studies*, (*The Assassination of Lord Mayo: The 'First' Jihad*—Helen James), Vol. 5, No. 2, 1-19, 2009, Penang, Malaysia, p. 6).

58. *Ibid.*, see also *Taameer-i-Haryana, (Jab Kala Pani Lord Mayo Ka Maqtil Ban Gaya*—Sayyad Asim Mahmood), Chandigarh, July-August, 2012, p. 36.
59. *TaAmeer-i-Haryana, (Jab Kala Pani Lord Mayo Ka Maqtil Ban Gaya-* Sayyad Asim Mahmood), Chandigarh, July-August, 2012, pp. 36-40.
60. *The International Journal of Asia Pacific Studies*, (*The Assassination of Lord Mayo: The 'First' Jihad-* Helen James), Vol. 5, No. 2, 1-19, 2009, Penang, Malaysia, p. 10, see also *Islamic Voice* (*Sher Ali Khan: A Forgotten Revolutionary-* Zubair Ahmed), Bangalore, March 2006
61. *Islamic Voice* (*Sher Ali Khan: A Forgotten Revolutionary-* Zubair Ahmed), Bangalore, March 2006.
62. *Indian Musalmans*, p. 27, see also Bakshi, S.R. and Chaturvedi, Ritu, *Bihar Through the Ages*, Vol. 3, New Delhi 2007, pp. 307-308.
63. *Ibid.*, pp. 30-38.
64. *Ibid.*, pp. 38-39.
65. *The International Journal of Asia Pacific Studies*, (*The Assassination of Lord Mayo: The 'First' Jihad-* Helen James), Vol. 5, No. 2, 1-19, 2009, Penang, Malaysia, p. 2.

Chapter 4

Faraizi Movement

The Faraizi Movement was started by Haji Shariatullah of Bengal just a few years after the martyrdom of Tipu Sultan. This movement was intended to follow the basic tenets of Islam or its fundamental duties (Faraiz), or rejection of all glosses and non-essential parts of Islam, reform in the society and more importantly to fight for independence from the British. In 1843, the Faraizi Movement attained such a dangerous position for the British Government, Hunter mentions that the Bengal Police reported that a single one of their preachers had gathered together some eighty thousand followers, who asserted complete equality among themselves, looked for the cause of each as that of the whole sect, and considered nothing criminal if done in behalf of a brother in distress. The Wahabi leaders, especially Yahya Ali, amalgamated the Faraizis of Lower Bengal with the Wahabis of Northern India. Hunter further writes, "during the past thirteen years they have been found side by side alike among the dead on the field of battle, and in the dock of our Courts of Justice."[1]

Haji Shariatullah

The founder of this movement, Haji Shariatullah, an eminent Islamic scholar of India, was born in 1781 in Faridpur of East Bengal in an ordinary farmer family. After attaining his early education from his village, he performed the Haj at the age of

18 in 1799 and resided in Mecca for about twenty years for the cause of his study. He studied in Madarsa al Rahimiya in Mecca and learnt Arabic and Persian from his teacher Maulana Basharat. It is likely that he was influenced with Wahabism, prevalent during that time in Mecca. After his return from Arabia in 1818, he saw Islam being crushed gradually from Bengal and his people downtrodden by Hindu and British landlords. He launched a movement to reform the religion as well as the society. Its chief aim was to remove un-Islamic practices from the Muslim society as well as to revive and restore Muslim rule once again by expelling the Christians from India. So this movement was strongly religious as well as political in character.[2]

During the passage of time, the Muslims became superstitious and gone astray. Islam was being invaded by non-Islamic religions, traditions, customs, and cultures. He asked the Bengali Muslims to give up un-Islamic customs and practices and to act upon the commandments of the religion called Faraiz or duties. Hence his followers came to be known as Faraizi. He called upon the Muslims to give up the Shii and Sufi Saint worship, forbade Tazia on the occasion of Moharram and singing and dancing at the time of wedding ceremonies. He also taught that Muslims should not perform communal prayers (Eid and Friday) as long as they did not have a legitimate Muslim ruler to govern them.[3]

Faraizi movement was also directed against the oppression of the Zamindars as well as the British planters. At that time, the condition of the Bengali Muslims in India was very miserable. The British agricultural and economic policies were having devastating effects upon the livelihood of the farmers and indigenous textile industry. British policy of distrust and oppression towards the local population which was mostly Muslims had grown restive under the British administrations' explosive land and taxation policies that favoured the British and Hindu landholders. Under them, the Muslims were economically and educationally crippled; and the oppression of the zamindars made their lives unbearable. Under these circumstances, the Faraizi Movement made a protest against the Hindu landlords and the British planters of indigo. Haji Shariatullah urged them to reject forced labour and not to pay their taxes. It was an attempt to free common people and farmers from oppression, injustice, and the atrocity of landlords. This movement declared a war against untouchability and discrimination on the basis of caste, creed, and colour as they were against the tenets of the Holy Quraan. The movement showed the light of hope to establish the democratic rights of the exploited people in Bengal. These reformist policies of the Faraizis made them most popular among the general masses and had its consolidating base among the backward and downtrodden people because of its teaching of equality.[4]

Haji Shariatullah also turned his movement against the British by calling *Jihad* against the British. He declared the country as *Dar ul-Harb* (abode of Infidels) and said that in this position, Eid and Friday prayers could not be offered. He said that it was an obligation on the part of all to wage a war against the British. With the announcement of this decree of war, more people, especially farmers and labourers joined the movement. Thus, he sowed the seeds of independence in Bengal. These activities of Faraizi Movement greatly alarmed the Hindu and British landlords, and eventually they exiled Haji Shariatullah to Nawabganj on the charge of spreading protest and disturbance in East Bengal. Later, he died in Dhaka district in 1840.[5]

Dadu Miyan

Haji Shariatullah was succeeded by his son Mohammad Mohsin, affectionately known as Dadu Miyan (1819-1862). He spent five years for schooling at Mecca. In 1838 he was called back due to his father's illness. He continued the Faraizi movement after his father's death in 1840. He was more learned and active in the movement than his father. Dadhu Mian popularized and strengthened the movement by organizing it in a systematic way. He divided the East Bengal into areas he called circles and appointed khalifas for each of them. The khalifas kept him informed about everything in their jurisdiction and were made responsible for all the social, political, and religious developments. He acquired great influence among the Muslim peasants and craftsmen of Bakarganj, Dhaka, Faridpur, and Patna districts. Dadu Miyan also declared India as *Dar-ul-Harb* as long as ruled by non-Muslims such as British and came into open clashed with the British authorities. He gave a new slogan *Al-Arzallah* (Allah's earth) and declared that nobody could rule it by virtue of legacy. He said that the British rulers had no right to collect taxes from farmers and appealed the people to resist the Government and landlords collecting the unjust taxes.[6]

Due to his anti-British policies, Dadu Miyan was implicated into many false cases, time to time, but he was always released and declared innocent. He was charged with house theft in 1838 and murder in 1841. He was arrested for holding public meeting without permission in 1844 and also arrested in the false charges of kidnapping and murder in 1846. During the Uprising of 1857, he was put under arrest for organizing the peasants of Faridpur districts against the British Government. He was set free from jain in 1861 and subsequently died in 1862 at Dhaka.[7]

Titu Mir

There was another movement working in Bengal at the time of Haji Shariatullah. Although it was not called as Faraizi Movement but it had the same goal as of Haji Shariatullah. It was led by a Muslim theologian Sayyad Mir Nisar Ali popularly known as Titu Mir. He also rebelled against the zamindars and British colonial system and put up an impressive armed resistance. Sayyad Mir Nisar Ali was born on 27 January 1782 in a small village named Chandpur, in the North 24 Parganas district of West Bengal. He was a good boxer, and family disturbances and a boundary dispute landed him in jail. After his release from the jail in 1822, Titu Mir went on Haj to Mecca where he met with Maulvi Sayyad Ahmad Barelvi. He took perhaps some guidance from the devout Maulvi and after returning from Pilgrimage, he devoted himself to the cause of his country.[8]

He took the cause with the peasants, who were oppressed by Hindu landlords. Among those landholders, one Krishna Chandra Rai, a large landholder levied a capitation tax of five shillings on each of his peasants who had embraced the new faith. Another proprietor threw one of his peasants into his private prison for destroying a shrine during the Moharram. Titu Mir organised the

Muslim peasants of his native village against the oppressing landlords who were generally Hindus and the British colonialists. Titu Mir opposed a number of discriminatory measures in force during that time which included taxes on keeping beards.[9]

As the rift between Titu Mir and local zamindars supported by the British rulers continued to widen, the armed conflict broke out at several places. Titu Mir prepared his men and trained them with martial art of the quarterstaff fighting hand to hand combat and the use of the bludgeon (lathi). His followers started physically attacking the zamindars and their followers and organized several armed loot and plunder in order to finance their movement. As his followers were mostly peasants, they stole horses from the stables of the zamindars and from the British Police Stations. The followers of Titu Mir were about 15,000 in number and on the 23d October 1831, the insurgents picked out a strongly situated village Narikelbaria, near the town of Barasat for their Headquarters, and erected a bamboo stockade (fort of bamboo) around it. He defeated the zamindar Krishna Roy Purwa and proclaimed the extinction of the English Rule and the re-establishment of the Muslim Power with his capital at Narikalbaria. The regions comprising the current districts of 24 Parganas, Nadia and Faridpur were under his control. The private armies of the zamindars and the forces of the British met by a series of defeats at the hands of his men as a result of his strike-and-retreat guerrilla tactics.[10]

The anti-British activities of Titu Mir provoked the British Government to send an expedition of 7,000 Sepoys to bring his followers under control. The British forces, armed with cannon and muskets, mounted a concerted attack on 14th November 1831, on Titu Mir and his followers. Within the couple of hours, the British were forced back. On the 17th November, the Magistrate got together some reinforcements, but the *Mujahideen* under Titu Mir met them, drawn up in the battle array a thousand strong, and chased the party to its boats on the river cutting down those who were slowest in the retreat.[11]

After a series of defeat of the British, it now became necessary to deal with the *Mujahideen* by Regular troops. A body of Native Infantry, with some Horse Artillery, and a detachment from the

Body Guard, hurried out from Calcutta. The *Mujahideen* under Titu Mir, disdaining the safety of their stockade, met the troops upon the open plain. A stubborn engagement decided their fate. According to Hunter, they were driven back pell-mell into their entrenchment, and the fortified camp was taken by storm. Titu Mir, the leader, fell during the action. Of the survivors (350 in number), 140 were sentenced by the Court to various terms of imprisonment; and one of them, Titu's lieutenant, was condemned to death.[12]

Muslim Discontent Against the British

In the Uprising of 1857, initially the Sepoys took the commands which were mostly Hindus of high caste by religion but within no time, the leadership shifted to the Muslim elites and even the Muslim masses took active participation throughout the northern and central India. The Uprising took a new turn when the literate Muslims, particularly the class of Ulema appealed the Muslim masses to wage a *Jihad* against the British infidels, to save their religion, and avail the opportunity of martyrdom.

Here the discussion needs the clear analysis that why the Muslims as a whole (leaving the few exceptions) arrayed against the British. Whether Islam religion was really in danger? Whether there was a need of *Jihad* against the British? Whether the Muslims in common were denied from their religious practices under British rule?

In order to get the answers of the above questions, there is a need of looking back history of the Indian Muslims. Initially, under the Muslim rulers (although the Islamic rule was not imposed), Muslim clerics were enjoying high Government posts, tax free lands, and a lot of unlimited rights. When British established their rule over Indian subcontinent, these high profile Muslims were denied from almost every right which they were enjoying since long.

According to William Wilson Hunter, "The educated Mohammadan, confident in his old training, sees himself practically excluded from the share of power and of the emoluments of Government which he hitherto had almost monopolized, and sees these and all the other advantages of life passed into the hands of the hated Hindu." While assessing the Muslim discontent, Hunter also blames the current modern system, which was responsible for completely excluding these Muslim elites from the mainstream. He further says, "But, indeed, from the highest official to the lowest, there is now a firm conviction that we have failed in our duty to the Mohammadan subjects of the Queen. A great section of the Indian population, some thirty millions in number, finds itself decaying under British Rule. They complain that they, who but yesterday were the conquerors and governors of the land, can find no subsistence in it to-day." Hunter also considers the Muslim intelligentsia responsible for not properly availing the opportunity provided by the Government. He says, "For this decay we are not entirely to blame. The Musalmans can no longer, with due regard to the rights of the Hindus, enjoy their former monopoly of Government employ. This ancient source of wealth is dried up, and the Mohammadans must take their chance under a Government which knows no distinction of colour or creed."[13]

The decaying position of the Muslims in every field was a matter of discussion among the Europeans and subsequently Bengal Government appointed a commission to enquire the Muslim participation in the English education and the Government services. The commission found that the Muslim element in the public service had gone on growing weaker every year, just as before.

William Wilson Hunter gives the following statistics to prove the deteriorating condition of the Muslims:[14]

> "In the highest grade in which the appointments dated from a previous generation, the Mohammadans had not much to complain of, as in April 1869 there was one Musalman to two Hindus; there is now but one Musalman to three Hindus. In the second grade there were then two Mohammadans to nine Hindus; there is now one Musalman to ten Hindus. In the third grade there were then four Musalmans to a total of twenty-seven Hindus and Englishmen; there are now three Musalmans to a total

> of twenty-four Hindus and Englishmen. Passing down to the lower ranks, there were in 1869 four Musalmans among a total of thirty of all creeds; there are now four among a total of thirty-nine. Among the probationers from whom the service is recruited, there were only two Musalmans in a total of twenty-eight; there is now not a single Mohammadan in this rank."

Hunter gives the statistics of lesser conspicuous departments in 1869,

> "In the three grades of Assistant Government Engineers there were fourteen Hindus and not one Musalman; among the apprentices there were four Hindus and two Englishmen, and not one Musalman. Among the sub-Engineers and Supervisors of the Public Department there were twenty-four Hindus to one Musalman; among the Overseers, two Musalmans to sixty-three Hindus. In the Offices of Account there were fifty names of Hindus, and not one Musalman; and in the Upper Subordinate Department there were twenty-two Hindus, and again not one Musalman."[15]

As Hunter has shown the above statistics, the proportion of Muslims to Hindus, was less than one-seventh. The proportion of the race which a century ago had the monopoly of Government, was fallen to less than one-twenty-third of the whole administrative body (Hindus and Europeans). Hunter says that in one extensive department the other day it was discovered that there was not a single employee who could read the Musalman dialect; and, in fact, there was scarcely a Government office in Calcutta in which a Muslim could hope for any post above the rank of porter, messenger, filler of inkpots, and mender of pens.[16]

It was really a grave situation for the Muslims to survive the system, which the British Government had imposed in India. The Muslims were bound to think about the old glorious days in which they were happy and prosperous. They considered the British system was brutally against the Muslims and tried to root out from India when they find chance during the Uprising of 1857. As the every aspect of life of a true Muslim was associated with their religion, they turned their struggle to the religious fold and issued many religious decrees to cover the entire Muslim population in this war against the infidel foreigner. Through this platform of Uprising, the Muslims used the weapon of *Jihad* and free the Indian subcontinent from the British control.

REFERENCES

1. *Indian Musalmans*, p. 100.
2. Campo, Juan Eduardo, *Encyclopedia of Islam*, New York, 2009, p. 226.
3. *Ibid.*
4. *Ibid.*, see also Tabassum, Farhat, *Deoband Ulema's Movement for the Freedom of India*, New Delhi, 2006, pp. 12-13.
5. Tabassum, Farhat, *Deoband Ulema's Movement for the Freedom of India*, New Delhi, 2006, p. 13.
6. *Ibid.*
7. *Ibid.*
8. *Indian Musalmans*, p. 45, see also Tabassum, Farhat, *Deoband Ulema's Movement for the Freedom of India*, New Delhi, 2006, p. 14.
9. *Ibid.*, see also Tabassum, Farhat, *Deoband Ulema's Movement for the Freedom of India*, New Delhi, 2006, p. 14.
10. *Ibid.*, p. 46, see also Tabassum, Farhat, *Deoband Ulema's Movement for the Freedom of India*, New Delhi, 2006, p. 14.
11. *Ibid.*, p. 47.
12. *Ibid.*
13. *Ibid.*, pp. 151-152.
14. *Ibid.*, p. 168.
15. *Ibid.*, pp. 168-169.
16. *Ibid.*, p. 170.

CHAPTER 5

Role of Ulema in the Uprising

The Uprising or war of 1857 was fought under the name of protection of religion and nation. Therefore, Muslims and Hindus both participated in this war and the Ulema led the revolt in various places. During the Uprising of 1857, the Ulema all over India particularly North India, waged a Holy War against the British. They issued the Fatwa of *Jihad* against the English, practically participated during the war, encouraged the *Mujahideen,* and led the revolutionary insurgents.

Most of the Ulema of that time were inspired by the teachings of Shah Waliullah as well as the Wahabi ideology. They remained on the forefront of Uprising and faced tremendous hardships at the hands of the rulers after the end to the war. In the events of 1857, a large number of Ulema issued Fatwa declaring *Jihad* against the infidel foreigners. A large number of Ulema were executed, and many of them were exiled to the Islands of Andaman for long spells of imprisonment at the end of the war.

It has already been said that the Ulema class was in the war with the British from many decades under the banner of Wahabis and Faraizis. However, when the British atrocities became unbearable in the fifties of the nineteenth century, the senior Ulema of India convened a meeting in 1856 to discuss the current grave situation of India. The Ulema, who attended the meeting, were Maulana Jafar Thaneseri, Maulana Wilaayat Ali, Haji

Imdadullah, Maulana Mohammad Qasim Nanautwi, Maulana Rashid Ahmad Gangohi, and Hafidh Mohammad Dhamin etc. In this meeting Maulana Nanautwi said, "Are you not aware that the British are sitting on our heads? They have laid their snare throughout the country. Be prepared for decisive battles. We shall either be cut to pieces or fight them to the end. We shall not allow the British to occupy this country."[1]

The meeting resulted in the organizing of the Muslim masses very effectively. The Ulema all over north India responded to the call and waged their war against the British. The most prominent Ulema who played the pivotal roles in the revolt of 1857, were Mohammad Baqar and his son Mohammad Hussain Azad, Maulana Ahmadullah Shah Madrasi, Mufti Sadruddin Azurda, Allama Fazle Haq Khairabadi, Maulana Faiz Ahmad Badayuni, Maulana Kifayat Ali Kafi Moradabadi, Maulana Wahajuddin Moradabadi, Mufti Inayat Ahmad Kakorvi, Moulana Rahmatullah Kairanvi, Maulana Dr. Wazir Khan Akarabadi, and Maulana Imam Baksh Sahbai Dehlavi etc. Although, they were not having sufficient arms to fight against the British who were armed with most modern weapons, even so, they had courage and belief in God which the enemy didn't possess. The poet Allama Iqbal captures the emotion:

> "*Momin hai to be tegh bhi larta hai sipahi*"
> (A true Muslim will fight; even he does not possess a sword).

After the failure of the Uprising, the British retribution started and thousands of Ulema were either hanged or burnt alive. According to sources dealing with the revolt, around fifteen thousand Ulema were martyred during the war. The British practically eliminated all the Ulema of India. By 1867, not a single Madrasa remained. In 1601 when the British first arrived in India, there were about one thousand Madrasas in Delhi alone. But the British did not leave a single Madrasa in the entire India. Madrasa Rahimiya, the Madrasa of Shah Waliullah Dehlavi was bulldozed into the ground by the English.

Maulvi Mohammad Baqar

Maulvi Mohammad Baqar, the father of, the Urdu poet and critic, Mohammad Husain Azad, was a Shia theologian of Delhi. He was a pioneer journalist and outspoken editor of '*Dehli Urdu Akhbar*' founded in 1839. He echoed this vision in slightly different and more explicitly Islamic language. Through this newspaper, he took active part in the Uprising of 1857. He called to the people to rise against the foreign rule and also published a pamphlet '*Risala-i-Jihad*' in which he called for a Holy War against the British to drive them out of India. He built a mosque known as Khojoorwali Masjid in Chhota Bazaar near Kashmiri gate in Delhi. After the fall of Delhi in September 1857, he was captured and shot dead by Major Hodson.[2]

At the outbreak of the Uprising, in May 1857 he wrote in his columns how the rebellion had been sent by God to punish the *Kafirs* for their arrogant plan to wipe out the religions of India. For him, the speed and thoroughness of the reverses suffered by the British was proof of miraculous divine intervention. Maulvi Mohammad Baqar quotes a dream of a person as follows:[3]

> "Our Prophet Mohammad (Praise Be Upon Him), said to Jesus that your followers have become an enemy of my name and wish to efface my religion. To this Lord Jesus replied that the British are not my followers, they do not follow my path, they have joined ranks with Satan's followers... Some people even swear that the day the troopers came here, there were camels (*Sandnis*-female bull) ahead of them on which rode green-robed riders... These green riders instantly vanished from sight and only the troopers remained, killing whichever Englishman they found, cutting them up as if they were carrots or radishes... Truly the English have been afflicted with divine wrath by the true avenger. Their arrogance has brought them divine retribution for, as the Holy Quraan says, God does not love the arrogant ones."

Through the writings in his *Dehli Urdu Akhbar*, he always

encouraged the revolutionaries of the Uprising. Apart from the encouragement, Maulvi Mohammad Baqar applauded the revolutionaries to bolster mutual solidarity and follow the instructions of central commanding forces during the war. He endeavoured to infuse loyalty to the Emperor there by invoking centripetal tendencies and joint action. He boosted the morale of the revolutionaries by calling them *Sipah-i-Hindostan* (the army of India) and appealed to 'fellow countrymen' (*ahli watan*) to rally in a united way against the British. He urged the Muslims to see through the light of the Quraan, and the Hadith and Hindus in the light of their own wisdom, Gyan, and dharma, (faith) to see that except God Almighty, nothing is permanent. Baqar made exemplary efforts to quote examples of great figures from history and mythology, epics and legends in order to inspire Hindu and Muslim solidarity during the war.[4]

Maulvi Mohammad Baqar whose bold and prompt reporting had unnerved the British in the course of the war was arrested on 15th September 1857 and shortly executed by Major Hodson without any proper trial.

Maulana Fazle Haq Khairabadi

Maulana Fazle Haq Khairabadi (1791-1861) was the son of Allama Fazle Imam Farooqi Khairabadi, the *Sadrus Sudoor* of Delhi. Allama Fazle Haq received his education in Islamic sciences from Shah Abdul Qadir and Shah Abdul Aziz, the *Muhaddith* (expert of the traditions of Prophet), of Delhi and in rational sciences from his father. At the age of 13, he completed his education and engaged himself in teaching. Then he took up service of the Government in 1815.[5]

Maulana Fazle Haq Khairabadi was a renowned philosopher, poet, religious scholar, but was most remembered as a freedom fighter. He was very close to the court of Mughal Emperor Bahadur Shah Zafar. He joined the services of the Nawabs of Jhajjar, Rampur, and Tonk and also served the Raja of Alwar. Finally, he went to Lucknow and became the *Sadrus Sudoor* and *Mohtamim-i-Huzoor-i-Tehsil* (official in charge of a tehsil). He also held a post of *Sar-Rishtadar* (an official) in Delhi and a similar post at Saharanpur.[6]

It is said that Maulana Fazle Haq Khairabadi was in conflict with other factions of the Ulema like Sayyad Mazhar Nabi and Noor Ahmad and jailed in 1851, and released in 1856. After his release he came in contact of Maulvi Ahmadullah Shah Madrasi who was already secretly engaged in the war against the British. Maulana Fazle Haq Khairabadi was very much influenced by the ideas of Maulvi Ahmadullah Shah Madrasi and fully engaged himself in the work of *Jihad* against the British. He toured the areas of Alwar, Mewat and Delhi and prepared a lot of freelancers against the British Government which were utilised in the Uprising of 1857.[7]

When the revolt broke out in 1857, he made his regular visit of Delhi from Alwar. On the arrival of General Bakht Khan along with his fourteen thousand soldiers from Bareilly to Delhi, Maulana Fazle Haq Khairabadi delivered a speech in front of the Ulema in the Jama Masjid after the Friday prayer. He prepared the decree *Jihad* which was signed by 35 renowned Ulema, including the Chief Qazi. As soon as the Fatwa was published, disturbance and tumult intensified throughout the country and as a result some ninety thousand Muslim freelancers gathered in Delhi. A British spy Turrab Ali wrote to his masters on 28th August 1857 as follows:[8]

> "Maulavi Fazle Haq is busy in instigating the citizens and Sepoys right from his advent in Delhi. He propagates that he had read a British Government proclamation from Agra Gazette that the Army was ordered to massacre the entire citizen of Delhi and dismantle the city in order to tell the future generation that there was a city inhabited on that place. Only one minaret of Jama Masjid will be spared."

After regaining control over Delhi by the British, Maulana Fazle Haq, following the other revolutionaries, also left Delhi and went to Awadh to continue the war. However, unfortunately, Maulana Fazle Haq Khairabadi was arrested and presented in front of the joint bench of Judicial Commissioner of Awadh, Mr. Campbell, and Judicial Commissioner of Khairabad

Division on 4th March 1859. On their decision they charged him as follows:[9]

1. He was the leader of the revolt during 1857-58 and instigated the people of Delhi, Awadh and other areas to revolt and murder.
2. In May 1858 he actively participated, in a meeting, with Mammu Khan, revolutionary leader of Bundi, and in the intention to murder he issued a religious decree

On 4th March 1859, the above said joint bench gave its decision to confiscate the property of Maulana Fazle Haq Khairabadi and sentenced him for life imprisonment in Andaman Nikobar popularly known as Kala Pani. His library was confiscated and brought to Calcutta. During his stay in prison, Maulana Khairabadi met a few Ulema like Mufti Inayatullah Kakorvi, Mufti Mazhar Karim Daryabadi, etc., who were already in the prison. He wrote two classical books in Arabic in the prison titled "*Al Sauratul Hindiya*" and Qasidas "*Fitnatul Hind*" on Indian Uprising. Qasidas "*Fitnatul Hind*" includes two qasidas, one "*Qasida Hamzia*" and the other "*Qasida Dalia*". These books are the best writings on the topic of Indian Uprising by any Indian Islamic scholar. These books particularly deal with the socio-economic conditions at that time, the cruelties committed by the British on Indian population and also the British plan to convert Indian people to Christinaity.[10]

It is said that Maulana Fazle Haq Khairabadi issued the famous Fatwa of *Jihad*. However, some scholars have doubted over his role in that very Fatwa. They take the plea that the Fatwa had the signature of 35 Ulema but there is no signature of Maulana Fazle Haq Khairabadi over it. Neither Maulana Fazle Haq Khairabadi had any mention of that Fatwa of *Jihad* in both his books "*Al Sauratul Hindiya*" and "*Fitnatul Hind.*" Contrary to this point Maulana Fazle Haq Khairabadi was always loyal to the British Government prior to the revolt of 1857 and even opposed the Ulema like Maulana Shah Ameer Ali, who was waging *Jihad* on the murder of 269 Muslims in Hanuman Garhi Ayodhya Mosque in 1855.[11]

It is also believed that Maulana Fazle Haq was imprisoned due to the crime committed by another Alim Fazle Haq Shahjahanpuri. The kinsmen of Maulana Fazle Haq Khairabadi appealed before the court to prove his innocence and at last became successful. His son Maulvi Shamshul Haq went to Andaman Nikobar with the order of release, but unfortunately, he reached when Maulana Khairabadi died on 20th August 1861, and his burial ceremony was being performed in the nearby area around the prison. Maulvi Shamshul Haq also attended the *Namaz-e-Janaza* of his father Maulana Fazle Haq Khairabadi.[12]

Maulana Fazle Haque Khairabadi writes in his '*Qasida Hamzia*, "O Allah fullfil my wishes and don't delay to release me from the enemies. I goaded the idle men to fight and when the war started I myself sat idle. I avoided such opportunities due to my laziness. I made a big crime of not responding when the virtuous people called me for sacrifice. I could not attain the martyrdom while the obedient people martyred (drink the *Jame Shahadat*).[13]

In his '*Al Sauratul Hindiya*, Maulana Fazle Haq Khairabadi writes, "The English prepared a scheme to Christianize all inhabitants of India. It was their belief that the Indians would not be able to find the help and cooperation from any class in this regard and therefore, would submit and obey, and they would not have the nerve of defiance. The English had thoroughly realized that the ruler's variance from the ruled based on religion, would be a great stumbling block in the way of domination and possession. Hence they began to indulge in all sorts of wiles and chicanery with complete diligence and assiduity, in their wilful attempt to obliterate religion and the sense of nationhood. To teach small children and the ignorant and to inculcate their language and religion, they established schools in towns and villages and made an all-out-effort to wipe out the old sciences and academic attainments."[14]

Maulana Fazle Haq Khairabadi was one of the first political prisoners of colonial times, who was, until the Uprising, in the Government job and resigned subsequently from the post of *Sadrus Sudoor* and *Mohtamim-i-Huzoor-i-Tehsil*. Maulana Fazle Haq Khairabadi is said to have not only issued a decree of *Jihad* against the British, but also had drafted the first constitution of independent India based on the principles of democracy under which the administrative council was running under Mughal Emperor Bahadur Shah Zafar during the Uprising.

Mufti Sadruddin Azurda Dehlavi

Mufti Sadruddin Azurda Dehlavi (1789-1868) was an accomplished Islamic Scholar and a renowned poet of Delhi whose ancestry was traced back to his Kashmiri forefathers. He received education from Hazrat Shah Abdul Aziz, the *Muhaddith* of Delhi. He was the Sadr Amin from 1827 to 1846 and *Sadrus Sudoor* from 1846 to 1857 in Delhi. Being a *Sadrus Sudoor* of Delhi under the English Government was the highest post for any Muslim, particularly an Alim.[15]

Maulana Abul Kalam Azad's father, Maulana Khairuddin Dehlavi and his grandfather, Shaikh Mohammad Hadi Dehalvi were Mufti Sadruddin Azurda Dehlavi's disciples. Yousuf Ali Khan, the Nawab of Rampur was also one of his disciples. The founders of Darul Uloom Deoband, Maulana Qasim Nanotvi and Maulana Rasheed Ahmad Gangohi, were also the disciples of Mufti Sadruddin Azurda Dehlavi. Mughal Emperor Bahadur Shah Zafar donated Madarsa Darul Baqa to Mufti Sadruddin Azurda Dehlavi and Mufti Azurda started teaching work in that madarsa. Madarsa Darul Baqa was established by Mughal Emperor Shahjahan, which was rendered desolate and deserted by the vagaries of time.[16]

Mufti Sadruddin Azurda Dehlavi gave a letter to Maulana Ahmadullah Shah Madrasi and sent him to Agra in 1846 where the latter formed the "*Majlis-i-Ulema*" (The Council of Ulema) and launched the campaign of purging India from the cruel hands of English. During the Uprising, Mufti Sadruddin Azurda Dehlavi was actively engaged in the war against the British, and he was one of the signatories on the religious decree or Fatwa, which was said to be issued by Maulana Fazle Haq Khairabadi. During the course of Uprising, Mufti Sadruddin Azurda kept visiting Bahadur Shah Zafar in the Red Fort, and the revolutionaries or *Mujahideen* came into his house for instructions and consultations.[17]

After failure of the Uprising and recapturing of the power by the British, a case was filed against him, and he was tried before a court for rebellion. He was imprisoned after the court's trial and after a great deal of pleadings, he was acquitted. However, a large part of his property was confiscated. He was most active in Delhi for the restoration of the religious places which were deliberately occupied and abused by the British, after the recapture of Delhi. The British also turned the great Delhi Jama Masjid into a stable. Mufti Sadruddin Azurda Dehlavi, along with the dignitaries from the city, made constant efforts for its evacuation and restoration. Consequently, the English according to an agreement evacuated the Masjid in November 1863. Mufti Sadruddin Azurda Dehlavi was 81 when he breathed his last in Delhi on 16th July 1868, and buried in Chiragh Dehli.[18]

Maulvi Ahmaddullah Shah Madrasi

Dilawar Jang Maulvi Ahmaddullah Shah Madrasi alias Ziauddin (1787-1858), born with the name Saiyyad Ahmad Ali Khan was the son of Mohammad Ali, the Nawab of Chinyapattam in the district of Poornamalli (Madras). He was the grandson of Nawab Umdat-ul Mulk Ameer-ul Hind Walajah Bahadur of Carnatic. He received the best education that was available at the time. He completed studies in classical languages and traditional Islamic sciences. As a prince he also received intensive training in the art of warfare. In the prime of his youth, he was inclined to saintly life and mysticism. He left his house at the age of 16 and after visiting Hyderabad and Madras, he traveled to England and Arabia. He also went to Egypt and Hajaz. After performing Hajj, he came back to India via Turkey, Iran, and Afghanistan. He became a disciple of Saiyyad Furqan Ali Shah, a saint of the Qadri order at Sambhar (Rajasthan) and remained with his pir for some time. It was by his *Peer* that he was called 'Ahmadullah Shah', a title by which he became known afterwards. He met Mehrab Shah Qalandar Gwaliori who granted him the Khilafah and ordered him to free India from the slavery of the English. Thus, he left Gwalior for Delhi in around 1846.[19]

In Delhi, he met the leading Ulema and Mufti Sadruddin

Azurda, who expressed his opinion, and advised him to go to Agra to make better and effective preparations for such a campaign. After reaching Agra, he met prominent scholars and leading personalities. His influence increased day by day. He formed a Council of the Ulema to unite and organize them. These Ulema, later on, proved helping hands to him. Maulvi Madrasi also visited Meerut, Patna, Calcutta, etc. besides Delhi and Agra and thus widened the scope of this campaign against the English. He visited different parts of the country and instigated people for the Revolt. It is said that during his travels, he formulated the novel scheme known as the Chapati Scheme. It was devised to disseminate the message amongst the rural population of the North India that a great Uprising would take place on the first favourable opportunity. The circulation of chapatis from hand to hand was easy and not likely to cause any suspicion.[20]

He was the most influential personality and Indian people, both Hindus and Muslims, had full faith in his command. In Savarkar's words, "Wherever this political saint went there was seen an extraordinary awakening among the people... He was loved by the masses in Awadh." Thus, he worked incessantly, preaching freedom and the destruction of the British power. Sayyed Zaheer Hussain Jafri writes that Ahmadullah Shah has won universal praise by modern writers who have studied this short but heroic phase of India's resistance against colonial domination. Historian R.C. Majumdar and political analyst V.D. Savarkar have used superlatives to describe his role. Tara Chand, S.N. Sen, Syed Moinul Haq, Abrar Husain Faruqi and Ghulam Rasul Mehr and also a host of Urdu writers have praised his leadership qualities.[21]

From Agra, he was followed by his disciples, moved to Lucknow perhaps in November of 1856. His arrival at the city was reported in the weekly newspaper of Lucknow, '*Tilism*', on 21st November, 1856, in the following manner:[22]

> "These days a person called Ahmadullah Shah in disguise of a faqir but having all the paraphernalia of royalty has arrived in the town... People... visit him in a large number on Mondays and Thursdays to take part in mystic

> gatherings (*majlis-i hal-o-qal*). A number of feats are performed at these gatherings...Such display takes place every morning and evening for the masses..."

On 30th January, 1857, the newspaper *Tilism* reported:[23]

> "Ahmadullah Shah... is very fearless in saying whatever he wishes to say and a large crowd is always there... Although he is unable to do anything, orally he always pleads for *Jihad*."

The British were also not behind in praising his great personality. They described him as tall, lean, and muscular, with large deep-set eyes, beetle brows, a high aquiline nose, and lantern jaws. Thomas Seaton described him, "as a man of great abilities, of undaunted courage, of stern determination, and by far, the best soldier among the rebels."[24]

In Lucknow, his call for *Jihad* was leaked to the British and this time the Kotwal (a police official) was sent asking him to give up the call of *Jihad* and to surrender his arms and ammunitions. Finally, Maulvi Ahmadullah Shah was forced to leave the town and go wherever he wanted along with his arms. Then Maulvi Ahmadullah Shah traveled to Bahraich and in the way he halted at Faizabad where he continued with his preaching of *Jihad*. Hardly, two or three days had passed that the authorities got alarmed, and the officer in charge of the city issued the necessary orders for his arrest. After Maulvi Ahmadullah Shah's refusal, an infantry company attacked them. Ultimately, Maulvi Ahmadullah Shah was arrested and after a brief trial, he was awarded the death sentence. He was imprisoned in the district prison at Faizabad but all of a sudden rebellion broke out on June 8, 1857 at Faizabad, and the rebellious Sepoys released him from the prison.[25]

About Maulvi's release, Malleson has very beautifully described, "But, before the sentence could be executed, Oudh broke into revolt, and, like many a political criminal in Europe, he stepped at once from the floor of a dungeon to the footsteps of a throne. He became the confidential friend and adviser of the Begam of Lucknow, the trusted leader of the rebels." At that time,

Faizabad was well protected by the British troops. The troops here consisted of a horse battery of native artillery, the 22nd Regiment of Native Infantry, the 6th Awadh Irregular Infantry, and a squadron of the 15th Irregular Cavalry; the whole commanded by Colonel Lennox, of the 22nd Native Infantry. Notwithstanding the heavy garrison, the Sepoys revolted and along with the people from that area chosen Maulvi Ahmadullah Shah as their leader; he commanded both the Hindus and the Muslims of that region.[26]

He joined Begum Hazrat Mahal, the ex-Queen of the imprisoned Nawab Wajid Ali Shah of Awadh, in fighting against the colonialists. Both the Begum and the Maulvi led the rebel soldiers against the English in the battlefield. Maulvi Ahmadullah Shah Madrasi fought pitched battles against the English at Lucknow, Faizabad, and Shahjahanpur. In the battle of Chinhat, he was a commander of forces and planned attacks against the British. This battle began when the British made their surprise attack in the morning of June 30, 1857. This battle ended after the defeat of the British. This battle was the most significant battle that Maulvi Ahmadullah Shah fought during his life time.[27]

After the battle of Chinhat, many people believed him invincible. Maulvi Ahmadullah Shah won universal praise. Maulvi Ahmadullah Shah emerged as perhaps the only visionary praised even by the British. The nobility of his character made both the Muslims and the Hindus accept him as the definite leader. His brilliant mind and tactical skills, which were proven during the Uprising, allowed him to succeed in all that he did. And, his virtues of chivalry and humanism make him one of the greatest visionaries to have ever lived.

Begum Hazrat Mahal, Maulvi Ahmadullah Shah, General Bakht Khan, Nawab Tafazzul Husain, Shahzada Feroz Shah, Nawab Ismail, Dr. Wazir Khan, Maulvi Faiz Ahmad Bareilvi, and Peshwa Nana Sahib gathered in Shahjahanpur after the capture of Fatehgarh by the British on 14th Jan, 1858. From thence they dispersed due to the arrival of the British force. Nana Sahib arrived at Shahjahanpur on 11th March, 1858, with 4,000 infantry and cavalry, encamped near the church in Dunday Bagh, and finally went to Bareilly on 24th March, 1858. Maulvi Ahmadullah Shah also fled towards Bareilly and from thence came to

Mohammadi, a few miles away from Shahjahanpur, with his companions, and declared himself an independent ruler. The coronation took place on 15th March, 1858, and he issued coins in his name. The *Khutba* (A Sermon from the Pulpit) of his name was also read. These verses were written on his coin:[28]

> "*Sikka zad bar haft kishwar khadim- i- Mehrab Shah*
> *Hami-i-din-i- Mohammad Ahmad Ullah Badshah*"
> (The slave of Mehrab Shah struck his Coins in the seven countries; the supporter of faith of Mohammad is King Ahmadullah)

Even after shifting himself at Mohammadi, Maulvi Ahmadullah Shah was continuously fighting against the British. He fought the battles such as Battle of Kankar, 6th April, 1857; Battle of Bachpooriya, 28th April, 1858; Battle of Sirsi, 22nd May, 1858; Battle of Hathaura, 18th May; Battle of Banni, 24th May, 1858; and Battle of Puwanyan, 8th October 1858.[29]

After victory at the Battle of Bachpooriya, on 28th April, 1858, he left for Bareilly leaving Colonel Hale at Shahjahanpur until 2nd May, 1858. On 3rd May, Ahmadullah Shah entered the city and suddenly attacked on the British camps and seized the city and Shahjahanpur fort. Nevertheless, after taking over the control of Bareilly, Sir Collin Campbell reached Shahjahanpur on 18th of May, and fought the Battle of Hathaura. After this battle, Maulvi Ahmadullah Shah fled to his kingdom, Mohammadi. At Mohammadi, he also joined the leaders like Azimullah Khan, Prince Feroz Shah, Nawab Bahadur Khan of Bareilly and Ismail Khan along with 16,000 people. Here at Mohammadi, Maulvi Ahmadullah again organized himself and established his formal Government. General Bakht Khan became his Wazir (Prime Minister). Maulvi Sarfaraz Ali Jaunpuri became his Qazi-ul-Quzzat (Chief Qazi) and Nana Sahib Peshwa was made Diwan (Chief Revenue Officer). The other members of the council were Maulvi Liaqat Ali Allahabadi, Dr.Wazir Khan Akbarabadi, Maulvi Faiz Ahmad Badauni, and Shahzada Feroz Shah.[30]

Maulvi Ahmadullah Shah created so much terror by his activities in the hearts of the English that Lord Canning had to offer a reward of Rs. 50,000 on his head. The Imperial proclamation, about the reward over his head, was as follows:[31]

> "It is hereby notified that a reward of Rs. 50,000 will be paid to any person who shall deliver alive, at any British Military post or camp, the rebel Moulvee Ahmed Molah Shah, commonly called "the Moulvee". It is further notified that, in addition to this reward, a free pardon will be given to any mutineer or deserter, or to any rebel, other than those named in the Government Proclamation No. 476 of the lst instant, who may so deliver up the said Moulvee".

Sir Collin Campbell attacked Mohammadi on 24th May, 1858, and Battle of Banni fought in which Maulvi Ahmadullah Shah was defeated. He left Mohammadi and wanted help from Raja Jagannath Singh of Puwanyan, which was situated just 25 miles away north-east of Shahjahanpur. The Rajah of this place was supposed to possess a certain amount of influence, and it was the Maulavi's object to induce him and others to join in a new league against the British. According to Mallesan, Raja Jagannath Singh was a fat unwieldy man, not given to martial feats, desirous to sit at home at ease, and particularly anxious to avoid giving offence to the British in the hour of their triumph. He, however, consented to grant the Maulvi a conference. Upon this the Maulavi pushed on to Puwanyan. On 5th June, 1858, Maulvi Ahmadullah Shah appeared in Puwanyan and went to the fort of the Raja riding on an elephant. The Raja shut the door and hid with his servants. Ahmadullah Shah dealt a few blows on the gate with his elephant. In this crisis, the Raja's brother Baldev Singh, inspired by the urgency of the occasion, seized a gun and shot the Maulavi dead. His followers at once turned and fled. The Raja's brother Baldev Singh cut off the Maulavi's head, and wrapping it in a cloth, drove to Shahjahanpur, thirteen miles distant. He placed it before the Collector G.P. Maney and received the reward. Maulvi's head was hanged at the gate of Kotwali, and the corpse was burnt.[32]

The murder of Maulvi Ahmadullah Shah was of course a treachery. It is said that the Raja had promised that when the

British army will face the Maulvi's forces, he would support Ahmadullah Shah along with a contingent of four thousand soldiers. However, the Raja acted on the instance of the British and got cash reward of Rs. 50,000. The martyrdom of Maulvi Ahmadullah Shah put an end to the war of independence not only in Awadh but in the whole country also. Although the revenge war continued for some time in Awadh and Rohelkhand it soon ended with despair.[33]

To take revenge for the hanging of the Maulvi Ahmadullah Shah, as Savarkar states, Nizam Ali Khan marched up to Pilibht; Khan Bahadur Khan with four thousand men ran into the field of action; the Farrukhabad men rose taking five thousand followers; Vilayat Shah took three thousand men to the field and, with five thousand men, Nana Sahib, Bala Sahib, Ali Khan Mewati, and other leaders started a tremendous campaign in Rohelkhand and Awadh. Seeing these great masses of troops marching in haste, and thirsting for his blood, the cowardly traitor of Puwanyan began to shudder with terror. The English immediately dispatched troops for his protection. Around that part, the revolutionaries were engaging in frequent and desperate encounters with the enemy.[34]

It was really a shame for an Indian Raja who had treacherously killed the great patriot to whom even the enemies have praised a lot and paid the tribute. In the words of Mallesan, "Thus died the Moulvi Ahmadullah of Faizabad. If a patriot is a man who plots and fights for the independence, tribute due wrongfully destroyed, of his native country, then to the most certainly the Maulvi was a true patriot. He had not stained his sword by assassination; he had connived at no murders; he had fought manfully, honourably, and stubbornly in the field against the strangers who had seized his country; and his memory is entitled to the respect of the brave and the true-hearted of all nations."[35]

Savarkar quotes the English historian Malleson, "The Maulvi was a very remarkable man...of his capacity as a military leader many proofs were given during the revolt, but none more decisive than those recorded in this chapter. No other man could boast that he had twice foiled Sir Colin Campbell in the field...."[36]

Maulvi Ahmadullah Shah, a true patriot and forgotten hero of 1857 Uprising, carried on systematic propaganda of *Jihad* in the present area of Uttar Pradesh, with considerable impact upon the popular mind, at least in Agra, Aligarh, Lucknow, and Faizabad divisions. He was perhaps the first popular leader of the Uprising, which had no personal benefit behind his involvement in the rebellion.

Maulana Faiz Ahmad Badayuni

Maulana Faiz Ahmed Badayuni was born in 1808 in Maulvi Mohalla, Badayun. His father was Maulana Hakim Ghulam Ahmad Usmani. When he was only three years old, his father died, and he received his education under the kind patronage of his maternal uncle, Allama Fazle Rasool Usmani Badayuni. He completed his education when he was only fourteen years old and in the fifteenth year he got permission to teach the students. He was a great and accomplished Alim of his age as well as a very good poet. After teaching at Badayun for a long time, he went to Agra, the capital of United Provinces. He was appointed a Peshkar (court official) at the Sadr-i-Nizamat of Agra and later became *Sar-Rishtadar* (an official) at the Board of Revenue. Sir William Muir, who was a military magistrate at that time, had learnt Arabic from him. Sir William Muir, was later on in 1868-1872, appointed as Lieutenant Governor of the United Provinces and Agra.[37]

Maulana Faiz Ahmad Badayuni was associated with Maulana Rahmat Ali Kairanvi in his theological debates with the Christian Missionaries in 1854. In this debate which lasted about three days, Reverend Padre Dr. C.C.P. Fonder, the head of the Christian Mission of India, having been defeated, fled away to Europe. In Agra, he came in contact of Maulana Ahmadullah Shah and was deeply influenced with his idea of *Jihad* against the British. He became an active member of the *Majlis-i-Ulema* (council of Ulema) formed by Maulana Ahmadullah Shah. He participated in the Uprising of 1857 with vigour and devotion. He came to Delhi soon after Bakht Khan's arrival at the capital and presented himself to Bahadur Shah Zafar, who assigned judicial duties to him. The famous Fatwa of *Jihad* issued by Maulana Fazle Haq Khairabadi bears the signature of Maulana Faiz Ahmad Badayuni. After the fall of Delhi, Maulana Faiz Ahmad and Dr. Wazir Khan went to

Lucknow to join Maulvi Ahmadullah Shah and to fight under his command. They fought the battles of Nawab Ganj and Alam Bagh. Following their defeat of the revolutionaries at Lucknow, both the scholars went to Badayun and joined the struggle under Shahzada Firoz Shah. Here in Badayun they fought the battle of Kakrala in which around one thousand *Mujahideen* martyred. Later, they rejoined Maulvi Ahmadullah Shah at Mohammadi. After the martyrdom of Ahmadullah Shah, Faiz Ahmad Badayuni disappeared, never to be heard of again.[38]

It is said that during his stay at Agra, Maulana Faiz Ahmad Badayuni made a long struggle to evacuate the Jama Masjid of Agra, a large portion of which was illegally occupied by the people. At last, he achieved success after litigations. The Masjid was evacuated and repaired. He formed a local agency at Agra to look after the management of the Masjid, and it gladly took up the responsibility. As a freedom fighter, he was always persuaded the people to wage *Jihad* against the British and also actively participated in many battles under the command of Maulvi Ahmadullah Shah and General Bakht Khan, etc. After the British control over northern India, he perhaps migrated to Nepal or Saudi Arabia. There is also some doubt that he might have martyred in any battle while fighting against British.

Maulana Rahmatullah Kairanvi

Maulana Rahmatullah Usmani Kairanvi (1817-1891) was born in Kairana, a place in the district Muzaffar Nagar in western UP. His father Maulvi Khalilullah was the Chief Agent of Maharaja Hindu Rao at Delhi. He was one of the descendants of Kabirul Aulia Makhdoom Jalaluddin of Panipat. Having received his primary education at Kairana, he went to Madrasa Hayaat in Delhi. Then, he travelled to Lucknow and learnt a few books (of higher studies) from Mufti Saadullah Moradabadi. He also learnt few books on Hadith from Shah Abdul Ghani Mujaddid Dehlavi. He also studied mathematics. In order to continue his family traditions, Maulana Kairanvi especially studied medicine. In the beginning, he taught the students in the Masjid at Kairana. When the Missionary schools and the Christians clergymen accentuated their activities and began raising objections against Islam, he wrote a voluminous book, "*Izaalatul Awhaam*" at the order of Shah Abdul Ghani Mujaddidi. This book provided satisfactory answers to all the objections put up by the Christians, particularly those raised by Padre Dr. C.C.P. Fonder, the Missionary, in his book, "*Meezaanul Haq*".[39]

A historic religious debate between Maulana Kairanvi and Reverend Padre Dr. C.C.P. Fonder, the head of the Christian Mission of India, took place at Agra on April 10, 1854, in which Maulana Kairanvi, with his substantial arguments, silenced the clergyman Dr. Fonder. The debating place was full of audiences including Government officials and Ulema as they were interested in the outcome of the debate. Dr. Fonder was assisted by Padre French. English knowing Dr. Maulana Wazir Khan Akbarabadi participated in the debate as special assistant of Maulana Kairanvi.[40]

When the Uprising of 1857 started, he put up a bold front against the English. Maulana Rahmatullah, along with Bahadur Shah Zafar and other *Mujahideen*, took active part in chalking out plans and guidelines for the war of independence. Maulana Yasin Akhtar Misbahi in the monthly *Jaam-e-noor* quotes that in the days of Uprising, it was proclaimed by beating *Naqqarah* (huge drum), on the steps of Jama Masjid Kairana after every *Asr* prayer (Afternoon prayer) that the land belongs to Allah and Command vests in Molvi Rahmatullah. He along with Maulvi Wazir Ahmad Khan Akbarabadi and Maulana Faiz Ahmad Badayuni participated in war waged during the Uprising of 1857. It is written in the Roznamcha (dairy) of Abdul Lateef that two hundred people of Najibabad, under the leadership of Maulvi Rahmatullah, had come to Delhi, waged war and then returned.[41]

Due to his engagement in the Uprising, the English filed a suit against him and announced that they would award one thousand rupees to a person who would capture Maulana Kairanvi and hand him over to them. Maulana Kairanvi could not be arrested, and he secretly migrated to Mecca in Saudi Arabia. His property and holdings at Kairana and Panipat were confiscated and then auctioned in meagre amounts. He started a madarsa in Mecca and breathed his last in 1891 and buried in Jannatul Maala, the famous graveyard of Mecca.[42]

Dr. (Maulana) Wazir Khan Akbarabadi

Dr. Wazir Khan Akbarabadi was from Akbarabad in Bihar Province. After he had received his primary education, his father, Mohammad Nazir Khan sent him to Murshidabad (Bengal) for English education. Then he was sent to England where he received education in medical science. He also learnt Greek and Hebrew and studied the Injeel (Taurah) thoroughly. He was appointed as an assistant surgeon in a hospital in Calcutta after he came back to India. Then, he shifted to Agra. After his transfer at Agra, he came in touch with Maulana Ahmadullah Shah it was the influence of the Maulana Ahmadullah Shah's company that Dr. Wazir Khan developed hatred for the English and love for freedom.[43]

Although he didn't have a Maulvi degree from any madarsa, he attained enough knowledge in Islamic learning and jurisprudence. On the basis of his Islamic knowledge and his friendship with the Ulema, the people generally called him Maulana. Due to his very deep knowledge in English literature, he became very useful to the Ulema for conversation with the Christian Missionary people.

He along with his friends, Maulana Kairanvi and Maulana Faiz Ahmed Usmani Badayuni, accepted the challenge of religious debate with the Missionary head Padre Fonder in 1854, at Agra. The Missionary, Dr. Fonder fled away after he was defeated at the end of the three days long heated debate.[44]

When the Uprising broke out, Dr. Wazir Khan Akbarabadi actively participated in different battles along with the army of *Jihadis*. He came in Delhi and was included in the "Council of Administration." He was associated with General Bakht Khan in almost all military campaigns. After the failure of Uprising in Delhi, Maulana Dr. Wazir Khan Akbarabadi along with General Bakht Khan and Maulana Faiz Ahmad Badayuni went to Lucknow. They all joined Maulana Ahmadullah Shah Madrasi and bravely fought against the British. After Lucknow, they all went to Shahjahanpur and finally dispersed. Maulana Dr. Wazir Khan secretly migrated to Mecca and joined Maulana Rahmatullah Kairanvi and settled over there.[45]

He set up a clinic at Mecca and came in touch with a Yamani, Shaikh Abdullah, while treating his wife. Indian Government asked the Khalifa of Turkey to hand him over to India. Khalifa asked the governor of Mecca, Sharif Abdullah, for the action but Yamani Shaikh Abdullah warned that his handover could be possible only after killing ten thousand people from his tribe. The governor conveyed the news to the Khalifa who wrote to the Indian Government that handing over a culprit under such circumstances was almost impossible. The Indian Government was compelled to keep quiet. Dr. Wazir Khan lived in Mecca for fourteen years. He breathed his last over there in 1873 and was buried at the Jannatul Maala the famous graveyard of Mecca.[46]

Maulvi Liaqat Ali Allahabadi

Maulvi Liaqat Ali was born on 5th October, 1817 in Mahgaon village of tehsil Chail, 30 kilometers away in the west of Allahabad. His father's name was Sayyad Mehr Ali and mother was Amina Bibi. His great grandfather Sayyad Gauhar Ali came to India from Khurasan during the reign of Shahjahan and was appointed a judge. He received his education under care of his uncle Sayyad Daim Ali, who was in the service of the British Army in Jhansi. Maulvi Liaqat Ali after completing his education and gaining profound scholarship in Arabic, Persian, and Urdu, joined the army service of the British Government. He started his life with a military job, but he was dismissed from service on the allegation of anti-Government activities. He returned to his village Mahgaon and started Islamic teaching in a mosque. He became very famous Qadri Silsila preacher and was a devout follower of the Sayyad Ahmad Barelvi' philosophy. Before the commencement of the Uprising, he was in the secret alliance with Nana Sahib and other revolutionary leaders. He was directly involved in the pre-planning of the Uprising.[47]

He issued two religious Fatwas of *Jihad* against the British, first was published in 1856 in *Risala-e-Jihad* of Maulvi Khurram Ali Bilhori, and the other was an appeal in the light of Quraan addressed to the people to fight against the British until their death. When the 6th Native Infantry in Allahabad mutinied on 6th of

June 1857 under the leadership of Ram Chander, Maulvi Liyaqat Ali also jumped in the Uprising and unanimously chosen as the leader of all the revolutionaries. He appealed to the people to join the *Jihad* by the name of religion and independence. On his appeal, many influential persons of that area like, Shaikh Nizam Ashraf, Ghulam Ismail, Mohammad Hussain, Chaudhary Miran Baksh, Maulvi Sayyad Ahmad Ali, Maulvi Ghulam Haider, Maulvi Amjad Ali, Hasan Ali Khan, Sher Khan, Shaikh Lutf Ali, Shaikh Fateh Ali, and Shaikh Najaf Ali, etc. joined the Uprising under him.[48]

Kaye quotes Fendall Thompson's Official Narrative about Maulvi Liaqat Ali, "There was a man known as the 'Maulvi', around whom the insurgent population gathered, as he proclaimed the restored rule of the Emperor of Dehli. Whence he sprung few people at the time could say. But it was known at a later period that he came from one of the Mohammadan villages in the Doab, which had gone into rebellion. Making great pretensions to sanctity, and investing himself with the character of a prophet as well as of a ruler of men, he stimulated the dormant fanaticism of the people, and told them to array themselves against the Firangis. Establishing his head-quarters in the Chasru Bagh—a spacious availed garden, in which were some tombs, held in high veneration—he simulated the possession of miraculous powers, by some obvious trickeries, which deluded his excited followers, and for a while he was recognised as Governor of Allahabad. It little mattered who or what he was, so long as he was strong in his hatred of the English, and could induce the Musalman population to believe that the Mohammadan dynasty would soon be restored. So for a little time he succeeded in setting up the likeness of a provisional Government, and the name of the Maulvi was on the lips of all the followers of the Prophet...."[49]

Under the leadership of Maulvi Liaqat Ali, the Uprising progressed in 1857. The inhabitants chose him as their ruler under the Mughal Emperor Bahadur Shah Zafar. His most trusted fellows in his mission were Ram Singh, Jai Chand, Ram Chander, Sher Khan, Sayyad Daim Ali, Aqiluddin Rahman, Qazi Mohsin Ali, Nawab Hikmatullah, and Allah Baksh, etc. Lieutenant Alaxander was killed and other Europeans were forced to leave Allahabad along with their families. He established his headquarter at Khusru Bagh, a spacious walled garden, in which were some tombs, held in high veneration. The Muslim landlords of Samadabad, Rasoolpur, Salori, Shadiabad, Minhajpur, and Bakshi, etc. supported whole heartedly Maulvi Liaqat Ali. He appointed Saifullah and Sukh Rai as Tehsildar, Qasim Ali, and Nemat Ashraf as Kotwal, Chaudhary Shahabuddin as Naib Kotwal, and Faizullah as an officer in the army.[50]

Maulvi Liaqat Ali also wrote a National Song which was sung by the revolutionaries, holding green flag in their hands. The National Song was as follows:[51]

> *Hindustan Hamara*
> *Ham Hain Iske Malik Hindustan Hamara*
> *Pak Watan Hai Qaumon Ka Yeh Jannat Se Bhi Pyara*
> *Hamari Yeh Milkiat Hindustan Hamara*
> *Unki Ruhaniat Se Roshan Hai Jag Sara*
> *Hindustan Hamara*
> *Kitna Nadeem Kitna Nafees Sab Duniya Se Nyara*
> *Karti Hai zarkhez se Yeh Gang-o-Jaman Ki Dhara*
> *Upar Barphila Parbat Hai Pahredar Hanmara*
> *Neeche Sahil Par Basta Hai Sagar Ka Jhalkara*
> *Hindustan Hamara*
> *Uski Kanen Ugal Rahi Hain Sona Hira Para*
> *Uski Shan-o-Shaukat Ka Hai Duniya Me Jaikara*
> *Hindu Muslim Sikh Hamara Bhai Pyara*
> *Ye Hai Azadi Ka Jhanda Ise Salaam Hamara*
>
> (India is ours. We are its owners India is ours. It's the holy country of all the nations and is beautiful than the paradise. It's our property; India is ours. The whole world is brightening by its spirit. India is ours. How friendly and better and different from the rest of the world. The water currents of Ganges and Jumna rivers make its land fertile. The snowy mountain to the top is our guard and in the bottom, there is beauty of sea. India is ours. Its mines are omitting gold, diamond, and mercury. There is the sound of victory of its splendor. Hindu Muslims and Sikhs are our dear brothers. This is the flag of freedom, and we salute it.)

Soon after the Native rule of a week, Colonel Gordon Neill advanced to Allahabad on 14th of June. In this fierce attack of Neill, Liaqat Ali made them kiss the dust and take refuge in the fort. However, Colonel Neil took military action on 16th June in Allahabad and its suburbs. The Pathan population of Sadiyabad and the Mewati Muslims of Rasoolpur became victims of the worst type of massacre. Colonel Neill tried to capture Khusru Bagh but could not succeed hence he spread news that he will undertake the massacre of the city of Allahabad. Liaqat Ali had seen the beastly act of British in Samadabad, Rasoolpur and other areas, so he decided to leave Allahabad with the hope that with his departure from Allahabad the innocent people of Allahabad may escape the massacre by British. Maulvi Liaqat Ali escaped with his 3000 followers to Kanpur to strengthen his position. In Allahabad Colonel Neill committed the inhuman atrocities, burnt the villages, tortured, and hanged the innocent population. According to Maulvi Liaqat Ali as quoted by John William Kaye, "not a house was tenanted, and not a light was to be seen in the city." The magistrate announced a reward of Rs. 5000 on the head of Maulvi Liaqat Ali.[52]

John Kaye quotes the report of Mr. Fendall Thompson, taken from "Perwannah addressed by the Maulavi Liaqat Ali, apparently to the King of Delhi-Supplement to Allahabad Official Narrative." The following is the Maulvi's account of the evacuation. "Some evil-minded men," he said, "who had sided with the 'accursed one,' urged that for a time the Fort would be a safe retreat, and that, if they would remain in it a few days longer, they (the evil-minded Natives) would contrive to spread abroad in the city fearful reports that the English were preparing the Artillery of the Fort to destroy the city, and that before dawn they would begin bombarding it with shot and shell. To show the sincerity of their advice, these men, with their followers, set off, giving out to all that they had left their houses and property to God's protection, and were going to save themselves by flight. On hearing this fearful report, the people, notwithstanding my repeated injunctions, commenced a precipitate flight, with their families and goods."[53]

Maulvi Liaqat Ali also fought a battle at Fatehpur against the Europeans. According to the Tatya Tope's narration as quoted by

John Kaye, "Sipahis were anxious that the Nana should accompany them to Fatehpur. "The Nana refused," Tatya Tope said: "I and the Nana remained at Kanpur, and sent Jwala Prashad, his agent, along with them to Fatehpur. Tika Singh, the 2nd Cavalry General, accompanied him. The Allahabad Maulvi also appears to have been with the Nana's party at this time." One of the witnesses, whose depositions have been published by Colonel Williams, when asked, "Who commanded at the battle of Fatehpur?" answered, "I myself saw Tika Singh, the General, and the Allahabad Maulvi and Jwala Prashad, going off to command. Many others went—small fry of lenders."[54]

After the failure of the rebellion, Maulvi Luiaqat Ali fled towards Nepal along with other freedom fighters, but he could not hide for long and left for Lajpur in Gujrat and then went to Bombay along with his family with the intension to go for Haj pilgrimage to Mecca, but he got arrested in 1872 before boarding to the ship. Liaqat Ali was brought to Allahabad, and there he was put to trial in the Court of Session Judge A.R. Pollack. The Judgment was as follows:[55]

> "Prisoner Liaqat Ali confessed that he did commit the offences charged against him, that he was the leader of the revolt and rebelled and waged war against Queen and the Government of the East India Company in the month of June 1857, at Allahabad, the Court finds that he is a guilty of an offence punishable under Section I Act XI of 1857 and directs the said Liaqat Ali transported for life."

According to the Judgment, he was transported to the Andaman (Kala Pani). His property was confiscated. He left his wife Hajra Bagum and a daughter to survive. He breathed his last in Andaman on 17th of May 1892.

Maulana Mohammad Qasim Nanautvi

Maulana Mohammad Qasim Nanautvi was an Islamic Scholar and one of the main people responsible for establishing the separate Deobandi ideology along with the basic principles of

Shah Waliullah or so-called Wahabi Movement. He was born in 1833 in Nanauta village of the district Saharanpur in UP, India. His father's name was Asad Ali. He completed his primary education in his hometown, and then he went to Saharanpur, where he remained with his maternal grandfather. In Saharanpur, he studied elementary books of Arabic grammar and syntax under Maulvi Nawaz. At the end of 1843, he went to Delhi where he completed his further studies.

Maulana Mohammad Qasim Nanautvi's most important efforts were the social and religious reformations among the Muslims, waging *Jihad* against the British and foundation of a Darul Uloom at Deoband. His like-minded Ulema which were called as Deobandi Ulema (although Darul Uloom was not established at the time of Uprising) never liked the British, and they were not willing to tolerate them on the soil of this country even for a moment. Maulana Qasim faced the opposition from his family in his revolutionary activities except his mother. Some of his associates also suggested that the war against the British will be suicidal in view of the strength and arms of the enemy but Maulana Qasim, and Haji Imdadullah decided to wage war against the British at any cost. They recruited an army of the *Mujahideen*, basically Ulema fighters, and Maulana Qasim became their Commander of the army and Maulana Rasheed Ahmad Gangohi as Qazi. The two other Ulema Maulana Mohammad Muneer and Maulana Mohammad Hafeez Zameer Ahmad were given charge of the two battalions. Nawab Shabbir Ali assisted him getting access to the Emperor Bahadur Shah Zafar. Undoubted their war was against the oppressive British Government which gave the war a national character. In this effort against the British, Maulana Qasim got the much-needed strength and confidence.[56]

The Ulema got further strength when the 4th Irregulars rose in revolt on June 21, and murdered their commanding officers as well as other Europeans, after which they marched off to Shamli, where the rebellious people galloped in a large number. Five days later, a party of the 3rd Cavalry arrived in the town; and on 1st July, Mr. R. M. Edwards came in from Saharanpur with a body of Gorkhas, and took charge of the administration of

Muzaffarnagar district. Vigorous measures were at once adopted to repress crime in the western parganas which were in open revolt led by mostly the Ulema. The Ulema decided to start the battle which was to be started from Thana Bhawan in Muzaffarnagar district and would end at Delhi after liberating from the British clutches. The revolutionary force, numbering about 30-40, under Haji Imdadullah, successfully attacked the British forces which were passing on the Bagh-i-Sher Ali Road and killed a British soldier and seized some weapons, including a canon on 21st of June 1857. The participation of Maulana Mohammad Qasim Nanautvi in this battle was doubtful but many oral sources testify his participation. The success of Bagh-i-Sher Ali attack enhanced the morale of the Ulemas and began to prepare for another fight with greater enthusiasm.[57]

When the news of Thana Bhawan incident reached to the Collector of Muzaffarnagar, Mr. Spankie, he immediately dispatched a force to revenge the revolutionaries to both the places of Thana Bhawan and Shamli. The British force accordingly surrounded the town of Thana Bhawan. However, the revolutionaries rushed to Shamli on hearing the rumour of British outrage. The success of the first victory of the Ulema also encouraged them to attack on Shamli. The Ulema and other revolutionaries in tens of thousands rushed towards Shamli, where a fierce battle ensued on 14th of September 1857. In this battle Maulana Qasim Nanautvi, Maulana Imam Rabbani, Maulana Rasheed Ahmad Gangohi, Maulana Hafeez Zamin Shaheed, Maulana Mohammad Mazhar Nanautvi, Maulana Rahmatullah Kairanvi etc. played the most important role. The Ulema and the revolutionaries became victorious by defeating the most advanced soldiers of the British. They massacred 113 persons in cold blood and plundered the office of the Sub-Collector Ibrahim Khan. In this battle, the Ulema were armed with traditional weapons while the enemy having the latest armaments fired sparsely upon the Ulema from all around. In this situation Maulana Nanautvi led his force more bravely and intelligently. The Ulema and the revolutionaries became victorious by defeating the most advanced soldiers of the British, but they lost one of their brave soldiers, Maulana Zamin Ahmad.[58]

Mr. Edwards received re-enforcement of Sikh and Gorkha Infantry and Cavalry from Meerut and Saharanpur and attacked Thana Bhawan on 16th of September 1857. However, in the fierce battle, British were forced to retreat with loss of seventeen killed and twenty five wounded, including two British officers. Later on at the end of September 1857, Mr. Edwards received further reinforcement of the British soldiers and occupied the town Thana Bhawan without resistance. In continuance of the attack, the British soldiers also occupied the town Shamli by killing thousands of revolutionaries.[59]

About the incident of Thana Bhawan, Robertson writes as follows:[60]

> "The *Ghazi* of Thana Bhawan, a place in the Muzzaffarnagar district, and on the southern borders of our own (Saharanpur), after murdering all the native officials of that place under circumstances of peculiar atrocity and treachery, had unfortunately succeeded in driving off a small party of Gorkhas and other troops, who had not been well managed when attacking him. This made matters serious as any slight defeat at that time ordinarily induced a general rising. A considerable force was consequently at once marched out from Meerut to attack Thana Bhawan. The place was abandoned, as usual by the rebels on seeing that the force opposed to them was more than their match, and they entered our district (Saharanpur) in considerable numbers, which necessitated my leaving Saharanpur rather hurriedly; to intercept them with some Sikh military mounted police under a native commandant."

After settling the matter of revolutionaries at Shamli and Thana Bhawan by the British, a manhunt of the revolutionaries was launched throughout northern India. The warrants were also issued, and rewards were announced at the head of the main target Maulana Qasim Nanautvi, Haji Imdadullah, and Maulana Rasheed Ahmad Gangohi and many other Ulema. Haji Imdadullah escaped to Mecca while Maulana Mohammad Mazhar went into hiding at Bareilly. Once a general amnesty was declared, he emerged from hiding and thereafter began teaching in his home. Maulana Nanautvi along with Maulana Gangohi after hiding three days went on roaming towards Deoband, Nanauta, Rampur, etc. and the British failed to track him. When people again begged Maulana Qasim Nanautvi earnestly to go underground, he said: 'To go into hiding for more than three days is not proven from the Sunnah, because the Holy Prophet too had remained hidden in the Cave of Thaur, at the time of migration, for three days only'.[61]

The story of Maulana Mazhar Nanautvi (one of the participants of Battle of Shamli), regarding the Battle of Shamli needs to be mentioned here. It is said that it was the habit of Maulana Mazhar Nanautvi that he would often lick his upper lip. Someone once asked him the reason for this, but the respected Maulana did not respond over him. When this person insisted, Maulana remarked, "When the battle against the British took place at Shamli, and the Muslims were being attacked, some of my comrades were dying and my leg was also hit by a bullet. In this state, I saw *Hurs* (Damsels of Paradise) with glasses in their hands. The glasses were filled with a special type of drink that they were giving to those of my fallen comrades who were dying, and had no chance of surviving. As this was happening, one of the damsels came towards me. She had just placed a glass against my mouth when another damsel took hold of her hands, pulled them away from me, and said, 'He is not among those who are to pass away.' A very small amount of this drink fell on my upper lip, the sweet taste of which remains until today. This is why I have this habit of licking my upper lip."

The role he played as a selfless leader, devoted to his righteous cause and aware of his avowed mission of defending Islam and protecting Muslims, cannot be forgotten. Although Ulema of Deoband were defeated in their armed struggle against the British, yet they fully succeeded in the ideological and religious war the British had initiated. Events that ensued proved that the establishment of Darul-Uloom in 1866 by Maulana Qasim Nanautvi and Rasheed Ahmad Gangohi proved far more useful than an armed struggle. This placid movement produced so many powerful stormy waves that forced the British to ultimately leave India.

REFERENCES

1. Ishaq, Abdul Hamid, *Ulema of Deoband*,, Madarsa Arabia Islamia, Azaadville, South Africa, 2011, p. 10.
2. Samiuddin, Abida, *Encyclopaedic Dictionary of Urdu Literature*, (Vol. I), New Delhi, 2007, p. 106.
3. *Dehli Urdu Akhbar*, 24th July, 1857.
4. *Ibid.*, 14th June, 1857.
5. Ahmad, Mohammad Masood, *Jange Azadi me Allama Fazle Haq Khairabadi ka Kirdar*, Malegaon, 2005, p. 2.
6. *Athara Sau Sattawan Ke Rahnuma (Sawanehy Khake)*, National Council for Promotion of Urdu Language, New Delhi, 2009, p. 171 see also Tariq, Shamim, *Ghalib, Bahadur Shah Zafar aur 1857*, New Delhi, 2008, p. 59, and Ahmad, Mohammad Masood, *Jange Azadi me Allama Fazle Haq Khairabadi ka Kirdar*, Malegaon, 2005, p.5.
7. *Athara Sau Sattawan Ke Rahnuma (Sawanehy Khake)*, National Council for Promotion of Urdu Language, New Delhi, 2009, p. 171.
8. Ahmad, Mohammad Masood, *Jange Azadi me Allama Fazle Haq Khairabadi ka Kirdar*, Malegaon, 2005, p.6.
9. *Ibid.*, p.7.
10. *Ibid.*, p.7 see also Tariq Tariq, Shamim, *Ghalib, Bahadur Shah Zafar aur 1857*, New Delhi, 2008, p. 55.
11. Tariq, Shamim, *Ghalib, Bahadur Shah Zafar aur 1857*, New Delhi, 2008, pp. 59-60.
12. *Athara Sau Sattawan Ke Rahnuma (Sawanehy Khake)*, National Council for Promotion of Urdu Language, New Delhi, 2009, p. 177 see also Tariq, Shamim, *Ghalib, Bahadur Shah Zafar aur 1857*, New Delhi, 2008, p. 83.
13. Maulana Fazle Haq praised the *Mujahids* of Sayyed Ahmad Shaheed and Maulvi Ismail Shaheed and the revolutionaries of the Uprising working under Bakht Khan. (Tariq, Shamim, *Ghalib, Bahadur Shah Zafar aur 1857*, New Delhi, 2008, p. 94).
14. *Ibid.*, p. 62.
15. *Jaam-i-Noor, Monthly, Millat Ka Tarjaman*, Delhi, 2007.
16. *Ibid.*
17. *Ibid.*
18. *Ibid.*
19. *India Perspectives*, Vol. 15, No. 3, March 2002, p. 21, see also Jafri, Saiyid Zaheer Husain, *The Great Uprising of 1857*, Delhi, 2009, p. 54.
20. *Radiance Viewsweekly*, Vol. XLIV, No. 28, 2006-12-31.

21. *India Perspectives*, Vol. 15, No. 3, March 2002, p. 21 see also *Radiance Viewsweekly*, Vol. XLIV, No. 28, 2006-12-31.
22. *Tilism*, Lucknow, 21st November, 1856 (Urdu translation was taken from *India Perspectives*, Vol. 15, No. 3, March 2002, p. 22).
23. *Ibid.*
24. Malleson, George Bruce, *Kay's and Malleson's History of the Indian Mutiny of 1857-8,* Vol. IV, London, 1911, p. 379.
25. Thurburn, Felix Augustus Victor, *Reminiscences of the Indian Rebellion of 1857-1858*, London, 1889, pp. 13-15.
26. Ghazi, M.A., *Islamic Renaissance In South Asia (1707-1867): The Role Of Shah Waliallah & His Successors*, Delhi, 2004, pp. 217-218 see also *India Perspectives*, Vol. 15, No. 3, March 2002, p. 22, *Radiance Viewsweekly*, Vol. XLIV, No. 28, 2006-12-31, and Malleson, George Bruce, *History of the Indian Mutiny of 1857-58, Commencing from the Close of the Second Volume of Sir John Kaye's History of the Sepoy War*, Vol. III, (Contemporaneous with Sir John Kay's Third Volume), London, 1878, p. 396, (Mallesan describes that the Maulvi travelled to the parts of India which subsequently proved the most susceptible to the revolt; that he was the confidential friend and adviser of a very prominent member of the deposed royal family of Lucknow. If, as I believe, the mutiny was in a great measure determined not less by the annexation of Awadh than by the sudden and treacherous manner in which that annexation was carried into effect—that the greased cartridges were simply a means used by the higher conspirators to force to revolt men who could be moved only by violence to their faith—the story of the action of the Maulvi only seems natural. Certain it is that in April 1857 he circulated seditious papers throughout Awadh; that the police did not arrest him; and that to obtain that end armed force was required. He was then tried and condemned to death. Malleson, George Bruce, *Kay's and Mulleson's History of the Indian Mutiny of 1857-8,* Vol. IV, London, 1911, p. 379).
27. *Radiance Viewsweekly*, Vol. XLIV No. 28, 2006-12-31.
28. *Shodh Sanchayan*, Bilingual Journal of Humanities and Social Sciences, (*The Great Uprising and Civil Rebellion in Shahjahanpur: (A Study of Anti-British Resistance in 1857*—Dr. Syed Mohd Ameer), Vol. 2, Issue 1 and 2, 15 Jan-15 July, 2011, pp. 2-3.
29. *Ibid.*, p. 3.
30. *Ibid.*, pp. 3-4.
31. *Radiance Viewsweekly*, Vol. XLIV, No. 28, 2006-12-31.
32. Malleson, George Bruce, *Kay's and Malleson's History of the Indian Mutiny of 1857-8,* Vol. IV, London, 1911, p. 380, see also *Shodh*

Sanchayan, Bilingual journal of Humanities & Social Sciences, (*The Great Uprising and Civil Rebellion in Shahjahanpur: (A Study of Anti-British Resistance in 1857*—Dr. Syed Mohd Ameer), Vol. 2, Issue 1 and 2, 15 Jan-15 July, 2011, p. 4.

33. *Radiance Viewsweekly*, Vol. XLIV, No. 28, 2006-12-31.
34. Savarkar, p. 416.
35. Malleson, George Bruce, *Kay's and Malleson's History of the Indian Mutiny of 1857-8,* Vol. IV, London, 1911, p. 381.
36. Savarkar, p. 370.
37. *Jaam-i-Noor, Monthly, Millat Ka Tarjaman*, Delhi, 2007.
38. Ghazi, M.A., *Islamic Renaissance In South Asia (1707-1867): The Role Of Shah Waliallah and His Successors*, Delhi, 2004, p. 217, see also *Jaam-i-Noor, Monthly, Millat Ka Tarjaman*, Delhi, 2007.
39. *Jaam-i-Noor, Monthly, Millat Ka Tarjaman*, Delhi, 2007.
40. *Ibid.*
41. *Ibid.*
42. *Ibid.*
43. *Ibid.*
44. *Ibid.*
45. *Ibid.*
46. *Ibid.*
47. Qasmi, Ataur Rahman, *Hindustan ki Pahli Jang Azadi 1857 me Musalmanon ka Hissa*, New Delhi, 2008, pp. 180-181 see also Pratap, Mahendra and Jafri, Saiyid Zaheer Hasan, *Region in Indian History*, (*Leadership of Maulvi Liaqat Ali: First Freedom Struggle of Allahabad-* Yusufa Nafees), New Delhi, 2008, pp. 261-262.
48. Pratap, Mahendra and Jafri, Saiyid Zaheer Hasan, *Region in Indian History*, (*Leadership of Maulvi Liaqat Ali: First Freedom Struggle of Allahabad-* Yusufa Nafees), New Delhi, 2008, pp. 262 see also Qasmi, Ataur Rahman, *Hindustan ki Pahli Jang Azadi 1857 me Musalmanon ka Hissa*, New Delhi, 2008, p. 181.
49. Kaye, John William, *Kay's and Malleson's History of the Indian Mutiny of 1857-8,* Vol. II, London, 1910, p. 196.
50. *Ibid.*, p. 261, see also Qasmi, Ataur Rahman, *Hindustan ki Pahli Jang Azadi 1857 me Musalmanon ka Hissa*, New Delhi, 2008, pp. 182-183.
51. Qasmi, Ataur Rahman, *Hindustan ki Pahli Jang Azadi 1857 me Musalmanon ka Hissa*, New Delhi, 2008, pp. 182-183.
52. Pratap, Mahendra & Jafri, Saiyid Zaheer Hasan, *Region in Indian History*, (*Leadership of Maulvi Liaqat Ali: First Freedom Struggle of Allahabad-* Yusufa Nafees), New Delhi, 2008, pp. 264 see also Kaye, John William, *A History of the Sepoy War in India, 1857-58,* Vol. II,

London 1874, p. 267 and Qasmi, Ataur Rahman, *Hindustan ki Pahli Jang Azadi 1857 me Musalmanon ka Hissa*, New Delhi, 2008, pp. 185-186.

53. John Kaye says that the whole city of Allahabad was evacuated due to the fear of British atrocity. They quotes Maulvi Liaqat Ali, "not a house was tenanted, and not a light was to be seen in the city." Maulvi Liakat Ali himself had escaped towards Kanpur. Kaye, John William, *Kay's and Malleson's History of the Indian Mutiny of 1857-8,* Vol. II, London, 1910, p. 201.
54. *Ibid.*, p. 273.
55. It was also remarked in the Judgment, "..... He acknowledges that he placed himself as the head of the body of the rebels .... Fought with the British force that came out of the fort and that subsequently when he found that the British Government becoming re-established at Allahabad, he fled to Kanpur and was present at that place in the Nana's camp at the time of Europeans in Wheeler's entrenchment were so cruelly massacred by the rebels and mutineers acting under Nana's order.... He is a man of extra ordinary respect and decoration by his co-religionist of Allahabad...." Pratap, Mahendra & Jafri, Saiyid Zaheer Hasan, *Region in Indian History*, (*Leadership of Maulvi Liaqat Ali: First Freedom Struggle of Allahabad*-Yusufa Nafees), New Delhi, 2008, pp. 265-266.
56. Tabassum, Farhat, *Deoband Ulema's Movement for the Freedom of India*, New Delhi, 2006, pp. 15-16.
57. Hunter, William Wilson, *The Imperial Gazetteer of India*, London 1907, p. 86, see also Tabassum, Farhat, *Deoband Ulema's Movement for the Freedom of India*, New Delhi, 2006, pp. 17-18.
58. Keene, Henry George, *British Administration during the Revolt of 1857*, New Delhi 1883, pp. 18-19, see also Tabassum, Farhat, *Deoband Ulema's Movement for the Freedom of India*, New Delhi, 2006, pp. 18-19.
59. Keene, Henry George, *British Administration during the Revolt of 1857*, New Delhi 1883, p. 20, see also Keene, Henry George, *Fifty-Seven: Some Account of the Administration of Indian Districts during the Revolt of the Bengal Army*, London, 1883, pp. 17-18.
60. Robertson, Henry Dundas, *District Duties during the Revolt in the North-West Provinces of India in 1857: With Remarks on Subsequent Investigations during 1858-59*, London 1859, pp. 165-166.
61. Tabassum, Farhat, *Deoband Ulema's Movement for the Freedom of India*, New Delhi, 2006, pp. 19-20.

CHAPTER 6

Muslim Luminaries of the Uprising

The pages of history are full of the heroic role of prominent Muslim personalities in the Uprising of 1857. Thousands of these leaders sacrificed their lives, family, and property for the sake of Indian independence. They need a separate book to highlight their courage, chivalry, and patriotism, but it is rather difficult to cover all the luminaries in a single work. Although the author has covered most of the luminaries under different topics and chapters categorized according to their role, works and beliefs. In this chapter only few of them has been mentioned with full details as could be possible according to the space. Here the author gives the tribute to those forgotten luminaries by quoting a couplet:

> "*Duniya mein bala se agar aaram na paya*
> *Hum ne yahi paya ke bura naam na paya*"
> (It does not matter if we enjoyed no comforts in this world, we have at least earned this distinction that we have been given no bad name).

Mughal Emperor Bahadur Shah Zafar

Abul Muzaffar Sirajuddin Mohammad Bahadur Shah Padshah-i-Ghazi (October 1775–7th November 1862), popularly known as Bahadur Shah Zafar was the octogenarian representative and the twentieth successor of the illustrious Emperor Akbar, the great

Mughal. He was the son of Akbar Shah II and Lalbai, a Hindu Rajput lady, and became the titular Mughal Emperor on 28th September 1837. He was seated at Delhi, which was the centre of the Hindustan, the richest country throughout the world. To sixty millions of Muslims in India and beyond the borders, Bahadur Shah Zafar was nevertheless, the symbol of ancient Muslim glory. Even the Hindus had recognised that Mughal Emperor was the only rightful person, after their local chiefs, to possess the land of Hindustan. Although he was a pensioner of the East India Company, but he enjoyed the sympathy of the whole Hindustan, spread from Himalayas to Kanyakumari.

From the centuries numerous invaders burst like a torrent over India, but the Muslims settled here permanently and made India as their homeland. They provided a friendly rule to their countrymen and worked for its prosperity to which India is still enjoying. Bahadur Shah Zafar, the last inheritor of Mughal Empire was representing the vast population of India, though nominally. He was considered best as the human being among the Mughal Emperors after Aurangzeb. He was a skilled calligrapher, a profound writer on Sufism, a discriminating patron of painters of miniatures, an inspired creator of gardens and an amateur architect. Most importantly he was a very serious mystical poet, who wrote not only in Urdu and Persian, but Braj Basha and Punjabi, and partly through his patronage there took place arguably the greatest literary renaissance in modern Indian history.

In spite of all the brilliant and extraordinary qualities, Bahadur Shah Zafar was still unaware of the developments that were taking place around him. He and the heir apparent alone were exempted from the jurisdiction of the Company's local courts, but were under the orders of the Supreme Government. He was allowed to maintain as many men at his service as he could pay. He was in receipt of a stipend of one lakh of rupees per mensem, of which ninety-nine thousand were paid at Dehli, and one thousand at Lucknow, for the subsistence of his family members living in Lucknow. He was also in receipt of revenue to the amount of a lakh and a half from the crown lands in the neighbourhood of Dehli. He also received a considerable sum from the ground rents of houses and tenants in the city of Dehli.[1]

Day by day, the British were curbing the sovereignty of Bahadur Shah Zafar and increasing their sphere of influence. No nobleman from outside Delhi could enter the Red Fort (3000 ft.× 1800 ft.) without the Resident's permission. To enforce his right to rent from his own lands, Emperor had to make an application to the British courts. He could not present gems from the crown jewels even to his own family members without first informing the Resident. Emperor was many times humiliated when the Resident asked the recipients to return the so-called unauthorized gifts. The British perhaps under-estimated the authority of the Emperor and handled him as a tool for their own sake. The humiliation of the Emperor tarnished the sentiments and ego of the Indian population irrespective of their caste and creed. The Europeans thought that the Emperor attained sympathy of only the people of his called court and the rest of the population generally hate the disguised old man. However, it amazed the British authority when the Sepoys after the outbreak of the Uprising directly rode towards Delhi and enthroned Bahadur Shah as their Emperor or rather Emperor of the whole of India. This was a reflection of the popular perception that the Mughal Emperor was the legitimate sovereign of India not a tool under British. The British Government due to their folly made Bahadur Shah Zafar as universally recognized Emperor of which position not even the great Mughal Emperors Akbar, Shah Jahan or Aurangzeb had enjoyed.

Before discussing the role of Bahadur Shah Zafar in the Uprising, it is must to introduce the political system under few of his predecessor of the last Mughal dynasty. After its victory in the Battle of Buxar in 1764, the East India Company had two masters to serve, one in Delhi, the Mughal Emperor, and the other in London, the British Government. From 1785, onwards Shah Alam came to the protection of Mahadji Sindhia, who was entrusted to administer the Delhi region. This was a challenge for the British and as a result in 1803, the East India Company's forces led by Lord Lake with a force of four thousand nine hundred captured Delhi after defeating the Daulat Rao Sindhia's fifteen thousand troops at the battle of Patparganj. Lord Lake entered Delhi on 14th September 1803, and provided protection to the Mughal Emperor. However, in October 1804, Maratha General Jaswant Rao Holkar along with his seventy thousand forces appeared near Delhi and met a severe defeat. Following this victory, the administration of Delhi and its adjoining areas was taken over by the British, and Emperor Shah Alam was placed in the protection and control of the Company and also assured of an income, amounting to about one lakh rupees per mensem. Besides this income, a token tribute of 101 gold coins was presented by Governor General to the Emperor on important occasions, but this practice was discontinued under Lord Hastings (1813-1823).[2]

However, it is also notable that the company acted as Subedar of the Emperor and it had to pay the Emperor not only a due portion of the revenue from the territories it held on behalf of the Emperor, and it had to do so with an annual ceremonial visit to Agra or Delhi, where successive Governor Generals paid homage and tribute to the Emperor in durbar and paid nazar, for which the Emperor in turn offered his servant, the subedari, gifts, robes of honour and his blessings. This practice the Company continued until 1833, annually confirming its subordination to the Emperor at a public ceremony. The Company explained about this practice to their own Government in England that it was the protector of territories of the Mughal Empire on behalf of Britain and that the nazar the Governor General paid annually at Delhi was only a pension for an improvident monarch. In December 1806, after Shah Alam's death, Akbar Shah became the nominal Emperor and enjoyed the more or less the same priviledges.[3]

On 20th September 1837, Akbar Shah died and was succeeded by Bahadur Shah Zafar, who was in his advanced age but never bowed upon the British terms and conditions. Although in 1835, the practice of stricking coins in the name of the Emperor was stopped but the other officials, including the Resident, continued to present the tribute down to 1844. In 1844, Lord Ellenborough gave the finishing stroke to the system of nazar-giving, or tributary present-making, to the King, by prohibiting even such offerings by the Resident. Whatsoever was the practice but full respect was outwardly shown for the Emperor's majesty right up to 1857. British officials strictly adhered to Mughal court etiquette.[4]

Before the Uprising of 1857, there was a complete revolutionary atmosphere in Delhi and the open discussion of revolution in Delhi and even in the palace was severely noticed. V.D. Savarkar quotes Mukund Lal, the Private Secretary of the Emperor of Delhi, who says, "Sitting at the doors of the royal palace, Mughals and others within the palace used to discuss the Revolution openly. The Sepoys would rebel soon; the army of Delhi would rise against the English; and then, all people, along with the army, would throw off the Firangi yoke and enjoy Swaraj—such definite opinions were current. All people were inspired with the hope that, when once the Raj was won, all power and all authority would remain in their own hands." Thus, in every cellar, in every house in Delhi, the disaffection only awaited a spark which should explode everything up.[5]

It was 11th May and 17th day of Ramadhan, the Meerut Sepoys comprising mostly Hindus, belonging to eastern part of Awadh (*Poorbea*), including the rabbles, arrived at Delhi and directly came to Red Fort. Roshan Ara, the youngest daughter of the Emperor cried, "Have I not spoken truly? These are the men who sacked Meerut. Scarce a Firangi lives there save those whom I have saved to good purpose. Admit your troops! Proclaim yourself their ruler. A moment's firmness will win back your empire." She almost dragged her father to the front of the balcony. The troopers recognized him with a fierce shout. A hundred sabers were waved frantically. "Help us, O King!" they cried. "We pray your help in our fight for the faith!" Captain Douglas, commandant of the palace guards, hearing the uproar ran to the King. He did not notice the girl Roshan Ara, who stood there like a caged tigress. "How dare you intrude on the King's privacy?" he cried, striving to overawe the rebels by his cool demeanor. "You must lay down your arms if you wish His Majesty's clemency. He is here in person and that is his command." However, the Begum made a signal with her hand which was promptly understood. For the time being, they dispersed towards Raj Ghat and started the massacre of the Europeans, but they again came and urged to the Mughal Emperor Bahadur Shah Zafar to lead them in this war and accept the throne of Indian Empire.[6]

Bahadur Shah Zafar was powerless to resist the Sepoys, being made the leader of an Uprising. The experienced and skilled Bahadur Shah Zafar knew from the start the fates of the action as the orderless armies of peasant-soldiers were set against the world's greatest military power. He was fully aware that the next intruder after the Sepoys would be the mighty British army. But he was surprised when he saw that there was no British following from Meerut. He was hardly to believe that there was no pursuit. He sent out a man on a sowaree camel along the Meerut road, who returned with the report that there were no European troops within twenty miles. Lastly, with a slight hesitation Mughal Emperor Bahadur Shah Zafar accepted their request.

The green Islamic flag was hoisted on the minaret of the Great Mosque. With the salute of guns and beat of drum the restoration of the Mughal rule was proclaimed. Next day, a silver throne was brought from its recess into the Hall of Audience. The Emperor Bahadur Shah took his seat upon it on 12th May, held his first formal audience (*Darbar*). The Sepoy officers passed before him, one by one, and as they bowed the Emperor put his hand on their head in acceptance of their allegiance. At the request of the soldiers, Mirza Mughal, one of the royal Princes, was made Commander-in-Chief, and other Princes were made colonels of regiments. A grand feast was given to the whole army. Emperor Bahadur Shah Zafar took the bold steps and ordered *Farmans* to several chiefs of India. Nevertheless, he was helpless to control the revolutionaries from massacre, loot, and plunder. When the officer in charge of the city reported that many European corpses were lying about the Emperor Bahadur Shah Zafar ordered a search to be made for the bodies of Mr. Simon Fraser (the Commissioner) and Captain Douglas (Assistant Resident and in charge of the Palace Guard), in order that if found they might be buried in the Christian burial ground; but all other bodies were to be thrown in the river. It was later reported to the Emperor Bahadur Shah Zafar that Sir John Metcalfe had not been identified among the killed.[7]

Emperor Bahadur Shah Zafar was dismayed by the attitude of the order less Sepoys and their looting the city people, but he was helpless to do anything. He was a puppet at the hands of the army. Orders were brought to him ready written out for his signature. He made a feeble attempt to assert himself, but his orders were set at naught. The cavalry stabled their horses in the royal gardens, and galloped about within the precincts of the palace, even up to the Hall of Audience, places which, as the Emperor pathetically complained, 'not even Nadir Shah or Ahmad Shah, or any of the British Governor Generals of India ever entered on horseback.' The soldiers turned the palace buildings into barracks, neglected to salute, appeared before the King without their turbans, and even crowded into the Hall of Devotion with their shoes on. On 16th May, Sepoys and palace servants killed 49 Europeans who had been held prisoner within the palace despite Bahadur Shah's protests. Over the attitude of the revolutionaries, the dispute was growing day by day between Emperor and the revolutionaries and on 16th, it rose on its height. On 17th of May, the mutineers elected Mirza Abu Bakr, the son of Mirza Mughal and the grandson of Bahadur Shah Zafar, as their Emperor in place of the old Emperor Bahadur Shah Zafar, whom they declared to be too old and infirm. Hakim Ahsanullah had an audience and represented that the mutineers were a treacherous, bloodthirsty class, on whom no dependence could be placed. The Emperor summoned many of the revolutionaries to his presence and spoke to them very severely.[8]

Emperor Bahadur Shah Zafar was fed up with the daily news of atrocities committed upon the people of Delhi by the Sepoys as well as the Princes. He expressed his anger to Mirza Mughal, Mirza Abu Bakr, and Mirza Abdullah, at their sympathy with the Sepoys (in their loot and plunder of the city as well as their looseness to fight against the British), warned them that one day they would be hanged, as soon as the English entered the city. "My fate," he said, may be thus expressed:

> "Kafan pahankar zindagi ke aiyyam, kisi bagh men guzar dunga."
> (For the rest of my life, 1 shall pass in the seclusion of some garden, Clothed in my burial sheet.)

Several *kaharies* and *khatris* petitioned the Emperor regarding the oppressions practised by the soldiers, and the stoppage of

Sepoy's entry to the city. Over the above issues and for public protection, the Emperor sent orders to the chief of the revolutionaries. He also threatened to take poison, unless greater discipline was enforced and the oppressions discontinued. The chief promised immediate compliancc, and assured that there would be no further occasion for similar complaints.[9]

Dehli Urdu Akhbar published the threatening of Emperor Bahadur Shah Zafar, "Earlier the Firangis.... Now you Tilangas are causing even more grief and trouble with your plundering .... I have no love for the throne or for the money, and give notice that I will proceed into retirement towards (the Sufi shrine of) Khwaja Saheb (in Mehrauli).... Hence I plan to migrate towards the Ka'aba and the Haram Sharif of Mecca, there to spend the rest of my days in prayer, repentance, and remembering the Almighty."[10]

After a lot of persuasion and negotiations, Emperor showed his readiness to continue to lead the revolutionaries. He issued a proclamation in the latter part of May, which was as follows:[11]

> "Be it known to all the Hindus and Mohammadans, the subjects and servants on the part of the officers of the English forces stationed at Delhi and Meerut, that all the Europeans are united in this point first, to deprive the army of their religion; and then, by the force of strong measures, to Christianize all the subjects. In fact, it is the absolute orders of the Governor General to serve out cartridges made up with swine and beef fat. If there be 10,000 who resist this, to blow them up; if 50,000, to disband them.... It is therefore necessary that all Hindus and Mohammadans should be of one mind in this struggle, and make arrangements for their preservation with the advice of some creditable persons.... If the infidels now become mild, it is merely an expedient to save their lives. Whoever will be deluded by their frauds, he will repent. Our reign continues. Thirty rupees to a mounted, and ten rupees to a foot soldier, will be the salary of the new servants of Delhi."

The experienced Emperor Bahadur Shah Zafar was still annoyed with the Sepoys for their inactivity and idle stay at the city. He served an order on 23rd June, 1857 'To all the officers of the Platoons and Sawars who had not gone into the trenches'. The order was as follows:[12]

> "Despite the fact that this war started over faith and religion, many of you have not gone to battle and instead while your time away in gardens or shops. Others are hiding inside their quarters, protecting their lives. His Highness the Emperor has made you all swear on his salt that all the platoons would go on the attack and annihilate the Kafirs, but you no longer show the will to do so, How sad that when this confrontation is about religion and faith, and when His Highness gave you his protection, you still refrain from going for battle. Remember, the platoon that does not go to battle, will have its allowances stopped from tomorrow, but those platoons and cavalry units who show courage and fortitude today and indeed have shown it before, will receive rewards, medals and honours from the Court. Moreover, His Highness the Emperor will be highly gratified."

As shown in the above orders, the Emperor seems active, firm to his duty, and willing to continue the war against the British. Nevertheless, perhaps the Sepoys show their inactiveness in fighting the British forces. Most of the Sepoys began to take the active part in court politics and enjoying the plundered booty of the local residents. Even some of the Sepoys passed their time in their quarters. Emperor goaded them to fight against the enemy both by alluring and threatening.

Regarding the role and position of the Emperor Bahadur Shah Zafar, there are a lot of historical writings, views, and opinions among the experts, mostly with general perception that the Sepoys showed naiveness by choosing the old, inexperienced, and British pensioner Bahadur Shah Zafar as their Emperor. However, by analyzing the whole fact and intentions of the Sepoys it becomes clear that they actually wanted to transform the character of the mutiny into the general Uprising or war of independence, and the Emperor was the only national symbol at that time. Their aim was to overthrow the East India Company's Government. The rebel Sepoys clearly understood that the colonial state could be successfully overthrown only by establishing an alternative source of authority with wide acceptability. The question of wide acceptability forced the Sepoys to accept Bahadur Shah Zafar as their nominal head and create their own state. Most of the rebel Governments in different parts of northern, central, and eastern India invariably sought the formal sanction of the Emperor to establish their legitimacy.

Most of the contemporary writers generally remarked the Emperor as inexperienced and foolish. The remark of Sir Syed Ahmad Khan about Bahadur Shah Zafar is needed to be quoted in this regard, He says, "...Such an imbecile was the ex-King that had one assured him that the angels of Heaven were his slaves; he would have welcomed the assurance, and would have caused half a dozen *farmans* to be prepared immediately. The ex-King had a fixed idea that he could transform himself into a fly or gnat, and that he could in this guise convey himself to other countries, and learn what was going on there. Seriously, he firmly believed that he possessed the power of transformation. He was in the habit of asking his courtiers in durbar if it were not so, and his courtiers were not the men to undeceive him." Sir Syed further says, "No one looked upon the King as sovereign or as consecrate; men used to flatter him to his face, and laugh at him behind his back. The people clung to him from no feeling of loyalty, but with a view to their own advantage."[13]

It is very strange and rather confusing that the Sepoys on the one hand, wanted to convert the Uprising into national war of independence; they frequently ridiculed their national symbol, Emperor Bahadur Shah Zafar, on the other. The contemporary writers have fully described the situation by calling the Sepoys as "*Purabea*" and harshly condemn their act and behavior. Bashiruddin Ahmad, in his *Waqiyat-i-Darul Hukumat Dehli,* quotes a wording of a Sepoy who says in his *Purabea* style, "*Bhayyan Ham Ja Manai Ke Sar Par Munda Rakh Dei Wahi Bas Sa Ho Jayi*" (That will be the Emperor on whose head we put our Shoes). In other words, the Emperor is under our shoes. He quotes another saying, "*Budhaoo Sasur Ke Goli Mar Do, Dusre Manai Ka Bas Sa Kar Di Jai*" (shoot the old abused fellow; we would enthrone another man as Emperor). According to Munshi Jeewan Lal, "they addressed him with such disrespectful terms, "I say, you King! I say, you old fellow!" (Ari, Badshah! Ari, Buddha!) "Listen," cried one, catching him by the hand. "Listen to me," said another, touching the old King's beard.[14]

No doubt these remarks were true as initially the position of the Emperor was too delicate, but after the arrival of General Bakht Khan on 1st July and later on setting up of Court of Administration, the normalcy among the royal forces and in the Delhi was restored. The Court of Administration was the main organ of the new and independent state. Bahadur Shah Zafar was formally the head of the state and had the right to be present for all sessions of the Court. However, the elected members of the Court were taking the actual decisions but on every decision the Emperor's approval was sought with his seal. Although the entire power was in the hands of the Court, Emperor tried to intervene in several decisions of the Court. Even the Court had to reconsider any decision that the Emperor did not approve of. In the *Peoples Democracy*, Ammar Faruqui has cited two instances of Bahadur Shah's intervention. First instance was when the soldiers had taken over the city, and the situation was chaotic, Bahadur Shah personally went around the city to instill confidence among the residents. The second was on the occasion of *Id-ul-Adha* in July 1857, to prevent the cow-slaughter. Faruqui mentions that there were enough evidences that the Emperor was actively engaged in consultations, deliberations, receiving petitions, hearing appeals, and recommending appointments.[15]

The most important and excellent work or rather greatest achievement of the Mughal Emperor Bahadur Shah Zafar was to maintain the pluralistic character and communal harmony among the Sepoys and the people. Under him, Hindu-Muslim unity found a powerful expression of anti-colonial movement in which Hindus and Muslims were united as the people of Hindustan. This attribute of communal harmony and non-partisanship towards any religion, Bahadur Shah Zafar inherited from Babar, the founder of Mughal dynasty.[16]

On 8th July, a great dissatisfaction arose due to the murder of five butchers who were caught taking meat to the English camp on a bed. In the audience of next day, the butchers of the city complained to the Emperor that five of their companions had been murdered. Mirza Mughal was ordered to inquire into the grievances. It was proclaimed by beat of drum that anyone caught cow-killing, would be blown away from a gun, and that anybody who was found objecting to the killing of a goat would be punished.[17]

Before the *Id-ul-Adha* festival (1st August), Mughal Emperor Bahadur Shah Zafar held an audience on July 29th and ordered that the letters to be written to the Generals and officers of the army that no cows were to be killed within the city during the forthcoming festival, and if any Mohammadan would defy the order, would be blown away from a gun; and whoever, on the part of a Musalman, helped to kill a cow, would also be killed. Thus, Emperor Bahadur Shah Zafar helped to maintain peace and tranquility among his subjects as half of Delhi population as well as the Sepoys consisted of Hindus and cow-slaughtering would have hurt their religious as well as emotional sentiments, resulting in their alienation from the resistance against the British.[18]

He also issued an order that all the town's cows should be registered, with *Chaukidar*s and sweepers of the different *Muhalla*s instructed to report to the local police station all "cow-owning Muslim households" and for each police station then to make out a list "of all the cows being bred by the followers of Islam" and to send it to the palace.[19]

In the month of September, the Emperor's position became so delicate to handle the war of independence. He was in urgent need of money and military support of the native Kings. In order to get their support Emperor dispatched letters to the Rajas of Jaipur, Jhodpur, Bikaner, and Alwar, that "the Emperor was in want of troops and was desirous of annihilating the English; but inasmuch as he had no reliable person to organize and administer the very important affairs of the empire at this juncture, federacy of States; and if the States he now addressed with these letters would combine for the purpose he would willingly resign the power into their hands."[20]

A lot of battles were fought between the revolutionaries and Europeans but on 14th of September, the British troops stormed Kashmiri Gate and blew it open by gunpowder and entered the city and started a general massacre of the innocent population. The Sepoys and the revolutionaries (*Mujahideen*) under Maulvi Sarfaraz came to the Emperor and told him not to lose the courage as the fighters and the peoples of Delhi are with him and would fight to oust the foreigners. On their request, the Emperor decided to go in person with them to lead the war but on the advice of Hakim Ahsanullah he returned to the fort.[21]

Here the Emperor deserves the ample criticism of being misguided by the Hakim Ahsanullah Khan, a suspicious personality to the revolutionaries. It was the fair chance for the Emperor to prove himself the real descendant of Taimur and Babar. He had to fight the war and meet his fate along with other revolutionaries, which was the only way to attain honour and respect among his Indian subjects. It was the opportunity for the last Emperor to earn honour and fame by fighting the British. If he had accompanied the royal army and boldly met his death on the battlefield, he would have surely attained unforgettable honour and respect from his countrymen.

Emperor Bahadur Shah Zafar committed another folly by trusting Mirza Ilahi Baksh, another suspected spy of the British, on the fateful occasion of fall of Delhi. Being misguided by Mirza Ilahi Baksh, he refused the request of his commander-in-chief General Bakht Khan to accompany the fleeing revolutionaries to another destination. Emperor Bahadur Shah Zafar could avail the second chance to lead the revolutionaries from another centre and proved his abitities, and to some extent, save his life from the wrath of British oppressors.

On 16th of September, when the war became almost one sided, the royal army under Bakht Khan decided to carry on the struggle from any other safest place rather than Delhi. He also requested the Emperor to accompany him to carry on the struggle from somewhere else, and promised to meet him in Humayun's tomb on the next day. However, Mirza Ilahi Baksh persuaded the

Mughal sovereign to accompany him to his house in the night. Having brought him there, he molded him to his purpose. He pointed out to him the hardships which would follow his accompanying the army, assured him of its certain defeat, and then, showing the other side of the shield, indicated that a prompt severance of his cause from the cause of the Sepoys would induce the victorious English to believe that, up to that moment, he had acted under compulsion, and that he had seized the first opportunity to sever himself from traitors.[22]

In the morning of 17th of September, Emperor left the fort without informing the Wazir Ahsanullah and Begum Hazrat Mahal. He, firstly, came to Shrine of Hazrat Nizamuddin Aulia and then left for Tomb of Humayun to take refuge. The other courtiers and family members also followed him later on. General Bakht Khan met the Emperor, his zenana, his sons, and his nobles at the tomb of Humayun on 19th September, represented to the Emperor that his only safety lay in flight, and begged him to accompany the Sepoy army and renew the war in the open country. The Emperor, however, rejected his advice, and, allowed him and the army to depart without him. John Kaye writes, "rather than undergo the fatigues, the perils, the uncertainties attendant on the prolongation of a contest which they had encouraged, they deliberately preferred to trust to the tender mercies of the conqueror. What those tender mercies were likely to be did not seem to trouble much the degenerate Mughals. They promised, at all events, a quick decision; a decision preferable to the agony of suspense."[23]

Mirza Ilahi Baksh now started communication with Maulvi Rajab Ali, the British spy of the highest order. Rajab Ali requested him simply to detain the royal family for twenty-four hours after the departure of the rebel army, at the tomb of Humayun, and to leave the rest to him. Rajab Ali further informed his chief, Hodson, and the whole tragic drama followed later on.[24]

Notwithstanding, in these grave situations, the remaining revolutionaries and *Mujahideens* never lose the courage and continued a street battle which lasted until the occupation of the Red Fort on 20th September 1857. The hideout of the Emperor was discovered by a British agent Maulvi Rajab Ali. Captain

Hodson along with 100 soldiers of his own rushed to the Humayun's tomb and invited the Emperor to surrender. Queen Zeenat Mahal implored the Emperor to yield on the condition of a promise of life. To this situation John Kaye has very beautifully described, "the mind of the old man, agitated by a dim recollection of the position he had inherited and forfeited, by despair of the present, by doubts of the future, was still wavering. Why had not he acted as Akbar would have acted, and accompanied the troops to die, if he must die, as a king? What to him were the few years of dishonour which the haughty conqueror might safe to him? Better life in the free plains of India, hunted though he might be, than life in durance for him, a king! But then rushed in the fatal conviction that it was too late. He had decided when he dismissed Bakht Khan! The Frank and his myrmidons were at his door!"[25]

After a few conversations, Hodson arrested the Emperor along with Zeenat Mahal and Jawan Bakht on 21st of September, 1857 amidst from thousands of armed dependents and so-called rabbles and put them in the Lal Kuan Haveli of Begum Hazrat Mahal (formerly the residence of Begum Samru) in strong confinement. Hodson himself writes, "I was fortunate enough to capture the King and his favourite wife. Today, more fortunate still, I have seized and destroyed the King's two sons and a grandson (the famous, or rather infamous, Abu Bukr), the villains who ordered the massacre of our women and children, and stood by and witnessed the foul barbarity; their bodies are now lying on the spot where those of the unfortunate ladies were exposed. I am very tired, but very much satisfied with my day's work, and so seem all hands."[26]

The occupation of the city by the British followed a large-scale murder, loot, and plunder, especially by European and Sikh soldiers. Griffiths describes that on September 14, the day of assault, until the solemn declaration, when Delhi was completely in their possession, much looting took place in the city. British troops, both European and Native, and especially the Sikhs, entered houses during those days and managed to secrete about their persons articles of value. Each and every house was searched carefully; the walls were raised; the floors were dug, and the furnitures were broken to find out the gold, silver and jewels. Many soldiers from the English regiments got possession of jewellery and gold ornaments taken from the bodies of the slain Sepoys and city inhabitants, and he (Griffiths) was shown by men of his regiment strings of pearls and gold mohurs which had fallen into their hands. The Europeans carried away the looted valuables where they fully demonstrated among their people.[27]

Griffiths describes about the Emperor's position after his imprisonment, "He was guarded by fifty men of my regiment, under command of a Lieutenant; and on the 22nd I went to see him, accompanied by our Adjutant. Sitting cross-legged on a cushion placed on a common native charpoy or bed, in the verandah of a courtyard, was the last representative of the Great Mughal dynasty. There was nothing imposing in his appearance, save a long white beard which reached to his girdle. About middle height, and upwards of seventy years old, he was dressed in white, with a conical shaped turban of the same colour and material, while at his back two attendants stood, waving over his head large fans of peacocks' feathers, the emblem of sovereignty a pitiable farce in the case of one who was already shorn of his regal attributes, a prisoner in the hands of his enemies. Not a word came from his lips; in silence he sat day and night, with his eyes cast on the ground, and as though utterly oblivious of the condition in which he was placed. On another bed, three feet from the King, sat the officer on guard, while two stalwart European sentries, with fixed bayonets, stood on either side. The orders given were that on any attempt at a rescue the officer was immediately to shoot the King with his own hand."[28]

Next day Captain Hodson again marched to the tomb and arrested his sons Mirza Mughal, Mirza Khizr Sultan and one grandson Mirza Abu Bakr, the son of Mirza Mughal, and mercilessly shot them near the Delhi Gate due to the bloody revenge, and their head were sent to the Emperor in the breakfast tray.[29]

In the words of Hodson, "...and then sent in one of the inferior scions of the royal family (purchased for the purpose by the promise of his life) and my one-eyed Maulvi Rajab Ali, to say that I had come to seize the Shahzadahs for punishment, and intended to do so, dead or alive. After two hours of wordy strife and very anxious suspense, they appeared, and asked if their lives had been promised by the Government, to which I answered' most certainly not, and sent them away from the tomb towards the city ...a large mob had collected, and were turning on the guard. I rode in among them at a gallop, and in a few words I appealed to the crowd, saying that these were the butchers who had murdered and brutally used helpless women and children, and that the Government had now sent their punishment: seizing a carbine from one of my men, I deliberately shot them one after another. I then ordered the bodies to be taken into the city, and thrown out on the 'Chabutara,' in front of the Kotwali, where the blood of their innocent victims still could be distinctly traced. The bodies remained before the Kotwali until this morning, when, for sanitary reasons, they were removed. In twenty-four hours, therefore, I disposed of the principal members of the house of Taimur, the Tartar."[30]

The question as to whether Hodson was justified in taking the lives of the princes has been much debated. The Hodson's plea to kill the princes, on the pretext of danger from the mob crowds, bears a lot of criticism from the historians and other intelligentsia. It was quite ridiculous that Hodson had scented no danger, in the distance, that lay between Humayun's tomb and the city. It was at the city gate that he realized the danger to his position. The day before, when Hodson brought the Emperor as a prisoner to the city, he apprehended no violence from the mob. Shortly afterwards twenty one princes of the Royal family were tried. They were tried for associating with conspirators and rebels and were all condemned, hanged and carted off the same day. The Emperor was surprisingly very calm when Hodson shot dead his sons Mirza Mughal, Mirza Khizr Sultan and one grandson Mirza Abu Bakr, who was barely 21 years of age. In the overall judgment, the shooting of the princes still remains one of the most painful episodes connected with the Uprising.

The whole city was converted into discarded waste where the streets were filled with broken furniture and corpses. There was no resident who could be seen in miles of distance except the British soldiery. Even the Great Mosque of Delhi was full of the infidel soldiers under Major Coke's Punjab Rifles, there were no worshippers to be found in the sacred building. *Grifiths* states, "A report spread at this time that it had been decided to blow up the mosque. I cannot vouch for the truth of this statement, and can only attribute the rumour to a belief that a large ransom would be paid by the Mohammedan population of India for the preservation of their temple had the authorities really intended to carry out the project. Its destruction would have been an act of vandalism quite at variance with the character of the British nation, and one which would have brought down on us the wrath and contempt of the whole civilized world."[31]

The trial of the imprisoned Emperor Bahadur Shah was started in his own Diwan-i-Khas by the Military Commission on 27th January 1858 and lasted until 9th March 1858. The Commission found him guilty of four charges:

> The first charge—"For that he, being a pensioner of the British Government in India, did, at Delhi, at various times between the 10th of May and 1st of October, 1857, encourage, aid, and abet Mohammad Bakht Khan, subahdar of the regiment of artillery! and divers others, native commissioned officers and soldiers unknown, of the East India Company's Army, in the crimes of mutiny and rebellion against the State."[32]
>
> The second charge—"For having at Delhi, at various times between the 10th of May and 1st of October, 1857, encouraged, aided and abetted Mirza Mughal, his own son, a subject of the British Government in India, and divers others unknown, inhabitants of Delhi, and of the North West provinces of India, also subjects of the said British Government, to rebel and wage war against the State."[33]
>
> The third charge—"For that he, being a subject of the British Government in India, and not regarding the duty of his allegiance, did at Delhi, on the 11th May, 1857, or thereabouts, as a false traitor against the State, proclaim and declare himself the reigning king and sovereign of India, and did, then and there, traitorously

> seize and take unlawful accession of the city of Delhi; and did moreover at various times between the 10th of May and 1st of October, 1857, as such false traitor aforesaid, treasonably conspire, consult, and agree with Mirza Mughal, his own son, and with Mohammad Bakht Khan, Subedar of the regiment of artillery, and divers other false traitors unknown, to raise, levy, and make insurrection, rebellion, and war against the State; and, further to fulfill and perfect his treasonable design of overthrowing and destroying the British Government in India, did assemble armed forces at Delhi, and send them forth to fight and wage war against the said British Government."[34]
>
> The fourth charge accused the Emperor Bahadur Shah Zafar, "of having, at Delhi, on the 16th of May, 1857, or thereabouts, within the precincts of the palace at Dehli, feloniously caused and become accessory to the murder of 49 persons, chiefly women and children of European and mixed European descent."[35]
>
> Lastly, on 9th March, the President of the Commission, Lieut. Colonel M. Dawes announced, "The Court, on the evidence before them, are of opinion that the prisoner Mohammad Bahadur Shah, ex-King of Dehli, is guilty of all and every part of the charges preferred against him."[36]

Kaye quotes the suggestion of the Chief Commissioner of Punjab, about the future disposal of the prisoner Mohammad Bahadar Shah, ex-King of Dehli, that the said prisoner be transported beyond the seas as a felon, and be kept in some island or settlement, where he will be entirely isolated from all other Mohammadans. As regards his wife, Zeenat Mahal, and his son, Jawan Bakht, no charges having been exhibited against them and the latter being only 17 years of age, but they both having been present at Dehli, the Chief Commissioner suggested that they be allowed the option of accompanying the prisoner to his place of transportation; and that, in the event of their declining to do so, they be confined as State prisoners somewhere in the Lower

Provinces of the Bengal Presidency. In the last, it was decided to send him to Rangoon, the capital of Burma.[37]

The mock trial of deceased Emperor Bahadur Shah was a process of humiliating the emblematic head of India and the charges of treason that were framed against the Emperor was nothing but to prove that the Company was the real sovereign power. The charges of treason were absurd on the part of the company and the whole process was the part of the terror which started in Delhi from September 1857 onwards. There needs a long discussion on this topic that who was the real rebel, Company or the Emperor Bahadur Shah Zafar, whose authority even the Company had recognized before 1857.

Emperor Bahadur Shah Zafar was a recognized ruler of India and the Indian people, including the Sepoys of every corner of India considered him as their only rightful ruler of India. The trial of Bahadur Shah Zafar was not only the humiliation of India as a nation but a serious injury to the millions of Indian people. Here it needs to be quoted the conversation of a Subedar of the mutinous British force at Awadh. The Subedar told to his officer, "Proclamations have been received from the King of Delhi, informing all that he is once more on the throne of his fathers, and calling upon the whole army to join his standard. Also that Raja Man Singh, under whose guardianship the (European) ladies at Faizabad placed themselves, had been appointed Commander-in-Chief in Awadh." The subedar further said, "You English have been a long time in India, but you know little of us. We have nothing to do with Wajid Ali or any of his relations; the kings of Lucknow were made by you. The only ruler in India empowered to give sunnuds is the King of Delhi; he was never made a King of Awadh, and it is from him only that we shall receive our orders."[38]

Undoubtedly, the Emperor Bahadur Shah Zafar was the great hero of the Uprising, and every point of his patriotism and sacrifice was proven during his trial. Charles Raikes writes, "I may here mention that I read several of the King's orders, written with his own pencil, and proving what an ungrateful old man he is. The English saved his family from the most cruel tyranny of the Marathas, gave them back royal rank, and bestowed an ample pension, yet this hoary-headed sinner orders all Christians to be murdered, etc. etc."[39]

Whatever Emperor Bahadur Shah Zafar, did as a ruler was certainly not a tyranny or infidelity towards the British. He was instead a marvelous ruler of India. Whatevcr he did was nothing other than patriotism to his nation and his duty of Kingship to protect the nation and its people from foreign marauders.

As a matter of fact, May 1857 was the time when the Sepoys joined with farmers, peasants, religious people, etc. and tried to overthrow the foreign yoke from Indian subcontinent. It was definitely a justified step as the Indian people were enslaved about a hundred years ago. Now they made the symbolic Mughal Emperor as their actual ruler with the assistance of a body known as Court of Administration purely on democratic pattern. It was unfortunate that the British again regained power by disturbing the existing political system and killing Delhites and relatives of the ruler. This shows that the so-called rebels were actually freedom fighters who were duty-bound to support the Emperor, and the Company was the rebel in the real sense, as its Government had no independent constitutional basis and derived from the various farmans issued by the Mughals. The act of trial was unjustified, highly condemnable and rather a blot on the so called most civilized race throughout the world.

Mughal Emperor Bahadur Shah Zafar died on 7th November 1862 in the Rangoon jail being buried in the night-time near his bungalow, so that none might know the resting-place of the last of the great Mughal Emperors. William Dalrymple says by quoting the British Commissioner, Captain H.N. Davis that the bier of the State Prisoner was accompanied by his two sons and an elderly mullah. The ceremony was brief. The British authorities had made sure not only that the grave was already dug, but that quantities of lime were on hand to guarantee the rapid decay of both bier and body. When the shortened funeral prayers had been recited, the earth was thrown over the lime, and the turf carefully replaced to disguise the place of burial. Captain H.N. Davis further reported, "...The death of the ex-King may be said to have had no effect on the Mohammadan part of the populace of Rangoon, except perhaps for a few fanatics who watch and pray for the final triumph of Islam. A bamboo fence surrounds the grave, and by the time the fence is worn out, the grass will again have properly covered the spot, and no vestige will remain to distinguish where the last of the Great Mughals rests."[40]

The remaining family members (*Shahzadas* and *Shahzadis*) of the Emperor Bahdur Shah Zafar met the grave fate. After long times' misery and suffering, Government fixed their monthly stipend as five rupees per month. But in course of time this was also discontinued. Bashiruddin Ahmad mentions that in Delhi, the persons who carry the bridegroom's cot in the marriage ceremonies called as *Shohda*. These *Shohdas* are actually the *Shahzadas* (princes) belonging to the royal Mughal family. They still swear that "If I tell a lie, then I could not get the throne".[41]

Khwaja Hasan Nizami has seen some princes who were beggars in his time. He especially mentions a blind man who was beggar in Jama Masjid area. Khwaja Hasan Nizami identified him as real son to the daughter (grandson or *niwasa)* of the last Mughal Emperor Bahadur Shah Zafar.[42]

Mughal Emperor Bahadur Shah Zafar was a freedom fighter rather than an Emperor. He was a true administrator and loyal to his subjects. Until 1857, he was the national symbol of united India. The following famous couplet of the Emperor proves his bravery and patriotism:

> *Ghazion men bu rahegi jab talak iman ki,*
> *Takht-e-London tak chalegi tegh Hindustan ki*
> (As long as there remains the least trace of love of faith into the hearts of our heroes, so long, the sword of Hindusthan shall be sharp, and one day shall flash even at the gates of London.)

The British were thc enemies of the Indian people, and they brutally punished the Emperor Bahadur Shah Zafar and annihilated his family. However, its rather chagrin to the nation that even after independence; the great national Emperor could not find the due place, and his ancestors are bound to beg in the streets.

Mohammad Bakht Khan

Mohammad Bakht Khan was born in 1797 in Bijnor in Rohelkhand. His grandfather Ghulam Qadir Khan (not Ghulam Qadir Rohilla) came from Afghanistan to Lucknow to make a living. His father Abdullah Khan got a job under Rohilla Government at Bijnore and was married to an Awadh Princess. Due to his close association to the Rohillas of Rohilkhand and his origin from Afghanistan, he was also known as Mohammad Bakht Khan Rohilla. It is also said that due to his mother's influence and relation to the eastern Uttar Pradesh, he was well versed in *Poorbea* language and culture.

He became a Subedar (native Captain) in the army of the East India Company, gaining forty years of experience in the Bengal horse artillery and seeing action in the First Anglo-Afghan War. He was belonged to No 15 Horse Light Field Battery. Subedar Bakht Khan was described by one of his British superiors of the Bengal Native Artillery as 60 years of age, forty years of which were spent in the Company's service. 5 ft 10 inches in height, 44 inches round the chest, barrel like chest, very fat thighs, bulging stomach, proud, sturdy, clever and good at gun drill, most intelligent, obsequious, fond of the society of Europeans etc. Mohammad Bakht Khan along with his forces mutinied on 31st of May on Sunday when the English were in church. It is also believed that this date was fixed for general insurrection but on 10th May, an untimely outbreak happened at Meerut. Bakht Khan and the Sepoys forced the British under Robert Alaxander, the Commissioner of Bareilly, to leave the city. He proclaimed Khan Bahadur Khan as the ruler of Bareilly in the capacity of the Subedar of the Emperor, and himself became commander of the troops. He organized, trained, and built up the Rohilla Sepoys. A Hindu, named Sobha Ram, who had served in the British Commissariat, was appointed Diwan of the district; other officials, Hindu and Musalman, were appointed to various posts. On the 11th June, Mohammad Bakht Khan along with the Sepoys left for Delhi and arrived in Delhi on 1st July 1857.[43]

On his arrival to Delhi, Mohammad Bakht Khan behaved not very well to the courtier or the Emperor; perhaps he was unaware of the Court etiquette. He also not handed over the treasury, which he had brought, except a couple of rupees into the hands of Emperor Bahadur Shah Zafar. Emperor presented him with a robe of honour. Bakht Khan was conferred upon the title of General by Emperor Bahadur Shah Zafar. Khushwant Singh his book, "*Delhi: A Novel*" very beautifully writes the conversation of the Emperor with General Bakht Khan. Khushwant Singh writes that on being conferred the title of General, Bakht Khan replied in rustic accent of Bihar. "*Badshah Salamat,*' 'I am no *jurnail-vurnail.* I am only a *subedar.* But I have ten thousand Ghazis with me. And we ask for nothing more than the honour to shed our blood for Your Majesty." He further writes that when Emperor virtually made him the Commander-in-Chief and wished that may Allah crown his sword with victory, Bakht Khan replied without decorum, "*Arre Bhai, Badshah,* 'your name is *Japhar,* isn't it? *Japhar* means victory, doesn't it? You will be *Japhar.* Anyone can any bet with me,' he said putting out his hands in challenge."[44]

As the Commander-in-Chief Mirza Mughal also called Mirza Zahiruddin was inexperienced in military affairs, Mohammad Bakht Khan was given the responsibility of virtually commanding the revolutionary forces while Mirza Mughal was still Commander-in-Chief in title. Bakht Khan's superior abilities quickly became evident, and the Emperor gave him the title of *Sahab-i-Alam Bahadur,* or Lord Governor General. He formed a Court of Administration composed of both soldiers and civilians of both the communities, Hindu and Muslim, so as to control and ensure smooth functioning of overall administration.[45]

M.G. Aggrawal in his book "*Freedom Fighters of India*" says that the Mughal army was unhappy with Emperor Bahadur Shah for promoting Bakht Khan to the rank of 'General' because neither did he take part in active fighting nor did he surrender his personal treasure to the Emperor. The Mughal High Command had become ineffective due to differences between General Bakht Khan and General Ghous on the one hand, and between Bakht Khan and General Sidhara Singh on the other. Agrawal emphasizes in his book that Sidhara Singh even suspected that General Bakht was secretly in league with the British. The Emperor seriously admonished Bakht Khan for his conduct.[46]

He formed the Military Coucil (Coucil of Administration) and also persuaded the Muslim Ulema to issue the *Fatwa* of *Jihad* and wage war against the British. In his able guidance, the mal-administration was ended and the people of Delhi were relieved from military oppression. Even he banned the illegal extortion by the Princes. His abilities created a jealousy among the officers of the Delhi administration and military men. It was perhaps a drawback on his part that he could not achieve the military success as he was expected. It was also his folly that instead of fighting on the battlefield against the British, he wasted his time in controlling the civil administration. All these drawbacks annoyed his colleagues and also the Emperor Bahadur Shah Zafar.

As he was the Commander-in-Chief, it was expected with him to continuously wage the war and defeat the enemy whose numerical strength was about one-tenth of the fighting force of Delhi. The Emperor was surprised that such a large fighting force composed of the experienced fighters of the British army and the suicide *Ghazis* are unable to crush the petty British, who were suffering over the Ridge. Emperor wanted the quick action, and nothing was being done according to his wishes. The Emperor Bahadur Shah Zafar was finally annoyed with the chief commander and administrator General Bakht Khan. The Emperor was so unhappy with Bakht Khan, whom he ordered to go out of the city and fight with the British otherwise he ould leave the city and go wherever he wanted to. The situation came to a head on 29th of August, when the Emperor ordered Bakht Khan to go to Najafgarh and rescue the brigade under siege of the British. Bakht Khan not only refused to obey the command but also added that he was totally independent in his actions.[47]

After the fall of Delhi, The Commander-in-Chief of the revolutionary army, the Bakht Khan, evacuated the city of Delhi, taking with him all the fighting men upon whom he could depend. Before his evacuation, Bakht Khan exerted all his eloquence to induce the King to accompany him. He represented to him that all was not lost, and though the English had gained their stronghold, the open country was before them, and that, under the shadow of his name and presence, it would be still possible to continue the war, always with a chance of success. However, his efforts could not become successful due to the interference of Ilahi Baksh Khan. Mohammad Bakht Khan after leaving Delhi went straight to Farrukhabad with all the few men he could keep together. Here he joined Moosun Ali Khan, one of the nazims of the Nawab of Furrukhabad, in opposing the British, and on being defeated at Khudagunj; he was making the best of his way across the Ganges and joined freedom fighters in Lucknow and Shahjahanpur.[48]

After the fall of Lucknow and other revolutionary centres of Northern India, the Heroes of the Uprising moved into the Terai area of Nepal border. General Bakht Khan along with his Brigade also followed the same. Most of them tried to take refuge in Nepal, but they were repulsed by the Gorkhas. They made their shelter in the Terai Jungle and continued their negotiation with the Gorkhas and their leader Jang Bahadur. The British force, 5th Punjab Infantry, under Colonel Vaughan was continuously chasing their hideouts. Charles Edward Stewarts writes that he was one of the officers who were following the revolutionaries in the Terai region near Rapti River of Sidhonia Ghat. In one of their encounters with the revolutionaries in June 1859, the British force killed eighty seven revolutionaries, outside of a village near Sidhonia Ghat. Among the dead, one was General Bakht Khan who was at that time commanding the Nasirabad Brigade. The remainders were driven into Nepal.[49]

It is general belief that Bakht Khan later on went to Nepal where he died in 1859 due to his wounds. Adam and Charles Black narrate a different story that Bakht Khan was killed in the battle of Nawabgunj in Lucknow. But according to some beliefs, General Bakht Khan was neither captured nor traced, and historians in Swat claim that it was there that he came when the war was lost. Bakht Khan spent his later life for the protection of the Akhund of Swat. General Bakht Khan was called 'The Prince' by Swati people, but they had no knowledge of his role as a freedom fighter. He kept his heroic past to himself to keep the British away. In 1859, he was mortally wounded and died and buried in the Graveyard of Nanser, Nanser (Koz Band) in Swat.[50]

Sir Syed Ahmad Khan

Sir Syed Ahmad Khan (October 17, 1817 – March 27, 1898) was born to Mir Mohammad Taqi and Aziz-un-Nisa in Delhi. It is said that his forefathers had migrated to India at the time of Mughal Emperor Akbar from Herat in Afghanistan. His ancestors from paternal and maternal side were closely attached to the Mughal administration from many generations. His grandfather Syed Mohammad Hadi came from Herat and settled in Hindustan. His grandfather Syed Mohammad Hadi was given the titles of Jowahid Khan and Javed-ud Daulah, a *mansab* of 1000/500, in the court of Mughal Emperor Alamgir II. Syed Ahmed Khan's father, Syed Mohammad Taqi, was a man of deep religious feeling, and on his father's death, declined all titles from the Mughal Emperor Akbar Shah II, though offered those of his father. His maternal grandfather Khwaja Fariduddin served as *wazir* in the court of Mughal Emperor Akbar Shah II.[51]

On his father's death in 1836, the Emperor Bahadur Shah Zafar bestowed upon Syed Ahmad Khan, the title of his grandfather, 'Javed-ud Daulah' with an additional title 'Aarif Jang'. He received education on the subjects like Persian, Arabic, Urdu, and Islamic jurisprudence at his home. He never received any formal instruction in English but through his own personal efforts, he gained some smattering of the language and could understand, speak, and write. In January 1837, he stopped his education, and, greatly against the inclination of his relatives, entered the British service as *Sar-Rishtadar* (an official) of the Criminal Department in the Sadar Amin's office at Delhi. In February 1839, he was transferred to Agra as Naib Munshi or deputy reader in the office of the Commissioner of that Division. In December 1841, he became Munsif or Sub-Judge of Fatehpur Sikri and was transferred to Delhi in January 1846. Here as Munsif in Delhi, he wrote his famous book, *Asar-us-Sanadid*, (Archeological analysis on the historical buildings of Delhi).[52]

In 1850, Sir Syed Ahmad Khan was posted to Rohtak as subordinate judge; and in 1855, he was transferred in the same capacity to Bijnor, where he remained until the Uprising broke out in May 1857. When the news of the Meerut mutiny reached

Bijnor on the 13th May, there were many European residents, whose lives were at stake. These were Mr. and Mrs. Shakespeare and their child; Mr. Palmer; Dr. and Mrs. Knight; Mr. R. Currie; Mr. and Mrs. Lemaistre, and three children; Mr. Johnson; Mr. and Mrs. Murphy, and four children; and Mr. Cawood. Mr. Shakespeare and Syed Ahmad Khan, in order to prepare them from any danger and to save the life of the Europeans, raised a body of 100 Pathan horse and foot for their protection and also arranged intelligence for the daily news regarding the progress of the Uprising.[53]

About the end of May, the Uprising erupted at Bijnor but Sir Syed Ahmad Khan convinced the Roorki mutineers to bye-pass the Bijnor and advised Mr. Shakespeare to hide the treasury in the well. However, after a few days Sir Syed Ahmad Khan heard that the Europeans, who were all in one house, were being surrounded by Mahmud Khan (nephew of Ghulam Qadir Khan who had put out the eyes of Emperor Shah Alam), and his 800 strong men. Sir Syed rushed to that place accompanied by Mir Turrab Ali, Tehsildar, Rahmat Khan, Deputy Collector, and Pratap Singh (later Raja) of Tajpur. Sir Syed urged to Nawab Mahmud Khan to save the life of Europeans and allow them to leave the city. On the other hand, he congratulated the Nawab on receiving the country of his ancestors. It was the trick, which Sir Syed Ahmad Khan applied to save the Europeans. The Nawab, after being fully convinced by the suggestion of Sir Syed Ahmad Khan, provided the Europeans the required carriage for departure. The Nawab thereupon gave them two elephants, a bullock cart and Rs. 3000 for necessary expenditure. All the Europeans departed from Bijnor and safely reached Meerut.[54]

Meanwhile, three Hindu landholders, the Chowdhries of Haldour and Tajpur, gathered their retainers together, and attacked and defeated the Nawab's forces. This created a political as well as administrative disturbance at Bijnor. Sir Syed Ahmad Khan was ordered by Meerut Commissioner to rule the district under the name of English with the assistance of Deputy Collector Mahmud Rahmat Khan and Tahsildar Turrab Ali. However, a month later the Choudhary of Haldour attacked and plundered at a Muslim village Nagina and slaughtered a number of inhabitants. The Muslim people urged the Nawab Mahmud Khan to take over the administration at the district as the English administration failed to provide them protection. The Nawab accordingly attacked and captured Bijnor. Unfortunately, Sir Syed Ahmad Khan fled to Haldaur which created suspicion among the Muslims that the Nagina attack was in connivance of Sir Syed Ahmad Khan. The Nawab attacked and took Haldour, and Syed Ahmad fled to another village, Chandpur, where he was surrounded by a crowd of Muslims who shouted out, "There is the man who brought about the massacre of Mohammadans at Nagina!" From Chandpur, Sir Syed Ahmad Khan, aided by some friends, escaped to Meerut at the end of September, after four months of anxiety and peril.[55]

Towards the end of September 1857, he visited his home at Delhi and heard that his mother had taken refuge in one of her horse attendant's houses. His biographer Graham wrote that on his calling out to her, she opened the door, crying out, "Why have you come here? All are being killed. You will be killed also!" Sir Syed Ahmad Khan came to know that his mother had been living on the horses' grain for five days, and was very weak. For three days, she had no water. He took his mother back with him to Meerut, but the shock and anxiety of mind that she had suffered during the siege and at the assault were too much for her, and she died a month afterwards. Sir Syed Ahmad Khan's uncle and cousin, whose house adjoined his at Delhi, were slain unarmed by the infuriated Sikhs three days after the assault.[56]

In July 1858, he was transferred to Moradabad as Principal Sadar Amin[57] or Native Judge and for his services during the revolt, he received a special pension of Rs. 200 per month and a *khil'at* of one cap of four cones, one *gashwara* or outer turban, one *neem astin* or jacket, one pair of shawls, one belt, one *jugha* or coat, one *surpech* or turban of honour, one pearl necklace and one sword. His loss in goods and chattels at Delhi and at Bijnor, he estimates at Rs. 30,384.[58]

During the Uprising, the British Government experience led them to beliave that happened due to the uprising Muslim religious war or *Jihad,* and after the revolt they massacred mostly the Muslim theologians and innocent population. The animosity between the British and Muslims before and after the rebellion of 1857 threatened marginalized Muslim communities across India. In this grave situation Sir Syed Ahmad Khan firmly stood to defend the Indian masses in general and Muslims in particular. He was the first person who declared that the British policies were the sole cause of the Uprising while defending the people of India. This knighted servant of the British Imperialism was, in the real sense, a first rebel in his own way, after the revolt of 1857.

In 1858, Sir Syed Ahmad Khan wrote a booklet *Asbab-e-Baghawat-e-Hind* (The Causes of the Indian Revolt) in which he rejected the common notion that the conspiracy was planned by Muslims. In this booklet, he blamed the British East India Company for its aggressive expansion as well as the ignorance of British politicians regarding Indian culture. Sir Syed advised the British to appoint the Indian people in their Legislative Councils. According to Sir Syed Ahmad Khan, there were five causes of Uprising, which compelled the Indian people to rise against the British rule. The causes were as follows:[59]

1. Ignorance on the part of the people: by which I mean misapprehension of the intentions of Government.
2. The passing of such laws and regulations and forms of procedure as jarred with the established custom and practice of Hindustan and the introduction of such as were in themselves objectionable.
3. Ignorance on the part of the Government of the conditions of the people; of their modes of thought and of life; and of the grievances through which their hearts were becoming estranged.
4. The neglect on the part of our rulers of such points as were essential to the good Government of Hindustan.
5. The bad management and disaffection of the army.

Sir Syed Ahmad Khan not only charged the British Government for their bad policies in India but also boldly defended the Indians and particularly Muslims who were more convicted in this regard. He tried a lot to save the Muslim community from the heavy hands of the British Government. As the Muslims and the Ulema class were the worst sufferers after failure of the Uprising, Sir Syed Ahmad Khan, while negotiating with the British authorities, deliberately hid the real facts as well as participation of the Muslims in the Uprising. While hiding the facts of the participation of Muslim clerics and masses, he wrote a letter to Sir John Key of India Office, London, in December 1869. In this letter, he boldly asserted that the people who participated in the Uprising were of three groups as follows:[60]

1. Robbers and dacoits who were kept down by the power and strength of the Government, now assembling in numbers, not only attacked way-farers but also plundered villages and even towns.
2. Some of the minor chiefs, whose families had fallen into decay, endeavoured the resuscitation of their ancestral power. This sort of mutiny occurred in four places only: Kanpur, Bareilly, Bijnor, and Farrukhabad. Some of these parties tried to have themselves restored, while others were compelled by the mutineers to make an effort.
3. Some of the lower classes, variously employed, entered the service of these rebellious chiefs.

In the same letter Sir Syed Ahmad Khan accused the British Army officers of Meerut for not handling the Sepoys properly which became a spark for the Uprising. He wrote, "It cannot be denied that the use of the greased cartridges did violence to the superstition of the Sepoys, who consequently determined not to bite the same. Almost all the Sepoys had unanimously resolved never to bite the cartridge, which determination was the only charge that could be brought against them, till a very severe punishment was inflicted upon them at Meerut, a punishment which produced a strong impression on the minds of those men, that they must either bite the greased cartridges or suffer the punishment of their disobedience. And it was then and not before that the discontent of the Sepoys grew into a military mutiny. I am strongly of opinion that if before the infliction of punishment the alternative either of biting the cartridges or resigning the service had been offered to them, the Sepoys would undoubtedly have peaceably withdrawn themselves from the Company's service."[61]

Sir Syed Ahmad Khan advocated that the British Government was not acquainted with the unhappy state of Indian people. He requested the Government that in order to know the public mentality Indians must be included in the Councils. Sir Syed Ahmad Khan says, "I only wish to say that they were misconstructed by people, and that this misconstruction hurried on the rebellion. Had there been a native of Hindustan in the Legislative Council, the people would never have fallen into such errors."[62]

The criticism of Sir Syed Ahmad Khan received the due attention of the British Government, and next year nominated Raja Narendra Singh (Rais Patiala), Raja Devi Narain (Rais Banaras), and Raja Dinkar Rao (Dewan of Gwalior) to the Legislative Council.[63]

His book *Asbab-e-Baghawat-e-Hind* was the first book of its kind about the Uprising of 1857, which boldly criticized the policies of the British Government and advised for reformation in the system according to the need of the time. His book first published from Agra, and he sent its copies to England and British Parliament.

His friend Rai Shankar Das advised him to burn the copies rather than put his life in danger. Sir Syed Ahmad Khan said that he was bringing these matters to the attention of the British for the good of his own people, of his country, and of the Government itself. He also said that if he came to any harm while doing something that would greatly benefit the rulers and the subjects of India alike, he would gladly suffer whatever befell him. When the Government of India had the book translated and presented before the Council, Lord Canning, the governor-general, and Sir Barthold Frere favourably accepted it as a sincere and friendly report. When the House of Commons discussed the pamphlet, Mr. Sale Beadon, the Foreign Secretary, vehemently opposed it and asked the Government to imprison such a revolutionary writer. However, Parliament did not support him. On the contrary, most of the British papers supported the views of Syed Ahmad and advised the Government to act upon the valuable recommendations made by him. The foreign secretary Sale Beadon, however, severely attacked it, calling it 'an extremely seditious pamphlet'. He wanted a proper inquiry on the matter and said that the author, unless he could give a satisfactory explanation, should be harshly dealt with. Since no other member of the Council agreed to his opinion, his attack did no harm.[64]

In addition to the *Asbab-e-Baghawat-e-Hind,* Sir Syed Ahmad Khan wrote another book *The Loyal Mohammadans of India,* in 1860, to save the Muslims from the cruelties of the British Government. He emphasized that during and for long after the Uprising, the Muslims were under a cloud. To them were attributed all the horrors and calamities of that terrible time; and that this prejudice was to a very great extent unjust, and that it was regretted and resented by the Muslims, is undoubted. In this book, he reminded the Government for the services rendered by the Indian Muslims during the memorable years of 1857-58.[65]

Defending his Muslim brethren, Sir Syed Ahmad Khan says in his book, *The Loyal Mohammadans of India,* "...Undoubtedly, if a man be guilty of a really culpable act, there can be no extenuation for it; but when he is enveloped by the sombre mantle of misfortune, even his good deeds are open to suspicion and misconstruction, and are either condemned in toto, or said to proceed from a latent sinister motive. Certainly, good and bad are to be found in every class and creed; but the proverb that 'a fish pollutes all water' has reference especially to a season of distress; for it is a peculiarity of the time, that if even one man has done ill, the entire class to which he belongs is held up to execration; and although a large number of that class may have done right well, nobody thinks of their good deeds, and they get no credit for them. Now the season of dire extremity to which I allude is that which befell the Mohammedans in 1857-58. There was no atrocity committed then of which the blame was not imputed to the Mohammadans, although the parties really guilty may have been Ramdin and Matadin.... There was no prickly thorn in those awful times respecting which it was not said that it was planted by a Mohammedan! There was no fiery whirlwind that was not raised by a Mohammadan".[66]

In 1876, when Hunter wrote a book *The Indian Musalmans,*

which defamed the Indian Muslims in all around, Sir Syed Ahmad Khan once again came forward in their defence. In 1872, he wrote a review of Hunter's book in which he answered the every aspect which had been discussed in that book. After their participation of the Uprising of 1857, the Indian Muslims were once again on the focus of British criticism. It was owing to three causes, viz., the Wahabi trials at Patna and Ambala, Dr Hunter's book on the 'Indian Mussulmans,' and the murder of the late lamented Chief-Justice Norman. Sir Syed Ahmad Khan writes, as quoted by Graham, "Articles sneering at them, or misrepresenting their thoughts and feelings, sink deep into their soul, and work much harm.... I had expected great things from Dr. Hunter's book. Alas that I should add one more to the long list of disappointed men! Friend to the Mohammadans as Dr. Hunter no doubt is, his friendship, as represented by this his last work, has worked us great harm. 'God save me from my friends!' was the exclamation which rose to my lips as I perused the author's pages...he has used his 'power of the pen' in a way calculated still more to embitter the minds of Englishmen against the already little-loved Muslims".[67]

At the time of crisis, Sir Syed Ahmad Khan, tried his level best to prove the Muslim community loyal to the British Government on the basis of the loyalty of a few people whose name he has mentioned in his book. However, the fact also could not be denied that the number of those people was like salt in the cooked food and it is evident that these were the Muslim *Jihadis* or *Mujahideen* who fought the war until their last breath.

After the war of 1857, when the British Government started the persecution of the Muslims, it appeared that Muslims would not stand upon their feet again. The Mughal Empire was finally liquidated in the terrible blood bath of 1857. Sir Syed bitterly lamented on the plight of Muslims and he thought that only modern education could improve their situation and change their mentality. That's why he established many schools wherever he was transferred.

In 1859, he founded a school in Moradabad, in 1863 in Ghazipur and finally in 1875 in Aligarh. In April 1864, Sir Syed Ahmad Khan got transferred at Aligarh where he continued his educational work of Scientific Society which he had already established at Ghazipur in the same year. The idea of establishing an English medium school was born in his mind at Aligarh. In 1867, he was transferred to Banaras and on 1st April 1869 Sir Syed Ahmad Khan, along with his two sons and servant Chajju, left for England to see the British system of education in England. Sir Sayed Ahmad Khan accompanied his sons Syed Mahmud and Syed Hamid, who were going to higher study in England, and after their return, they were appointed High Court Judge and Superintendent of Police in the North-West Provinces. Traveling across England, Sir Syed Ahmad Khan visited its colleges and was inspired by the culture of learning established after the Renaissance.[68]

Sir Syed returned to India towards the end of 1870 with determination to build a 'Muslim Cambridge' and resumed his duties of Native Judge at Banaras. Soon after his return from England, Sir Syed started a journal called the '*Mohammedan Social Reformer*,' and wrote a series of articles combating the religious prejudices of his fellow-countrymen against the acquisition of modern science and art. Graham quotes, "He saw the weakness that had crept over Mohammadans through their estrangement from the thoughts and aspirations of the nineteenth century, and he proposed to himself the great task of makings Mohammadans change, not their dogmas, but their policy, so that independence of mind and political liberation should no longer be accounted as symptoms of heterodoxy."[69]

At Aligarh, the Mohammadan Anglo Oriental College was opened on 24th May 1875, but the actual work commenced from first June of the same year. On 12th November, the Governor of United Provinces, Sir William Muir visited the College and after a long address congratulated Sir Syed Ahmad Khan. In 1876, after thirty-seven years' service, Syed Ahmad retired on his pension, and took up his abode at Aligarh and continued the work of educational uplift of the nation. On 8th January 1877, Honourable Edward Robert Lytton, Viceroy and Governor General of India laid the foundation stone of the College which was already running from 1875. At this occasion, Sir Syed Ahmad

Khan gave expression to his earnest hopes that this College may expand into a University, whose sons shall go forth through the length and breadth of the land to preach the gospel of free enquiry, of large-hearted toleration and of a pure morality. Only to uplift the community Sir Syed Ahmad Khan accepted the membership of the Viceroy's Council for two terms from 1878-1882, but it crowned his long and honourable career.[70]

Through his articles in his journal Mohammadan Social Reformer and modern scientific ideology, Sir Syed Ahmad Khan was dubbed as an atheist. When the MAO College was started a Mohammedan wrote to Mecca asking the priests as to their opinion on Syed Ahmed's proposed college. He said, "What is your opinion (may your Excellence continue) regarding the legality of an institution established by a man who does not believe in the existence of an Evil One; who denies the bodily night-journey of the Prophet to heaven; who does not believe the story of Adam; ...his institution was a school to teach atheism and spread irreligion, ...let me know whether it is religiously lawful for Mohammadans to aid this college or not." The Mecca priest accordingly wrote, "In this case no assistance is allowable to the institution. May God destroy it and its founder. No Mohammadan is allowed to give assistance to or countenance the establishment of such an institution. It is, moreover, the duty of the faithful to destroy it if it be established, and to chastise to the utmost those who are friendly to it." After this religious decree Sir Syed Ahmad Khan received numerous anonymous letters. One of the letters was quoted as, "Sher Ali, who assassinated Lord Mayo, was an idiot for doing so, as he could have ensured Paradise for himself by killing Syed Ahmad!"[71]

Sir Syed Ahmad Khan faced boldly all the hindrances came on his way and showed the right path of uplift and development to his Muslim community. Perhaps educationally upgrading the Muslim community was the only tribute to the Muslim martyrs of the Uprising of 1857. His efforts strengthened the Muslim community to cope with every future engagement and take active part in nation building by educating themselves in modern science and technology.

Mirza Asadullah Beg Khan Ghalib

Mirza Asadullah Beg Khan, popularly known as Ghalib, (27th December, 1797– 15th February, 1869) was born at Agra at Kala Mahal, which is now converted as Indrabhan Girls Inter College. His grandfather, Mirza Qoqan Beg Khan immigrated to India from Samarqand during the reign of Mughal Emperor Ahmad Shah (1748–54) and obtained a minor rank in his army. His father Mirza Abdullah Beg Khan was first soldiered for the Nawab of Awadh, then for the Nizam of Hyderabad, and finally joined the service with the Raja of Alwar, Bakhtawar Singh in 1802. In the battle of Laswari which was fought at Alwar by the combined armies of British East India Company and Alwar Raja Bakhtawar Singh with the Marathas, Mirza Abdullah Beg Khan died in this battle in 1803. At that time, Ghalib was a little over five years of age. He was raised by his uncle Mirza Nasrullah Beg Khan.[72]

Mirza Nasrullah Beg Khan was in marriage to the sister of Nawab Ahmad Baksh Khan of Firozepur Jhirka. Mirza Nasrullah Beg Khan was the governor of Agra under the Marathas. However, in 1803 due to the efforts of Lord Lake, he changed the side and was appointed as an officer of 400 cavalry in the British army and also the monthly salary of Rs. 1700.00 was fixed. Mirza Nasrullah Beg Khan was also awarded the two parganas in Mathura district worth more than one hundred thousand rupees. Nevertheless, after his accidental death in 1806, the British took away the parganas and fixed the pension as Rs. 10,000.00 per annum to his dependents which was to be paid from the revenues of Nawab Ahmad Baksh Khan of Firozepur Jhirka. Mirza Ghalib got his education through private tutoring in various subjects such as Urdu, Persian, and Arabic. It was a setback for him when Nawab of Ferozepur Jhirka reduced the pension to Rs. 3000.00 per year to all the orphans of Mirza Nasrullah Beg Khan. Mirza Ghalib's share in this amount was Rs. 750.00 per anum (Rs. 62 and eight Annas per month). Mirza Ghalib grew up at Agra and in 1810, he was married to the eleven years old Umrao Begum, daughter of Nawab Ilahi Baksh, younger brother of Nawab Ahmad Baksh of Ferozepur Jhirka and Loharu. At the age of fifteen, he moved to Delhi and settled the rented house of Gali

Qasim Jan. Mirza Ghalib received that amount in full only until 1827; after 1827, thanks mainly to the antagonism of his own relatives, he had to struggle hard to get his due share. He went to Calcutta, petitioned the Governor General and the Queen.[73]

His diary, the *Dastamboo* was written by Mirza Ghalib, as a frightened man, who was looking for avenues of safety, and forging versions of his own experience in order to please his oppressors. Whereas his letters, which were the private documents, are more real in the expression of what Ghalib was, in fact, feeling at the time. His contradictory attitudes or rather dilemma in both documents which were meant for public and private needs to be analyzed to better understand the complex intellectual responses of Mirza Ghalib. Mirza Ghalib was a frequent visitor of the Red Fort and a court poet and tutor of Emperor Bahadur Shah Zafar after Ustad Ibrahim Zauq. However, when Uprising broke out and the revolutionaries fully controlled the city in May 1857, Ghalib slowly detached himself from the court. He was confined in his rented house of Late Hakim Mohd Hasan Khan whose descendents were in the service of a close British ally Raja Narender Singh of Patiala. After the victory of the British army some of the Patiala forces guarded the building in which Mirza Ghalib was living as a tenant. Mirza Ghalib in his house started writing his diary which was known as *Dastamboo* in Persian and was meant to please the British.[74]

Ghalib was a chronicler of this turbulent period from the very beginning until the end. It records the events from May 11, 1857 to July 31, 1858. The book not only carries chapters from Ghalib's personal life, but it also speaks about the situation of Delhi and the British troops. In fact, Ghalib wrote *Dastamboo* to show his loyalty to the British, that's why he criticizes to the revolutionaries and tried to prove the British as fair, impartial, and morally correct. His diary *Dastamboo* is a pro-British document, criticizing the British here and there for excessively harsh rule but expressing, generally, horror at the tactics of the revolutionary forces.

During the uprising of 1857, Mirza Ghalib was not happy with the native planning and administration of his master Bahadur Shah Zafar. Eventually, he detached himself from the court. Like most of the elites of Delhi Mirza Ghalib was not sure about the success of the revolutionaries and their administrative capabilities. Perhaps Mirza Ghalib had sensed a defeat of the revolutionary forces on the hands of the British as the rebellion was neither well-organised nor powerful enough to counter the military might of the foreigners. One more thing, which could not be ignored, is his faith in British Government, administration, justice, and western scientific thought. The new cultural influences, especially the introduction of western science and technology undoubtedly excited his imagination as has been shown in his couplet:

> *Iman Mujhe Roke Hai Joh Kheenche Hai Mujhe Kufr;*
> *Kaa'ba Mere Peeche Hai, Kaleesa Mere Aage.*
> (Faith holds me back while infidelity attracts me. The Kaaba is behind me, and the church ahead beckons me.)

For Mirza Ghalib, this couplet was not an admission of his attraction to the Christian faith but a sign of his open mindedness towards the new system. Actually, Mirza Ghalib, who was fully imbued with Muslim aristocracy and feudalism, became attracted to the British mind after his visit to Calcutta, first modern city of India, in 1829-30. In Calcutta, he saw municipal system and cleanliness, good city planning, etc. and perhaps wanted the city of Delhi to be adorned on the same style. Whatever may be the reason, but it is the hard sane fact that Mirza Ghalib was very much impressed with the British administration, constitution, and rule of law. He praises the British for eliminating the city from the loot and plunder of the neighbouring Mewatis and Goojars.[75]

His 1857 diary to which Mirza Ghalib claims to have written during the turbulent period was actually the later work. In fact, it was a chronicle which was written after the occupation of British troops on Delhi and restoration of normalcy to some extent. That's why the dairy had the only motive to please the British Government and release the pension. In this diary in order to praise the British, Mirza Ghalib tried to hide the facts and justified the brutal oppression of the British army, and he reached at the height of flattery by writing his own brother Mirza Yousuf's death was due to the fever. Nevertheless, the fact was that his brother, already suffering from mental illness, was shot dead by the British army.[76]

Kunwar Mohammad Ashraf in his '*Ghalib and the Revolt of 1857*' has rightly defended Mirza Ghalib that he depended for his living in a pension and before the authorities could be persuaded to restore it, he had to prove his *bona fides*. This was all the more necessary to the case of one who belonged to the aristocracy and had been a tutor, a courtier, and a friend of Bahadur Shah, the Mughal King of Delhi. Kunwar Mohammad Ashraf further says that Mirza Ghalib should not be blamed for arguing his carefully prepared defence before the authorities concerned. He pleaded that his family had always been loyal to the British, and that he had been granted a life pension on that very score; he had kept himself severely aloof both from the royalists and the rebels during the days of the Uprising. Kunwar Mohammad Ashraf continues that Mirza Ghalib took good care to see that his diary was not used either against himself or against those of his friends who had taken a leading part in the Uprising.[77]

In his diary, *Dastamboo*, Mirza Ghalib has written unequivocal and exhaustive account of the grisly dance of death and destruction by the revolutionaries. He starts his diary with message that "Since the rush of the torrent may not be checked by the aid of straw, each one (among the supporters of the British) found himself helpless and sat down (in the solitude of) his home to mourn (at the turn of events). Count me as one of these mourners."[78] Mirza Ghalib says that everywhere the land was coloured with the blood of Englishmen and the revolutionaries never spared their innocent ladies and children.[79]

Mirza Ghalib further says, "Those sinful and tyrant killers have stayed place to place in the city. In the Red Fort, they have converted the Imperial Garden as a stable and sleeping place to the *Nasheman-e-Sultani*. By and by, news came pouring in from far-off cities that hotheads of every regiment in each cantonment have killed their (British) commanders. And just as the dancing girl is roused to sing by the tune of music, the ungrateful soldiers and workmen in their thousands joined heartily, and far or near, even without uttering a single word among themselves, they got down to their respective tasks.... These unmanly troops of skilled fighters have a bond of solidarity of their own like a broom. On their march they make a fine display without the usual exercise and fight the battles even without proper command."[80] Mirza Ghalib openly criticizes the revolutionaries and says that they freed the prisoners who were busy in loot and plunder in the daylight and spent their nights in silky bed.[81]

Mirza Ghalib also comments about the worsening conditions of the aristocracy by saying that the revolutionaries laid into dust the honour and the mansions of those who were distinguished for wisdom and good name, while those who had neither power nor pelf shot into prominence. He further says, "my painful condition is mere a story for you but the stars will have tears of blood by listening this."[82]

Mirza Ghalib also narrates that as soon as they (revolutionaries) arrived in Delhi, the various detachments of troopers first handed over the gold and silver with them to the royal treasury then put their foreheads on the threshold of the King and later moved about with a martial air over the city. Mirza Ghalib further added that there emerged from every nook and corners a soldier, from every pathway a platoon and from each direction, an army and all began to move about on the land. These are wonderful times and hour of those who have triumphed. They also freed the prisoners of Delhi. The prisoners also put their forehead of the King and demanded the Jagirs. Just now within and without the city of Delhi, there have gathered something like 50 thousand cavalry and infantry.[83]

Mirza Ghalib narrates that during these periods of onslaught, British forces were encamped on a hillock in the west of Delhi. He expresses his rejoice and called it the greatest day when the British army attacked on Kashmiri Gate on 14th September 1857. Mirza Ghalib says that in face of the British onslaught on the Kashmiri Gate, the Indian forces had no choice but to retreat. In the words of Mirza Ghalib, "...The reign of terror was ended and the period of justice came back....Delhi was evacuated from the insane and wise British has bravely occupied."[84]

While narrating the commentary of British occupation and people's resistance, Mirza Ghalib says that when the British occupied the city from the hands of the popular army, the common people joined the soldiers and took to street fighting. Some from among the hoodlums and the rabble of the city now began to engage the stout-hearted occupation troops. Ghalib further says that for two or three days every nook and corner of the city from Kashmiri Gate onwards was converted into regular battlefield and three outlets of Delhi Darwaza, Ajmeri Darwaja and Turkman Darwaza remained in the hands of the rebel soldiers. As a result when Delhi was finally occupied most of its population escaped from the city.[85]

Mirza Ghalib describes that fire and fury of the British army in such a way that daring lions (victorious British army) advanced through the passage in front of Kashmiri Gate, which leads to the market, and killed whomsoever they could find on the road. Nobody spared from the gentry and sobers. The people shut themselves in their houses. Mirza Ghalib in his narration had justified the killings of the innocents and burning their houses. Mirza Ghalib also justified their terror by saying that victorious army generally does the same.[86]

When Delhi was totally overpowered by the British forces, the neighbouring area of Mewat was still under the control of the revolutionaries. According to the Mirza Ghalib, "..the Mewatis of Sohna and Nuh have created the uproar in such fashion that you would imagine lunatic had broken loose from their chains. A tumultuous named Tula Ram is still at large in Rewari and has now joined his forces with those of the Mewatis on the Devil's instigation and operates under him. This group, in those hilly and forest regions has its own independent plan of fighting the British rulers. In the word you might say that very elements in India are in ferment."[87]

About the arrest and death penalties, Mirza Ghalib says that Delhi looks like a big prison. In this city, the prison is situated outside the town and the police lockups arc within. They have crowded these two places with so many people that you almost feel that one human being is packed into other. The Angel of Death alone knows the number of those from these two prison houses who have died on the gallows from time to time. The Muslim residents in the city do not now exceed a thousand; they are either relations of the prisoners or otherwise, pension holders.[88]

The heart-broken Mirza Ghalib lastly narrates the condition of Delhi and its people in such a way that he was once known to thousands had a companion in every home and friend in every home and establishment. But now the city was empty of Muslims. In the darkness of the night, their homes are without light and by day the chimneys of their walls emit no smoke. In this hour of desolation and despair, Mirza Ghalib saw nothing but death and starvation facing the Muslims as a community.[89]

Mirza Ghalib was also questioned by a British officer Colonel Burn. Mirza Ghalib appeared before Colonel Burn wearing a Turkish style headdress. On asking the British Officer if he was a Muslim? Mirza Ghalib answered that he was a half Muslim and explained that he drinks wine and doesn't eat pork, and as a result he was freed. However, Mirza Ghalib in his diary *Dastamboo* tried to hide the conversation and praised the British Officer Colonel Burn.[90]

The conversation between Mirza Ghalib and Colonel Burn was the sign of the British fear and terror which could be easily felt. Although he was living an Islamic way of life, he felt hesitation of showing himself as Muslim before the British Officer. Mirza Ghalib's position as Muslim can be understood by his following couplet:

> *Ye Misaale Tasawwuf, Ye Tera Bayan Ghalib*
> *Tujhe Ham Wali Samajhte, Jo Na Baada Khwaar Hota*
> (Your matter is mystic; your style is inimitable. I would have called you a Prophet, were you not so fond of wine.)

By October 1858, he had completed his diary *Dastamboo*, published it, and presented copies of it to the British authorities, mainly with the purpose of proving that he had not supported the insurrections. Although, his life and other possessions were spared, however, he was still suspected of having his loyalties towards the Emperor Bahadur Shah Zafar. The suspicion was on the report of the British agent Gauri Shankar. Mirza Ghalib was charged to write a "*Sikka*" (a verse or couplet to be written on coin at the occasion of Emperor's enthronement). The *Sikka* was as follows: [91]

Bazur Zad Sikka-e-Kashoor Stani...Sirajuddin Bahadur Shah Sani

Actually this *Sikka* was written by Hafiz Ghulam Rasul Veeran the disciple of Ustad Ibrahim Zauq. The famous writer Malik Ram also proves this fact by quoting the Urdu newspaper '*Sadiqul Akhbar*' in which the Sikka was published in the name of Hafiz Ghulam Rasul Veeran. In a letter of October/November 1859, to Abdul Ghafoor Saroor, Mirza Ghalib says that he is charged for writing two *Sikka.* Although, Mirza Ghalib repeatedly denied the writing of the *Sikka* but in his letter of June 1859, written to Nawab Yousuf Mirza he firmly admits that he wrote the *Sikka* to save his life and honour (from Mughal Emperor Bahadur Shah Zafar). He continues that writing the *Sikka* is not such a grave sin which could not be removed by Queen's proclamation. By his own writings, it can be rightly concluded that he had written at least one *Sikka* for Mughal Emperor Bahadur Shah Zafar for which he repeatedly denied perhaps this time to save his life and honour from the British power. It was only in March 1860, Mirza Ghalib's British pension reinstated most probably with the help of Sir Syed Ahmad Khan or Nawab of Rampur. The arrears Rs. 2250.00 was also paid to Mirza Ghalib.[92]

His thought and feelings about his experiences during the Uprising, however, can be found not only in *Dastamboo* but in his letters, which were written with comparably greater freedom and boldness. In his letters, his attitude toward the British shows quite contradictory by comparing his diary *Dastamboo*. Whatever admiration he had ever felt for the British was seriously brought into question by the events of that onslaught of 1857, more particularly, by the mercilessness of the British in their dealings with those who participated in or sympathized with the revolutionaries. It was obviously impossible for him to reconcile this conduct with whatever humanity and progressive ideals, he had ever expected the British to have possessed. His letters tell of his terrible dissatisfaction and dilemma. In his letters, Mirza Ghalib boldly describes the advent of the British army into the city of Delhi that how the victorious army went on killing everyone in sight, looting people's property as they advanced. Many of his friends were also hanged, deprived of their fortunes, exiled from the city, or detained in jails. In his letters, Mirza Ghalib openly sympathized with the sufferings of his revolutionary friends and the fallen aristocracy in general.

In his letter to Hakim Ghulam Najaf Khan on 19th January 1858, Mirza Ghailb writes:[93]

> "I am here with grace, until this time I am living with my wife and kids. Nobody knows what will happen after a moment. By holding the pen in my hand, I want to write enough but could not write anything. We will talk if we sit together otherwise *Inna Lillahe Wa Inna Ilaihe Rajeoon* (To Allah we belong and to Him we shall return)."

In a letter to Nawab Anwaruddaula Saaduddin Khan Bahadur Shafaq in August-November, 1858, Mirza Ghalib writes:[94]

> "I beat my face and head in perplexity that I could not write what I want...."

In another place Mirza Ghalib writes to Shiv Narain Aram on 19th April, 1857:[95]

> "...Bhai the light has gone out of India. The land is lamp less. Lakhs have died and among the survivors, hundreds are in jail...."

In another place, Mirza Ghalib writes to Mir Mehandi Majrooh on 2nd December, 1859:[96]

> "What do you ask...Red Fort, Chandni Chawk, everyday's Bazaar of Jama Masjid, every week's roaming on Yamuna Bridge, yearly *Phool Walon Ka Mela*. These fives are not now, then where is Delhi? Yes! It seems that there was a city of this name in India...."

His letters, however, are some of the most graphic and vivid accounts of British violence. On the basis of his diary, he could not be considered as pro-British or anti-revolutionary. Actually, Mirza Ghalib was fond of lavish style of living and it could only be achieved through the rising sun like British. That's why he not only praised to the British but also to their spies like Maulana Sayyed Rajab Ali, Mirza Ilahi Baksh, etc. The analysis of his whole writing shows his leanings towards the revolutionaries and hate for the foreigners. His love for India needs to be quoted here in his couplets:

> *Hindustaan Ki Bhi Ajab Sar Zameen Hai,*
> *Jis Men Wafa-o-Mehr-o-Mohabbat Ka Hai Wafoor.*
> *Jaise Ki Aaftaab Nikalta Hai Sharq Se,*
> *Ikhlaas Ka Hua Hai Isi Mulk Se Zahoor.*
> *Hai Asl-i-Tukhm Hind Se Aur Is Zameen Se,*
> *Phaila Hai Is Jahaan Me Ye Mewa Door Door.*
> (Wondrous is the Indian soil, fruitful and fertile.
> Faith, kindness and love, bloom on every side.
> As the East is the source of sun and light,
> India is the home of sincerity undefiled.
> It was here the seed was sown, here it fructified,
> And from here the fruit spread to distant shores of Isles.)

REFERENCES

1. Handcock, Arthur Gore, *The Siege of Delhi in 1857: A Short Account*, Allahabad, 1897, p. 6, see also Kaye, John William, *Kay's and Malleson's History of the Indian Mutiny of 1857-8,* Vol. II, London, 1910, pp. 8-9.
2. Ahmad, Bashiruddin, *Waqiyat-i-Darul Hukumat Dehli*, Vol. I, Urdu Academy Delhi, 2012, pp. 455-459 see also *Peoples Democracy*, Vol.XXXI, No.24, 17 June, 2007.
3. Kaye, John William, *A History of the Sepoy War in India, 1857-58,* Vol. II, London 1874, pp. 9-10.
4. *Ibid.*, pp. 11-12.
5. Savarkar, p. 66.
6. Tracy, Louis, *The Red Year; A Story of The Indian Mutiny*, New York 1907, p. 44, see also *Secular Qayadat*, Delhi, 21 August, 2007 (Mughal Emperor was perhaps doubtfull about the success of the

Uprising and lawless Sepoys. That's why he informed to the British officers at Agra about the details of Delhi crisis. John William Kay writes, "A message from Agra, dispatched on the 14th, stated, on the authority of a letter from the King of Delhi that the town and fort and his own person were in possession of the insurgents; and it was added that Fraser, the Commissioner, and many other English gentlemen and ladies, had been murdered. Then, at last, it became apparent that the King himself had cast in his lot with the insurgents, that the rebel standard had been hoisted in the palace of the Mogul, that Englishmen and Englishwomen had been ruthlessly massacred in the streets of the city, and that the mutiny of a few regiments, by thus concentring at Delhi, was beginning to simulate a national rebellion." Kaye, John William, *A History of the Sepoy War in India, 1857-58,* Vol. I, London 1875, pp. 596-597).

7. Adam and Charles Black, *History of the Siege of Delhi,* Edinburgh, 1861, p. 89, see also *Two Native Narratives*, p. 91, and Aitchison, Charles, *Rulers of India: Lord Lawrence*, Oxford, 1892, p. 88.
8. Aitchison, Charles, *Rulers of India: Lord Lawrence*, Oxford, 1892, p. 89 see also *Two Native Narratives*, p. 95.
9. *Ibid.*, pp. 111 and 123 (Imani Begum, wife of Mirza Bulahi, attended the audience of the Emperor, and represented that the night before Abu Bakr, in a state of intoxication, came to her house with several sowars to seize her, and fired several shots with rifles and pistols, and beat a number of people of the Mohalla. Emperor issued orders to all the sardars to note that he had disgraced the Princes and they were to be treated as ordinary persons if they were found committing any oppression. Aitchison, Charles, *Rulers of India: Lord Lawrence*, Oxford, 1892, p. 138).
10. *Dehli Urdu Akhbar*, 24th May, 1857.
11. Mead, Henry, *The Sepoy Revolt: Its causes and its Consequences,* London, 1858, pp. 107-108.
12. *Mutiny Papers*, Collection 60, no.'s 213-14, 23 June, 1857. (National Archives, New Delhi).
13. *Asbab-e-Baghawat-e-Hind*, pp. 4 and 11.
14. Ahmad, Bashiruddin, *Waqiyat-i-Darul Hukumat Dehli*, Vol. I, Urdu Academy Delhi, 2012, p. 459 see also *Two Native Narratives*, p. 87.
15. *Peoples Democracy*, (*Bahadur Shah Zafar and the 1857 Revolt*- Amar Farooqui) Vol. XXXI, No. 24, 17 June, 2007.
16. Babar addressed to his son Humayun as "So, this nation Hindustan has different religions. Thank Allah for giving us this Kingdom. We should remove all the differences from our heart and do justice to each community according to its customs. Avoid cow slaughter

to win over the hearts of the people of this land and to incorporate the people in the matters of administration. Do not damage the places of worship and temples, which fall in the boundaries of our rule. Evolve a method of ruling whereby all the people of the Kingdom are happy with the King and the King is happy with the people. Islam can progress by noble deeds and not by terror. Ignore the differences of Shiya and Sunni, as this is the weakness of Islam. Keep the people following different customs integrated into a single whole, so that no part of the body of this Kingdom becomes diseased". (Puniyani, Ram, *Communal Politics Facts Versus Myths*, Sage Publication, New Delhi, p. 54.

17. *Two Native Narratives*, p. 144.
18. *Ibid.*, p.170.
19. *Biblio*, Vol. XII, No. 3 and 4, March-April 2007, p. 8.
20. *Two Native Narratives*, pp. 219-220.
21. *Secular Qayadat*, Delhi, 21 August, 2007, see also Norman, Henry Wylie, *Delhi - 1857; The Siege, Assault, and Capture as given in the Diary and Correspondence of the Late Colonel Keith Young*, London 1902, p. 296.
22. Malleson, George Bruce, *Kay's and Malleson's History of the Indian Mutiny of 1857-8,* Vol. IV, London, 1911, p. 51.
23. *Ibid.,* see also Handcock, Arthur Gore, *The Siege of Delhi in 1857: A Short Account*, Allahabad, 1897, p. 23.
24. *Ibid.*, p. 52.
25. *Ibid.*, p. 53.
26. *Secular Qayadat*, Delhi, 21 August, 2007, see also Norman, Henry Wylie, *Delhi-1857; The Siege, Assault, and Capture as given in the Diary and Correspondence of the Late Colonel Keith Young,* London 1902, p. 296, and Hodson, George Herbert, *Hodson of Hodson's Horse or the Twelve Years of a Soldiers Life in India: Being Extracts from the Letters of the Late Major W. S. R. Hodson*, London, 1889, p. 221 (Hodson narrates the story of the Emperor's arrest, "During this time messengers were coming in constantly, and among the rest one from Zeenat Mahal (the favourite Begum), with an offer to use her influence with the King to surrender on certain conditions. These conditions at first were ludicrous enough—viz, that the King and the whole of the males of his family should be restored to his palace and honours; that not only should his pension be continued, but the arrears since May be paid up, with several other equally modest demands. I need not say these were treated with contemptuous denial.... General Wilson, who at last gave orders to Captain Hodson to promise the King's life.... King asked whether he was

"Hodson Bahadur," and if he would repeat the promise made by the herald? Captain Hodson answered that he would, and repeated that the Government had been graciously pleased to promise him his life, and that of Zeenat Mahal's son, on condition of his yielding himself prisoner quietly, adding very emphatically, that if any attempt was made at a rescue he would shoot the King down on the spot like a dog. The old man then gave up his arms, which Captain Hodson handed to his orderly, still keeping his own sword drawn in his hand." Hodson, George Herbert, *Hodson of Hodson's Horse or the Twelve Years of a Soldiers Life in India: Being Extracts from the Letters of the Late Major W.S.R. Hodson*, London, 1889, pp. 226-227).

27. Griffiths, Charles John, *A Narrative of the Siege of Delhi with an Account of the Mutiny at Firozpur in 1857*, London, 1910, pp. 232-233.
28. *Ibid.*, pp. 201-202.
29. Tariq, Shamim, *Ghalib, Bahadur Shah Zafar aur 1857*, New Delhi, 2008, pp. 45-46.
30. Hodson, George Herbert, *Hodson of Hodson's Horse or the Twelve Years of a Soldiers Life in India: Being Extracts from the Letters of the Late Major W.S.R. Hodson*, London, 1889, pp. 223-224, (Hodson arrested three Princes from the Humayun's Tomb, Mirza Mughal, Mirza Khizr Sultan and Mirza Abu Bakr, the later was the grandson of the Emperor. In the words of Sir T. Seaton, "There was an immense crowd surging round them which was increasing every moment, closing in and pressing on his men. Hodson stopped the carriage and made the three prisoners descend. The wretches, seeing that something was about to happen, put up their hands and fell at his feet, begging that their lives might be spared, and that an investigation might be made into their conduct. All that Hodson said was, '*Chup raho* (be silent); take off your upper garments,' and they did so. 'Get into the ruth!' They obeyed. Hodson, then putting out his hand and taking a carbine from one of his men, shot Mirza Moghul, and immediately after, the two others." Edward, Gilliat, *Heroes of the Indian Mutiny; Stories of Heroic Deeds*, London 1914, pp. 90-91).
31. Griffiths, Charles John, *A Narrative of the Siege of Delhi with an Account of the Mutiny at Firozpur in 1857*, London, 1910, p. 207.
32. Malleson, George Bruce, *Kay's and Malleson's History of the Indian Mutiny of 1857-8,* Vol. V, London, 1911, p. 322.
33. *Ibid.*, p. 324.
34. *Ibid.*, p. 326.

35. *Ibid.*, p. 329.
36. *Ibid.*, p. 350.
37. *Ibid.*, p. 361, see also Norman, Henry Wylie, *Delhi-1857; The Siege, Assault, and Capture as given in the Diary and Correspondence of the Late Colonel Keith Young*, London 1902, p. 334.
38. Mead, Henry, *The Sepoy Revolt: Its causes and its Consequences*, London, 1858, p. 121.
39. Raikes, Charles, *Notes on the Revolt in the North-Western Provinces of India*, London, 1858, p. 80.
40. Frazer, R.W., *British India*, New York 1896, p. 303, see also *New Statesman*, 16th October, 2006.
41. Ahmad, Bashiruddin, *Waqiyat-i-Darul Hukumat Dehli*, Vol. I, Urdu Academy Delhi, 2012, pp. 459 and 467.
42. Tariq, Shamim, *Ghalib, Bahadur Shah Zafar aur 1857*, New Delhi, 2008, pp. 27-28.
43. Keene, Henry George, *Fifty-Seven: Some Account of the Administration of Indian Districts during the Revolt of the Bengal Army*, London, 1883, pp. 129-131, see also *Defence Journal*, Vol. 3, No. 9, Islamabad, December, 1999, Savarkar, p. 140, and Ramchandani, Indu, *Students' Britannica India*, Volume-1, Delhi, 2000, p. 150, (Savarkar quotes the Native Narratives by Metcalfe, p. 60, "The bridge of the Jumna is repaired; for, the arrival of the Rohelkhand troops is expected. The Emperor with a telescope viewed the approaching army of Rohelkhand while it was still far away. On the morning of the 2nd of July, Nawab Ahmad Kuli Khan, with all other nobles and citizens, went forth to receive the array of Rohelkhand. Hakeem Ahsanullah Khan, General Samad Khan, Ibrahim Ali Khan, Ghulam Kuli Khan, and other leaders, too, were present. Mohammad Bakht Khan, the commander of the forces of Rohelkhand, requested the Emperor to accept his services. When Bakht Khan pressed his request to know the desire of the Emperor, the Emperor said: 'It is my ardent desire to see that the people are completely protected, that the security of life and property is maintained, and that the extermination of the British foe is triumphantly carried out.' The general then said that, if the Emperor wished, he was ready to act as the commander-in-chief of the Revolutionary forces. At this, the Emperor pressed the hand of the general with affection. Then, the different heads of the different regiments were called together and they were asked whether they would elect Bakht Khan as commander-in chief. All of them voted 'aye' and took military oaths of obeying the general as their commander-in-chief. After the levee was over, the Emperor

again granted a private interview to the general. All over the city, the order went forth that Bakht Khan would act as the commander-in-chief. He was presented with a shield, a sword, and the title of General. The Prince Mirza Mogul was appointed adjutant-general. Bakht Khan informed the Emperor that, even if any of the princes of royal blood would continue looting in the city, he would not hesitate to cut off his ear and nose at once. The Emperor replied, 'You are invested with supreme authority. Do whatever you think best, without the least hesitation.' The Kotwal of the city was ordered that if there was any row or looting through his negligence in the city he would be hanged. Bakht Khan reported that he had brought with him four infantry regiments, seven hundred cavalry, six horse guns, three field-pieces, etc., etc. As this part of the army had been given its pay for six months in advance and as the general had with him four lakhs of Rupees in cash, the Emperor was assured that he need have no anxiety about money or pay. Not only this, the Emperor was informed that further captures of money would at once be sent to the Royal Treasury. The Emperor distributed sweet-meat worth four thousand Rupees amongst the Sepoys. The Sepoys of Agra, the regiments of Nasirabad, of Jallundhar, all are under the command of Bakht Khan. The general ordered that every citizen in the city should be armed. All householders and shopkeepers should keep arms. And those who had none should, at once, ask for them at the Supreme Thana and they would be given them free. But none should be found without arms. Any Sepoy who would be found looting would be deprived of his hand. Bakht Khan went to the armoury and, after examining it, got the arms and powder-magazines properly arranged. At eight in the night, the general went to the palace. The Emperor, with the Begum Zeenat Mahal, Hakeem Ahsanullah Khan, and Ahmad Kuli Khan, discussed the state affairs. In the general parade on the 3rd of July, nearly twenty thousand Sepoys were present." Savarkar, V.D., *The Indian War of Independence of 1857*, London, 1909, pp. 244-245).

44. Singh, Khushwant, *Delhi: A Novel*, New Delhi 1990, p. 288.
45. *Defence Journal*, Vol. 3, No. 9, Islamabad, December, 1999 and Ramchandani, Indu, *Students' Britannica India*, Volume-1, Delhi, 2000, p. 150.
46. Agrawal, Lion M. G., *Freedom Fighters of India*, Volume 3, Delhi 2008, p. 70.
47. *Ibid.*, p.71.

48. Robertson, Henry Dundas, *District Duties during the Revolt in the North-West Provinces of India in 1857: With Remarks on Subsequent Investigations during 1858-59*, London 1859, p. 193, see also Malleson, George Bruce, *Kay's and Malleson's History of the Indian Mutiny of 1857-8,* Vol. IV, London, 1911, p. 50.
49. Stewart, Charles Edward, (Edited by Basil Stewart), *Through Persia in Disguise with Reminiscences of the Indian Mutiny,* London, 1911, pp. XVIII and 39-40.
50. Adam and Charles Black, *History of the Siege of Delhi,* Edinburgh, 1861, pp. 137-138, see also *The Express Tribune,* Karachi, January 27th, 2011.
51. Graham, G.F.I., *The Life and Work of Sayed Ahmed Khan*, Edinburgh, 1885, pp. 1-2.
52. *Ibid.*, pp. 6-8.
53. *Ibid.*, pp. 18-20.
54. *Ibid.*, pp. 20-25.
55. *Ibid.*, pp. 25-27.
56. *Ibid.*, pp. 27-28.
57. The Native Commissioners were of three kinds—Sadar Amins, Amins and Munsifs who were subordinate to the District Judge. Sadar Amins sat at the headquarters of the Judge and Magistrate and were empowered to dispose of suits of which the subject matter did not exceed Rs. 100 in value, referred to them by the Judge. The Amins were nominated by the Judge and confirmed by the Sadar Diwani Adalat. They sat in the interior of the district. Each had a jurisdiction of about 10 square miles and could hear suits of which the subject matter did not exceed Rs. 50 in value referred to him by the Judge. A Munsif was appointed for each Thana and had an original jurisdiction in the case of suits of which the subject matter did not exceed Rs. 50. The Munsifs could receive plaints whereas Sadar Amins and Amins could only take up cases referred to them by the Judge. (Dewar, Douglas, *Hand-book to the English Pre-mutiny Records in the Government Recordrooms of the United Provinces of Agra and Oudh*, Allahabad (ND), p.1).
58. Graham, G.F.I., *The Life and Work of Sayed Ahmed Khan*, Edinburgh, 1885, pp. 28 and 31.
59. *Ibid.*, pp. 202-204.
60. *Asbab-e-Baghawat-e-Hind*, pp. 15-16, see also Graham, G.F.I., *The Life and Work of Sayed Ahmed Khan*, Edinburgh, 1885, p. 39
61. *Ibid.*, p. 114.
62. *Ibid.*, p. 113.
63. *Ibid.*, p. 16.

64. Mohammad, Shan, *Writings and Speeches of Sir Syed Ahmad Khan*, Bombay, 1972, p. 20.
65. *Ibid.*, p. 15.
66. Graham, G.F.I., *The Life and Work of Sayed Ahmed Khan*, Edinburgh, 1885, p. 58.
67. *Ibid.*, pp. 205-207.
68. *Ibid.*, pp. 59-60.
69. *Ibid.*, pp. 95-98 and 116.
70. *Ibid.*, pp. 194 and 201.
71. *Ibid.*, pp. 252, 259, 267, 275 and 289-290. Finally the dream of Sir Syed Ahmad Khan became true and in 1920 this MAO College was elevated to the Muslim University, after his death. See also, Ahmad, Aijaz, *Aligarh Muslim University: An Educational and Political History, 1920-47*, Ghaziabad, 2005, pp. 17-18.
72. *Annual of Urdu Studies,* Vol. 18, Madison, USA, 2003, p. 3.
73. Ghalib, Mirza Asadullah Khan, *Dastamboo*, Urdu Trans. Khwaja Ahmad Faruqi, New Delhi, 2000, pp. 44-45, see also Tariq, Shamim, *Ghalib aur Hamari Tahrik Azadi*, (3rd Ed.) Mumbai, 2011, p. 207 and *Annual of Urdu Studies,* Vol. 18, Madison, USA, 2003, pp. 9-10.
74. Anjum, Khaliq, *Intkhab-e-Khatoot-e-Ghalib*, (16th Ed.) New Delhi, 2011, p. 106.
75. Naim, C.M., *Urdu Text and Contexts, Selected Essays*, Delhi, 2004, p. 258.
76. Tariq, Shamim, *Ghalib aur Hamari Tahrik Azadi*, (3rd Ed.) Mumbai, 2011, p. 140.
77. Joshi, P.C., *Rebellion 1857*, New Delhi, 2007, pp. 266-267.
78. Mirza Asadullah Khan Ghalib, *Dastamboo*, Urdu Trans. Khwaja Ahmad Faruqi, New Delhi, 2000, p. 22.
79. *Ibid.*, pp. 22-23.
80. *Ibid.*, p. 24.
81. *Ibid.*, pp. 24-25.
82. *Ibid.*, pp. 26-27.
83. *Ibid.*, pp. 28-30.
84. *Ibid.*, p. 36.
85. *Ibid.*, p. 37.
86. *Ibid.*, pp. 37-38.
87. *Ibid.*, pp. 55-56.
88. *Ibid.*, pp. 70-71.
89. *Ibid.*, p. 82.
90. *Ibid.*, p. 54.

91. Tariq, Shamim, *Ghalib aur Hamari Tahrik Azadi*, (3rd Ed.) Mumbai, 2011, p. 152.
92. *Ibid.*, pp. 206-207, *see* also Tariq, Shamim, *Ghalib, Bahadur Shah Zafar aur 1857*, New Delhi, 2008, p. 58.
93. *Ibid.*, p. 186.
94. *Ibid.*, p. 187.
95. Devy, G.N., *Indian Literary Criticism: Theory and Interpretation*, Hyderabad, 2002, p. 135.
96. Anjum, Khaliq, *Intkhab-e-Khatoot-e-Ghalib*, (16th Ed.) New Delhi, 2011, p. 129.

CHAPTER 7

Uprising and the Role of Urdu Press

There are a lot of contemporary sources mainly British scholars, regarding the happenings of 1857 and almost all the sources proves the rising as the mutiny. However, journalism in native languages, particularly Urdu, was the only source which declares the rising as a national revolt or war of independence. Most of the historians generally based upon the British sources give a lot of confusing remarks and different conclusions regarding the Uprisings such as referring to it as Mutiny, Rebellion, General Uprising, Sepoy Revolt, Sedition, etc. It was only due to the non availability of contemporary Urdu newspapers which contains the real facts of day-to-day happenings of the Uprising. The historians who used, these basic documents have rewritten the history of the Uprising and boldly proved it as the war of independence.

In 1857, a lot of Urdu newspapers were active in promoting national feeling and Hindu-Muslim unity such as *Dehli Urdu Akhbar, Sadiqul Akhbar, Tilism, Gulshan-e-Naubahaar, Sultanul Akhbar, Habibul Akhbar, Umdatul Akhbar,* etc. in different parts of India. These newspapers regenerated new spirit of freedom among the revolutionaries through their writings. During the war, these newspapers were free to publish anti-British news and statements and aroused a new enthusiasm and spirit of their freedom and independence among the Indian people and encouraged them to fight against the British. The great historian of that period, Malleson, also agreed that at the time of Uprising, the tone of the native press almost immediately changed. He writes that possibly the supineness which they witnessed made them believe that the fatal day for the English had arrived, just as their fathers had seen that day overtake the Mughals, the Marathas, and the Sikhs. Nevertheless, whatever may have been the reason it was at least undeniable that from the time of the arrival in Calcutta of the news about the Meerut outbreak, the tone of the native press changed. It began to speak out against the Government, and to show very plainly that it had sympathy for the revolutionaries.[1]

Although Lord Canning was aware that the native press was encouraging sedition and rebellion, he opined on banning the native press that 'remedy was worse than the diseases'. However, later on he ordered the Legislative Council on 13th June, 1857, to pass an act for the restriction of the native press, known thenceforth as the Gagging Act. Even the British authorities were unsatisfied or rather furious with the European press, who were disclosing the weak points of the Government.[2]

Definitely, the Urdu press played a sterling role in the Uprising. The native press filled the patriotic feelings and communal harmony in both the Indian communities of Hindus and Muslims. The historic religious unity, which was first seen in India and undoubtedly, the last as well, was due to the restless efforts of the native press, particularly in Urdu languages.

Dehli Urdu Akhbar

The newspaper *Dehli Urdu Akhbar,* although, historically started in 1837 published on every Saturday by Maulvi Mohammad Akbar, the father of Maulvi Mohammad Baqar with the name of *Dehli Akhbar*, which later changed its name as *Dehli Urdu Akhbar* in 1840. On 12 July 1857, its name again changed as *Akhbar-uz-Zafar* and started to be published on Sunday in defiance of the Christian decree that opposed the idea of a newspaper being issued on Sunday. According to Maulana Mohammad Hussain Azad, this newspaper was printed in the Lithographic Press which Maulvi Mohammad Baqar bought from Dr. Sprenger, the Principal of the Delhi College. Nevertheless, this statement seems to be exaggerated. In the beginning or before 1850s, the names such as Khwaja Ahmad Faruqui, Sayed Moinuddin, Mirza Imdad Beg, and Moti Lal were attached with the newspaper *Dehli Urdu Akhbar*.[3]

The surviving copies of *Dehli Urdu Akhbar* 1840, 1852, and 1857 are preserved in the National Archives, New Delhi as the mirror of social and political life of Delhi and the rest of India. Before 1857, it also covered the news of Europe and England but after the stoppage of the postal system it carries the news stories of Delhi people, Royal Court, native states, East India Company, etc. In 1857, this newspaper gained much popularity under the editorship of Maulvi Mohammad Baqar, which was printed and published by Sayyed Abdullah, the Manager of *Dehli Urdu Akhbar* Press. This newspaper gives the eye witness account of Delhi and neighbourhood rebel regime. Maulvi Baqar gave more stress on the authenticity and asked the correspondents not to rely on hearsay and rumours. It frequently called the Tilanga to the rebel Sepoys and Angrez to the British.[4]

In its issue of 10th May, the newspaper gives the detailed account of Meerut and Lucknow and discontent among the Sepoys. On the basis of a report of 8th May, this newspaper writes that "there is a riot in Meerut city and there is no night spent when the rioters not have burnt the bungalows of British officers. There is also a burning fire in the hearts of the Sepoys due to the use of new greased cartridges." In the same issue on the basis of Lucknow reporting of 4th May, the newspaper writes that in addition to the greased cartridge issue, there is also a rumour that the British Government provides flours mixed with grounded bone.[5]

In its issue of 17th May, the newspaper writes its entire first page with the gallantry of the Sepoys and does not show even a little sympathy for the Europeans who were killed by the Sepoys. This issue creates a history by setting the first example of the spot reporting. Maulvi Baqar says, "The present scribe too came out of his house to see things for himself, inspired as he was by a regard to the glory of his faith and hearing the sounds of gunfire. I was confronted by the strange sight that the people were running from Kashmiri Gate side into the market. Personal safety was no doubt in danger but dearer to me than my personal safety was the desire to see unusual sights and the other equally strong desire to give a faithful eye witnessed accounts of events to my readers. As I moved forward, I heard gunshots near the bungalow of Sikander Sahab. A little ahead I saw that Sahab Bahadur was running for his life, sword in hand and followed by the Tilangis with their guns close at the heel. In the rear was a crowed of common people, some with sticks in their hands, other with bamboos, chasing the beleaguered Englishmen at the hot speed. They hunted down from Zeenat Bara towards the canal. I moved towards Naseerganj."[6]

Newspaper of this issue also writes that some Tilangis killed the Europeans who were hided in the Fakhrul Masajid. Maulvi Baqar further reports, "I saw that two hundred or three hundred cavaliers and Tilangis are standing at a place and spread in the groups and asks the each and every people that where are the Englishmen? ...and seen that two or three Englishmen were laid dead in every lane. They killed every Englishman with his family by hunting from their bungalows (*Kothis*)." The reporter also expresses pleasure on the killing of Nixon, head of the Chancellery and Taylor, the Principal of the Delhi College. It also reports that most of the Englishmen were killed, and some fled towards Ambala, but they were attacked in Panipat and Karnal, and only three survivors could reach the destiny.[7]

In the issue of 24th May, the newspaper published a poem of Mohammad Hussain Azad under the title of *A History of Instructive Reversals* that vividly reflected the popular sentiments aroused by the first war of independence. The poem recalls, "the great rulers and conquerors like Soloman and Alaxander, cruel tyrants like Hajjaj, Changez, Halaku and Nadir, great epic heroes and sages have all disappeared...Yesterday the Christians were in the ascendant; world-seizing, world-bestowing; the possessors of skill and wisdom; the possessors of splendour and glory; the possessors of a mighty army. But what use was that; against the sword of the Lord of Fury? All their wisdom could not save them; their schemes became useless; their knowledge and science availed them nothing; the Tilangas of the East have killed them all. O Azad, learn this lesson: For all their wisdom and vision; the Christian rulers have been erased; without leaving a trace in this world."[8]

This newspaper of the same issue expresses grief over the

robbery and loot by the anti-social elements of Delhi and outsiders. In these days, most of the victims were wealthy and honourable persons of the society. Even the royal officials' and princes' involvement was also noticed. It was moreover reported that lower caste people in the uniform of Tilangis generally looting the public and British houses. Emperor Bahadur Shah Zafar warned the peoples, Tilangis and other officials that if they did not stop loot and plunder, then he would leave for Mecca. After his warning normalcy restored to many extent.[9]

In the issue of 31st May, the newspaper reports that many Muslim clerics aroused the religious sentiments of the people. Maulvi Baqar quotes the words of a cleric, "O Muslims, congratulations; the Islamic progress is compulsory on you. Stay on your faith and believe in the trueness of divinity and honour of Almighty and don't be misguided to believe in the knowledge skill, wisdom, and character of the Christians..." This newspaper also reports that the Tilangis became so rich by looting the havelis of Englishmen. They went to the mahajans to convert their rupees into gold coins (*asharfis*). They purchased the *asharfis* in 20-25 rupees while the current rate was 16-17 rupees. Many Tilangis were befooled many times by the fake mahajans. This newspaper also showed its unhappiness over the killing of a Kshatri horseman and injuring a vegetable vendor in Chandni Chauk.[10]

The issue of 14th June of this newspaper basically preaches the Hindus and Muslims to remain firm to their respective religions and be inspired by its laws and personalities and also remain united against their common enemy the Europeans. To the common enemy the Europeans, Maulvi Mohammad Baqar compared to Ravana, the demon king, in the Hindu epic the *Ramayana*. Maulvi Mohammad Baqar appeals to Hindus and Muslims that God is great and except Him everything would perish in this world. All were appealed to unite, if Muslims, take the name of the God and Prophet and follow the Holy Quraan and Hadeeth, if Hindus, pray *Parmeshwar* and *Narayan* and see their books of *Dharam Katha* and through their religious personalities pray for favour and end the hardships. The Sepoys are to follow the examples of Bhim, Arjun, Rustam, Changez, Halaku, Taimur, and Nadir Shah to defeat the English. It also appealed that the English being

Christians and so believing in the Trinity of God are now held to polytheist and infidels while Hindus being believers in *Adipurush* share the basic belief of one God with Muslims and so are close to them. So both Hindus and Muslims were therefore called upon to fight against the British.[11]

In the same issue, the editor continues writing on the same subject, "O my countrymen, looking at the strategy and devious cleverness of the English, their ability to make arrangements and to order the world in the way they wish, the wide expanses of their dominions and their overflowing treasuries and revenues, you may feel disheartened that such a people could ever be overcome. But my Hindu brothers, if you look in your Holy books you will see how many magnificent dynasties have come into being in the land of Hindustan, and how they all met their end. Even Ravana and his army of demons were beaten by Raja Ramchandra (the Hindu God King Ram).... Except the *Adipurush*, the primeval Deity, nothing is permanent.... If God brings all these magnificent kingdoms to an end after a short period, why do you not comprehend that God has sent his hidden help (to defeat) this hundred year old kingdom (of the British) so that this community (the Christians) who regarded the children of God with contempt, and addressed your brothers and sisters as 'black men,' have now been insulted and humiliated? Realise this, and you will lose your fear and apprehension. To run away and turn your back now would be akin to denying divine help and favour..."[12]

The newspaper of 21st June, by feeling the anxiety of the people it encourages them to not be afraid of Englishmen's strength and gunfire and recalls that only those die whose time has elapsed. It tries to remove the phobic reactions due to heavy arms and armament of the British forces while recalling that how the Angels helped the Muslims in Battle of Badar. It says that the English rulers are not only of a different religion but also of a different race and speaking a different language. They did not spend the wealth to this country of Hindustan and deprive this country from its own wealth. The newspaper also informs that some of the pro-British natives were supplying the ration to the British camps. The Tilangas had caught intelligently some of them who were carrying the ration, to the British, tied like the corpse on the cot.[13]

In the issue of 5th July, the British tried to create the rift among Indians on religious grounds by pasting a copy of the *Ishtihar* (Public Notice) on the Jama Masjid which described the rebellion as the handiwork of some unfaithful servants of the East India Company who not only imprisoned women and children but also captured the Emperor Bahadur Shah Zafar. The Notice called upon Muslims to wage a 'holy war against Hindus', for the Christians were the natural allies of Muslims as 'People of the Book' according to the *Shariat* (Muslim Law). It asserted that the use of pig-tallow in the greased cartridges was a totally false rumour. The editor Maulvi Baqar gave a point by point rebuttal and declared this notice as a conspiracy, the handiwork of enemies of both '*Dharm*' and '*Iman*' (the faith of Hindus and Muslims). He said sarcastically that the English could not try to deceive anyone by invoking the *Shariat* and urged, "Now brother countrymen and especially those who serve the army, let us beware of these attempts to divide us. We are united as part of the body. Let us sacrifice all our comforts in the task of liberating ourselves from fears."[14]

The *Dehli Urdu Akhbar* issue of 12th July changed its name as Akhbar-uz-Zafar, the title suggested by Emperor Bahadur Shah Zafar. In this issue, the editor informs that the so-called mighty Englishmen are escapping to the safest places in Indian ladies' dress and also perform bowing salute to strangers. It also says that there is a continuous flow of the forces combined with the *Jihadis*. Maulvi Baqar instigated the Indians that how in the Battle of Khandak, the unarmed Muslims were supported by the Angels of Almighty God and finally, the infidels fled with much loss.[15]

In the issue of 19th July, Maulvi Baqar urges the Hindus and Muslims to unite and consider each other's body organs as their own and fight against the Englishmen. He recalls the Almighty's help that how the five cavalrymen in green dress were fighting before the Tilangis and later on became invisible. The newspaper also gives the details of court proceedings of Emperor Bahadur Shah Zafar and his instructions to punish the Tilangis who kills the innocents.[16]

The newspaper of 9th August says that the royal forces were in doubt that wazir Hakim Ahsanullah was in alliance with the

British and finally arrested him and also looted and burnt his house. It is said that the gunpowder factory which was blown, and many hundred men were slain was due to his conspiracy. However, it is also said that the factory was blown due to the pebble in the grind stone.[17]

In the issues of 16th August, 23rd August and 13th September, the newspaper generally discourages the pro-British feelings, loss of faith by Indians and their hope of reoccupation by the British. The newspaper also informs that at many places where British have set their administration started killing of innocent population, particularly the Muslims. Nevertheless, Maulvi Baqar encourages the *Jihadi* and other martial men to believe in Almighty as most of the Englishmen were killed and routed with the Divine help.[18]

Almost all times from the beginning of the Uprising to the re-occupation of the British over Delhi, the newspaper *Delhi Urdu Akhbar* continuously encouraged the revolutionaries to fight the accursed Europeans by maintaining Hindu-Muslim unity. Its editor Maulvi Baqar was brutally shot dead by nefarious Hodson after the occupation of Delhi by the British.

Sadiqul Akhbar

The newspaper *Sadiqul Akhbar* was a true source of the Uprising of 1857. Its editor Maulana Jamiluddin Hijr played almost the same role as Maulvi Baqar of *Dehli Urdu Akhbar*. The newspaper *Sadiqul Akhbar* was started, firstly, in Persian in 1854, and after two years in 1856, it was converted into Urdu newspaper. It not only planted the seeds of the revolt but aroused the feelings and emotions of the people during the Uprising. In open anti-British tune, it generally published the news of war between Iran and England and also published that the armies of Iran and Afghanistan were coming to attack on the British during the Uprising. A news of this newspaper is needed to be quoted as follows:[19]

> "A friend tells us that according to the report of a messenger from Peshawar, several thousand soldiers have

> killed many Englishmen and put the Governor of Swat, Sayyed Mohammad Akbar, who is most devout of the royal throne, and after setting him well they proceeded to surround Lahore. Now the people of Lahore are besieged. We are certain that the victorious and brave army would be triumphant and the remnants of the whites who are on the verge of their graves would be buried in the graves."

This newspaper writes with great delight that the King of Iran would soon conquer India and present the throne of India to King of Delhi. Another news of this paper which further inflames the Uprising is being quoted as follows:[20]

> "See, when God chose to make the English nation fortunate, from the east to the west, north etc. They could conquer countries without waging wars. Wherever they raised the banner of war, the kings were terrified into seeking peace. Conditions do not remain unchanged for everyone. What exists today can also become naught. God has been kind for the people of India so that the English had been destroyed by their own army, otherwise their evil intensions would have caused a lot of suffering to Indians. It has happened several times that the army has crowned whomever it has favoured...thousands of white from all parts came here; the Europeans have tried all kinds of strategies to conquer Delhi, but the bravery of the whites was in the vein; before fate, all devices failed. In every place and every field their heads were cut down. The few that survived were also swept away with the broom of the curse of Almighty, and the King has started wielding authority all over the country."

When British recaptured the city of Delhi, the editor Maulana Jamiluddin Hijr met the same fate of imprisonment, a sentence of three years for aiding the rebels. This newspaper was especially placed before the court in the trial of Bahadur Shah Zafar.

According to a Government witness Chinni Lal, this newspaper was foul-mouthed and was popular among all classes to the people of Delhi.[21]

While *Dehli Urdu Akhbar* mainly focused the Hindu-Muslim unity and appealed them to fight for their religion and nation, filled hatred against the Europeans, the *Sadiqul Akhbar* tried to maintain the enthusiasm of the revolutionaries by assuring the support of the forces of Iran and Afghanistan. Maulvi Jamiluddin assured the revolutionaries that the Almighty God has fixed the decay of the British paramountcy and emotionally goaded the revolutionaries to avail the chance by fighting with the British and ousting them from India.

Tilism

The publication of the Urdu Weekly, *Tilism*, was started in 1856 from Lucknow by Maulvi Yaqub Ansari, five months after the deposition of Nawab Wajid Ali Shah. It gives a vivid account of the conditions of the people of Awadh. The contents of the paper were filled with the anti-British sentiments. Due to its bold content and courageous criticism of the British rulers, the paper acquired a respectable position among the contemporaries. The policy of newspaper was a reflection of courage and boldness. The paper truly mirrored and heavily criticized the deteriorating circumstances of the state of Awadh after coming under the British administration. It clearly reflects the public resentment over the annexation of Awadh.

As quoted by Saiyid Zaheer Husain Jafri, *Tilism* records three secret attempts of resentment after the annexation. Firstly, it quotes that a saint named Qadir Ali Shah secretly raised an army of 12000 persons, and a date of 11th September 1856 was fixed for Uprising against British rule at Lucknow. However, the conspiracy was foiled by the alertness of the authorities.[22]

Secondly, the paper quotes that Maulvi Ahmadullah Shah arrived in Lucknow in November 1856, and gave a call of Holy War against the British Government. By the intervention of the British authorities, he went away to Faizabad where he continued the call of Holy War against the British. A battle ensued between the Maulvi and the British forces in which some of his supporters were killed and he himself was greatly wounded and eventually arrested.[23]

Thirdly, the paper quotes that in December 1856, another Saint settled near Tari Wali Kothi in Lucknow and began to preach among his followers that his mission was to restore the King to the throne. However, authorities took the strict action and expelled the Saint from the city.[24]

In its issue of January 16, 1857, the newspaper *Tilism* report about mis-management under the British rule in Awadh, "Saturday instability has come to Lucknow. Robbers have created a havoc. Every incident is a matter of wonder; at the slightest nap, the headgear is missing.... The Government turns a blind eye to all this. There is an undeserving rule of the roost. There are strange happening everyday."[25]

This newspaper gauged the sentiments to the people of Awadh on the deposition of their Nawab Wajid Ali Shah in following words:[26]

> "The ups and downs of the world have brought this most unfortunate time. All the subjects were crying; their heart sickness was really distressing. Those who saw were deeply hurt but what could the helpless people do? They simply looked at each other wept bitterly."

No doubt, according to the report of this newspaper, the people of Awadh and the forces employed in the British army were much annoyed with the annexation by British, and it was one of the main reasons of the Uprising in Awadh and eastern areas of UP and also the Delhi region. Lucknow was the most sensitive place of Uprising. That's why the Sepoys and other revolutionaries continued their fight at Lucknow and other eastern areas even after the fall of Delhi. The newspaper *Tilism* fully covered all the happenings and also public feelings during the Uprising. It was forced to close down after the War.

REFERENCES

1. Malleson, George Bruce, *History of the Indian Mutiny of 1857-58, Commencing from the Close of the Second Volume of Sir John Kaye's History of the Sepoy War*, Vol. III, (Contemporaneous with Sir John Kay's Third Volume), London, 1878, p. 18.
2. *Ibid.*, pp. 18-19.
3. This information was based on the report of Mohammad Hussain Azad, the son of Maulvi Mohammad Baqar. The report does not seem true as Dr. Sprenger came to Delhi in 1842 and introduced the Press in Delhi College. It also notable that Maulvi Baqar's name never attached to this newspaper until 1850s. (*The Annual of Urdu Studies*, Vol. 18, 2003, Madison, USA, pp. 119-120 and pp. 17-18).
4. *People's Democracy*, (*Rebel Journalism: Dehli Urdu Akhbar, May-September 1857*- Shireen Moosvi), Vol. XXXI, No. 17, April, 29, 2007.
5. *Dehli Urdu Akhbar,* 10th May, 1857.
6. *Ibid.,* 17th May, 1857.
7. *Ibid.*
8. *Ibid.,* 24th May, 1857.
9. *Ibid.*
10. *Ibid.,* 31st May, 1857, (Munshi Jeevan Lal in his Roznamacha also narrates the same story; "the mutineers had possessed themselves of much money and were buying gold mohurs at 32 rupees apiece.... The demand for gold increasing, many of the soldiers were duped by the city Budmashes, who, leading them to one of the Mohallas, invited them to sit down while they brought them the coveted gold mohurs. Then taking the money to buy the gold, they decamped by another way and left the soldiers to deplore their loss. The soldiers revenged themselves upon the innocent people of the Mohalla. *Two Native Narratives*, pp.100-101).
11. *Dehli Urdu Akhbar,* 14th June, 1857.
12. *Ibid.*
13. *Ibid.,* 21st June, 1857.
14. *Ibid.,* 5th July, 1857.
15. *Ibid.,* 12th July, 1857.
16. *Ibid.,* 19th July, 1857.
17. *Ibid.,* 9th August, 1857.
18. *Ibid.,* 16th August, 23rd August and 13th September, 1857.
19. Engineer, Asghar Ali, *They Too Fought for India's Freedom: The Role of Minorities*, Gurgaon, 2006, p. 124.
20. *Ibid.*, p. 125.

21. *Secular Qayadat*, Delhi, 21 August, 2007.
22. Jafri, Saiyid Zaheer Husain, *The Great Uprising of 1857*, Delhi, 2009, p. 49, quoted from *Tilism*, Nos. 9 and 10, dated 19 and 26 September, 1856.
23. *Ibid.*, quoted from *Tilism*, Nos. 18, 21, 28 and 33, dated 21 November, 12 December 1856 and 30 January and 6 March 1857.
24. *Ibid.*, quoted from *Tilism*, Nos. 20 and 21, dated 5 and 12 December, 1856.
25. Engineer, Asghar Ali, *They Too Fought for India's Freedom: The Role of Minorities*, Gurgaon, 2006, pp. 125-6.
26. *Ibid.*, p. 126.

CHAPTER 8

Conclusions

The Uprising of 1857 was the result of all the British policies right from the Battle of Plassey to the eventful year of 1857. Last two years 1856 and 1857 were the most exciting years which added much violent anger among the people of India. The last two years Canning rule further refreshed the wounds given by the infamous Lord Dalhousie. The Missionary activities were most active in 1856-57; the other related grievances of Indian masses were also on peak; in such a situation the bombastic rumour of the greased cartridges alarmed the people to wake for the sake of their religion and country. Overall, the wrong policies of the British Government created resentment among the Indian people.

Although, the peak period of the war of 1857 was short-lived and lasted for less than two years, but it was in existence in Indian masses right from the martyrdom of Tipu Sultan until the formation of Indian National Congress. However, it was controlled and managed by Indian Muslims by the name of Wahabi and Faraizi movements. It also may not be the exaggeration to say that the Uprising of 1857 was the maturity phase of that very War of Independence which was waged by the Wahabis and Faraizis of Indian Muslims. During the eventful years of the Uprising, the people *en masse* without the distinction of caste and creed participated with full vigour.

The policies of the East India Company, including religious persecution and wont of independence by the Indian people forced them to rise against the Europeans. As the Muslims were already in fighting, the Hindu population of this country found additional courage and enthusiasm in 1857, which enabled them success in many fronts against the British. The activities of the Christian Missionaries and other religious issues related to both the major communities of India further united them against the British.

No doubt the Missionary activities were a great threat for the both religions of Hinduism and Islam, but the political factor was also gaining the ground as most of the Indian States and Principalities were liquidated and annexed into the paramountcy of the British Empire. The religious factor aroused the hatred against the British and united the diverse Indian population for the common cause which was none other than nationalism. The religious feelings, more rapidly, became the main excuse of national unity and setting India free from the foreign yoke. Both the Hindus and the Muslims frequently used the green flag and used the common term of *Jihad* against the British. Here the term *Jihad* or Holy War against the British could not be separated from the Indian nationalism of 1857, as it was the main force which goaded both the major communities of India against the foreigner.

In the Uprising of 1857, the national enthusiasm spread, such an extent that the Sepoys frequently used the same Enfield rifle and the greased cartridges, against the British, for which once they had mutinied in their regiments and cantonments. The atmosphere was really amazing and perhaps first time in Indian history the world had seen such a type of national unity and valorous martyrdom in which every revolutionary was bent upon to lay his lives for the cause of his religion and nation. The revolutionaries chose the 82 years old Mughal pensioner as their national symbol and enthroned him on the seat of the Emperor of India and waged a war against the common enemy, the British, the most powerful in the world. Every revolutionary was the army man of the nation and joined the group or leader wherever he could find. Delhi, Meerut, Barrielly, Jhansi, Kanpur, Lucknow, Faizabad, Jagdishpur, Allahabad, Banaras and even the Frontier, every area was the battlefield of the revolutionaries against the one and only common enemy, the British.

As far as the theory of *Jihad* or the Holy War is concerned, the Muslim Ulema or theologians played the most important role. They issued religious decrees to awaken the Indian Muslims to wage war against the British as their compulsory duty. They also appealed their Hindu brethren to fight against the British in light of their religion following the example of their cherished gods, goddesses, and historical figures. The Muslims responded quickly and flocked to their nearby centres either Delhi or Lucknow as freelance *Jihadis* or *Ghazis*. They were unpaid warriors, filled with religious passion, whose only aim was to attain martyrdom for their religion and nation. The British considered the *Jihadis* as most dangerous as they had no love with their lives and property. The British saw the first time very typical type of people who fought with the swords in open fields in front of the heavy guns and rifles. The British gave them the name of freelance suicide *Ghazis* who were more dangerous than the trained Sepoys and other class of the revolutionary fighters.

The Sepoys who were in the habit of receiving regular pay for service to the British Government started drifting away to their home towns as their leaders failed to pay them their salary. When the Uprising prolonged, the Ulema or the Maulvis collected religious funds, recruited suicide *Ghazis*, by the name of religion and nation, from various parts throughout the country, and took the command of war in their own hands. Even the Sepoys who remained to fight for their national cause began to fight under the command of the Maulvis. These Maulvis or *Ghazis* also fought under the regional leaders like Tatya Tope, Rani Luxmi Bai, Kunwar Singh, Bakht Khan, etc. Their enthusiasm never dimmed even after desertion of the trained Sepoys and empty treasure. They were bound with the religious decree of *Jihad,* and nothing could deter them except death or martyrdom. So the *Jihad* played the most pivotal role in the Uprising which arrayed the unpaid army to fight against the British until their last breath.

The most well organized Wahabi and Faraizi Movements and its workers could not be detached from the Uprising startting from May 1857, and mingled with their men and money. These were the people, whose efforts prolonged the national struggle even after abandoning by the Sepoys.

In India, Shah Waliullah Dehlavi felt the need of the religious revival of Islam, which was at that time filled with unnecessary innovations. His disciples, along with other likeminded theologians, continued to preach the philosophy after his death. However, this religious revivalist movement turned anti-British, due to the policies of the British Government, about two decades before the great upheaval of 1857. This movement gained much public support and greatly alarmed the British. They falsely dubbed this movement as the Wahabi Movement which was much prominent in Arabia. From that time, this Waliullahi Movement was generally called as Wahabi Movement and the people attached to the movement were known as Wahabis. So these were, undoubtedly, the Muslim Ulema who felt the pain of slavery and raised the call for freedom by overthrowing the British Government. In order to emotionally attach the Muslims as a whole, the Wahabi leaders issued religious decrees and bound them to fight against the British tyrant.

These so-called Wahabis were undoubtedly the real source of inspiration, for the revolutionaries and *Mujahideen,* during the whole period of Uprising. They taught the chapter of *Jihad* by their speeches and physical involvements in the battles. Particularly, Maulvi Peer Ali's words before his execution, "You might hang me, you might hang other men like me; but, you cannot hang our ideal. If I die, thousands of heroes will rise out of my blood and will destroy your kingdom" were a talisman for almost all revolutionaries of the Uprising. The daring act of Sher Ali Afridi listed him the first revolutionary in the list of Bhagat Singh, Ashfaqullah, and Chandrashekhar Azad, etc. Afridi was definitally considered an ideal for the second phase freedom struggle.

The other similar movement known as Faraizi Movement was also a religious revivalist movement which preached among the Muslims to follow the basic tenets (*Faraiz*) of Islam, similar to that of Wahabis. Faraizis also turned anti-British and fought gallantly a lot of battles like the Wahabis. These movements led the creation of British mindset that the Muslim community as a whole is a thorn for the British Empire in India and without their subjugation, it would be impossible for the British to rule peacefully in India.

Some Ulema who were not associated to the Wahabi or Faraizi movements were also very much active in the Uprising, and fought, lead the war, against the British. The full details of their lives and works are given in different chapters of this book. They had no religious pretext like Wahabis and Faraizis and had only motives for the freedom of their country. They not only sentimentally bound the Muslims to fight against the British, but they also appealed their Hindu brethren to unite in that holy cause. They opined that every citizen is religiously bound to protect his country or motherland. The Hindus of that time also had shaken their hands with the Muslims without any hesitation and fought shoulder to shoulder with the Muslims commonly against the British. This third group of the Ulema later on made their stronghold at Deoband and formed a religious institution.

There was another group of Ulema who also played very influential role was belonged to the Shia community of Islam. Maulana Mohammad Baqar and his son Maulana Mohammad Hussain Azad were prominent among them. They also laid their lives and property for their motherland like the other Sunni Ulema of Wahabi, Faraizi, and Deobandi.

It is really interesting and noteworthy that all the Ulema floated the slogan that the religion is in danger and appealed to the public to fight against the British for the religion. Here the question arises that whether Islam was really in danger? Was it necessary to call the Muslims for *Jihad*? The answer is certainly not. It is evident that in India, the Muslims were free in their religious practices equally as their Hindu brethren. There was not a single instance which proves the religious persecution or forcible conversion by the British Government. All the communities of India lived with peace and tranquility. Although there was racial discrimination but that too was not a taboo in their religious practices. If there was persecution, tyranny, any type of retribution and exploitation that was related to the political, administrative, and financial policies of the British Government. If the Muslim Ulema were free to follow their religion, then what forces compelled them to wage a war of religion or Holy War against the British? It was none other than pain of slavery and certainly the hope to gain independence from the British yoke. Wahabi or

Faraizi, whatever it may be dubbed, but these were the national movements against the British. It is really unfortunate that the British ideologies regarding these movements were generally raked up by Indian peoples even after the Independence of India.

In the retributions following the Uprising of 1857, thousands of Ulema were hanged and burnt alive. They were brutally crushed with the hope to never rise again. The remaining Ulema hid themselves for the few years but in order to re-establish themselves, some of them like Maulana Qasim Nanotawi and Rasheed Ahmad Gangohi, founded a madarsa at Deoband. They never dared to involve in any anti-British activity, but they could not remain calm for long and in the late years of the first quarter of the twentieth century, they again raised their head for the India's freedom movement, and founded 'Jamiatul Ulama-i-Hind' as the sister organisation of the Indian National Congress. It was surprising that these Ulema opposed the partition of India and after its partition they fully contributed to the development of India by joining the Indian National Congress.

Apart from the Ulema, there were a lot of Muslim luminaries who participated directly or indirectly in the Uprising. However, due to the lack of spaces, only few of them have been widely described in this book. The main figure in this category was the only national symbol of that time, the Mughal Emperor Bahadur Shah Zafar. He was very experienced and advanced in age. He was doubtful about the success of the Uprising as it was started by the regularly paid Sepoys of the British army. He was sure that these Sepoys would not stand long in lack of their monthly payment. Notwithstanding all the presumptions, Bahadur Shah Zafar not only became ready to lead the war against the world's most mighty power but also appealed the other Indian Rajas, Nawabs, bankers, and money lenders to join hands for the common cause of ousting the British from India. He even showed his readiness to evacuate the throne and handover it to any Raja unanimously chosen to lead the war and rule the country. In order to maintain the communal harmony, he imposed ban on the cow slaughter even on the occasion of Bakrid festival. He regularly instructed the Princes to effectively lead the battles which were being fought with the British. Emperor Bahadur Shah Zafar was several times annoyed with the Sepoys for their loot and plunder in the city and sitting idle in the walled city rather than fighting at the front.

General Bakht Khan was another eminent person who revolutionized the war and the imperial administration after his arrival. Due to his efforts, a Military Council or Council of Administration was formed including both civil and military persons. As a Commander-in-Chief, he led most of the important battles in Delhi and other parts of India. Apart from the formation of the council, his most important achievement was uniting the Sepoys and religious people on one platform. His abilities and qualities promoted him on the height of eminence and in other words, next to the Emperor Bahadur Shah Zafar. He was a real hero of the Uprising and a true Indian patriot who didn't lose his heart even after the fall of Delhi and moved forward to assist the revolutionaries of Lucknow and other centres of revolt.

The next contemporary personality Sir Syed Ahmad Khan unwillingly supported the British Government in the Uprising. He severely opposed and criticized the British policies, more surprisingly, being in the service of the same Government. Through his book *Asbab-e-Baghawat-e-Hind* he advocated that the Indians were not the traitor, but the British Government was responsible for the Uprising in India due to its policies. Being in the service of the British Government, his daring advocacy, for the Indian people, could not be ignored. At that time when Indian intelligentsia was silent on the matter Sir Syed Ahmad Khan was the only intellectual who publicly abused the British policies and demanded the reformation in the system. When this matter was discussed in the House of Commons, many Parliamentarians urged for punishing Sir Syed Ahmad Khan severely but the majority of them more intelligently accepted their folly and suggested that his points were not baseless and reformation was a must in the Indian administration. The failure of the Uprising taught a lesson to him that without getting modern scientific education and advancement, the mighty British Empire would not be challenged. For that very purpose Sir Syed Ahmad Khan opened schools to educate the innocent Indians. So he cleverly prepared a ground for Indian independence, more surprisingly, with the cooperation of the British Government.

Mirza Asadullah Khan Ghalib, however, didn't openly criticize the British Government in the hope of releasing his pension, but his writing in his letters and diary, *Dastamboo*, speaks the truth of the misery and sufferings of the innocent Indians. At the time of Uprising he was the trusted court poet and tutor of the Emperor Bahadur Shah Zafar. Mirza Asadullah Khan Ghalib was the first man who wrote *Sikka* in the Mughal Emperor's name. When the Delhi siege began, Mirza Asadullah Khan Ghalib more cleverly changed the side in the hope of resuming his pension, the single source of his livelihood. He shut himself in his house and wrote the daily happenings in his letters and diary. As an Urdu poet and writer, he has given the full details of the plights of the Delhi residents. Massacre, burning down the houses, loot, and plunder has sometimes compelled him to criticize the Sepoys and revolutionaries. Although taking U turn after the siege of Delhi, his pain for his country and people could be easily felt through his writings.

In the last of the book, the role of the Urdu press during the Uprising has been discussed in detail. The first and foremost among them was *Dehli Urdu Akhbar* of Maulana Mohammad Baqar whose name was later on changed as *Akhbar-uz-Zafar*. It not only gives the full details of the daily happenings from the beginning to the revolt to the siege of Delhi but also prepares a ground to fight against the British. It frequently aroused the sentiments of both Hindus and Muslims to follow the examples of their ancestors and fight commonly to oust the tyrant foreigners. It also assures Divine help to the Sepoys and revolutionaries. When the Sepoys indulged themselves in loot and plunder, the *Dehli Urdu Akhbar* reminds them their high moral character in the light of their religion. For the whole period of Uprising it served as the source of inspiration and moral courage to the revolutionaries.

The other Delhi newspaper *Sadiqul Akhbar* of Maulana Jamiluddin was also a good source inspiration and promotion and aroused the feelings and emotions of the people during the revolt of 1857. It boosted the power of the revolutionaries by publishing the news of war between Iran and England and also published that the armies of Iran and Afghanistan were coming to attack on the British during the Uprising. It also wrote that the King of Iran would soon conquer India and present the throne of India to King of Delhi. It published that it was the God who made the British prominent and now is the time of their fall by the wish of the same God. The newspaper *Sadiqul Akhbar* was undoubtedly an aid and a definite source of inspiration to the revolutionaries during the Uprising of 1857.

The other Urdu Weekly, *Tilism*, was started in the reaction of annexation of Awadh and the deposition of Nawab Wajid Ali Shah. It was started by Maulvi Yaqub Ansari in 1854. The contents of the paper were filled with the anti-British sentiments. Due to its bold content and courageous criticism of the British rulers, the paper acquired a respectable position in the civil and military population of Lucknow. The policy of newspaper was a reflection of courage and boldness. It also gives full details of the anti-British activities of Maulvi Ahmadullah Shah and other saintly people of Awadh. The paper truly mirrored the misery and suffering of the people of Awadh after the annexation by the British. It clearly reflects the public resentment over the annexation of Awadh.

In the last month of 1858, the war of independence was over except a few skirmishes in the areas of northern portion of Awadh. The prophecy that the Company's rule would vanish after a hundred years became true with the famous proclamation from the queen of England in November 1858, which published throughout India. According to the proclamation, everyone who fought openly against the English in the war was given a full pardon as soon as he lay down his arms; a promise was given that his property would not be confiscated. However, some Muslim theologians, popularly called Wahabis by the British, didn't avail the opportunity of the proclamation and continued the national struggle until their final persecution after the murder of the Lord Mayo, the Governor General of India.

Bibliography

Journals, Newspapers, Magazines and Gazetteers

1. *Annual of Urdu Studies,* Vol. 18, Madison, USA, 2003.
2. *Biblio*, Vol. XII, No. 3 and 4, March-April, 2007.
3. *Dawn*, Karachi, 26 January, 2008.
4. *Defence Journal*, Vol. 3, No. 9, Islamabad, December, 1999.
5. *Dehli Urdu Akhbar,* 10th May, 1857, 17th May, 1857, 24th May, 1857, 31st May, 1857, 14th June, 1857, 21st June, 1857, 5th July, 1857, 12th July, 1857, 19th July, 1857, 24th July, 1857, 9th August, 1857, 16th August, 1857, 23rd August, 1857, 13th September, 1857.
6. Hunter, William Wilson, *The Imperial Gazetteer of India*, London 1907 Delhi, 2006.
7. *India Perspectives*, Vol. 15, No. 3, March, 2002.
8. *Islam and Muslim Societies—A Social Science Journal*, (Zafarul Islam- Book Review, *Excavation of Truth- Unsung Heroes of 1857 War of Independence* by Khan Mohammad Sadiq Khan) Vol. 4, No. 1, New Delhi, 2011.
9. *Islamic Voice* (*Sher Ali Khan: A Forgotten Revolutionary*—Zubair Ahmed), Bangalore, March, 2006.
10. *Jaam-i-Noor, Monthly, Millat Ka Tarjaman*, Delhi, 2007.
11. *Leidschrift*, Leiden, Netherlands, No. 24, December 3, 2009.

12. *Mutiny Papers,* Collection 60, Nos. 213-14, 23 June, 1857. (National Archives, New Delhi).
13. *Naya Daur,* (*Brijis Qadr: The Last King of Awadh-* Mirza Qaukab Qadr) Awadh Number, a Monthly Urdu Journal published by the Information and Public Relations Department of the Government of Uttar Pradesh, Lucknow, February-March, 1994.
14. Nevill, H.R., *District Gazetteers of the United Provinces of Agra and Oudh,* Vol. IV, Allahabad, 1904.
15. *New Statesman,* 16th October, 2006.
16. *New York Daily Tribune,* July 15, 1857, August 4, 1857.
17. *People's Democracy,* Vol. XXXI, No. 41, October 14, 2007, Vol. XXXI, No. 18, May 6, 2007, Vol. XXXI, No. 10, March 11, 2007, Vol. XXXI, No 17. April, 29, 2007, Vol. XXXI, No. 04, January 28, 2007.
18. *Radiance Viewsweekly,* Vol. XLIV No. 28, 2006-12-31.
19. *Secular Qayadat,* Delhi, 21 August, 2007.
20. *Shodh Sanchayan,* Bilingual journal of Humanities and Social Sciences, (*The Great Uprising and Civil Rebellion in Shahjahanpur: (A Study of Anti-British Resistance in 1857*—Dr. Syed Mohd Ameer), Vol. 2, Issue 1 and 2, 15 Jan-15 July, 2011.
21. *Social Scientist,* Vol. 26, No. 1-4, January-April, 1998.
22. *Taameer-i-Haryana, (Jab Kala Pani Lord Mayo Ka Maqtil Ban Gaya-* Sayyad Asim Mahmood), Chandigarh, July-August, 2012.
23. *The Annual of Urdu Studies,* (*Kaala Paani: Twarikh-e Ajib,* Mohammad Jafar Thanesari, Eng. Tr. S. Kamal Abdali), Vol. 26, Madison, USA, 2011 and Vol. 18, Madison, USA, 2003.
24. *The Express Tribune,* Karachi, January 27th, 2011.
25. *The Guardian,* 10th May, 2007.
26. *The International Journal of Asia Pacific Studies,* (*The Assassination of Lord Mayo: The 'First' Jihad*—Helen James), Vol. 5, No. 2, 1-19, 2009, Penang, Malaysia.
27. *The Living Age,* Volume 0055, Issue 702, New York, November 7, 1857.
28. *Tilism,* Lucknow, 21st November, 1856.
29. *World Policy Journal,* (*The Hidden Roots of Wahhabism in British India*—Charles Allen), Vol. 22, No. 2, Massachusetts, USA, Summer, 2005.

Books

1. Adam and Charles Black, *History of the Siege of Delhi*, Edinburgh, 1861.
2. Agrawal, Lion M.G., *Freedom Fighters of India*, Volume 3, Delhi, 2008.
3. Ahmad, Bashiruddin, *Waqiyat-i-Darul Hukumat Delhi*, Vol. I, Urdu Academy Delhi, 2012.
4. Ahmad, Aijaz, *Aligarh Muslim University: An Educational and Political History, 1920-47*, Ghaziabad, 2005.
5. Ahmad, K.J., *100 Hundred Great Muslims*, San Francisco, 1987.
6. Ahmad, Mohammad Masood, *Jange Azadi me Allama Fazle Haq Khairabadi ka Kirdar*, Malegaon, 2005.
7. Aitchison, Charles, *Rulers of India: Lord Lawrence*, Oxford, 1892.
8. Allen, Charles, *God's Terrorists: The Wahabi Cult and the Hidden Roots of Modern Jihad*, Massachusetts, USA, 2006.
9. Anderson, Clare, *The Indian Uprising of 1857-8: Prisons, Prisoners and Rebellion*, London, 2007.
10. Anjum, Khaliq, *Intkhab-e-Khatoot-e-Ghalib*, (16th Ed.), New Delhi, 2011.
11. Argyl, Campbell, George Douglas, Duke of, *India Under Dalhousie and Canning*, London, 1865.
12. *Athara Sau Sattawan Ke Rahnuma (Sawanehy Khake)*, National Council for Promotion of Urdu Language, New Delhi, 2009.
13. Bakshi, S.R., and Chaturvedi, Ritu, *Bihar Through the Ages*, Vol. 3, New Delhi, 2007.
14. Beveridge, Henry, *A Comprehensive History of India*, Vol. III, London, 1962.
15. Campo, Juan Eduardo, *Encyclopedia of Islam*, New York, 2009.
16. Cunningham, Henry Stewart, *Earl Canning*, Oxford, 1891.
17. Devy, G.N., *Indian Literary Criticism: Theory and Interpretation*, Hyderabad, 2002.
18. Dewar, Douglas, *Hand-book to the English Pre-mutiny Records in the Government Record rooms of the United Provinces of Agra and Oudh*, Allahabad, (ND).
19. Dodd, George, *The History of the Indian Revolt and of the Expeditions to Persia, China, and Japan, 1856-7-8*, London, 1859.

20. Edward, Gilliat, *Heroes of the Indian Mutiny; Stories of Heroic Deeds*, London, 1914.
21. Engineer, Asghar Ali, *They Too Fought for India's Freedom: The Role of Minorities*, Gurgaon, 2006.
22. Fanshawe, H.C., *Delhi Past and Present*, London, 1902.
23. Forbes-Mitchell, *Reminiscences of the Great Mutiny, 1857-59*, London, 1894.
24. Forrest, G.W., *A History of the Indian Mutiny; Reviewed and Illustrated from Original Documents,* Vol. I, London, 1904.
25. Forrest, G.W., *A History of the Indian Mutiny; Reviewed and Illustrated from Original Documents,* Vol. II, London, 1904.
26. Forrest, George W., *A History of the Indian Mutiny; Reviewed and Illustrated from Original Documents,* Vol. III, London, 1904.
27. Forrest, George W., *Selections From The Letters Despatches and other State Papers Preserved in the Military Department of the Government of India 1857-58,* Volume III, Calcutta, 1902.
28. Forrest, Robert Edward, *Eight Days; A Tale of the Indian Mutiny*, London (ND).
29. Frazer, R.W., *British India*, New York, 1896.
30. Ghalib, Mirza Asadullah Khan, *Dastamboo*, Urdu Trans. Khwaja Ahmad Faruqi, New Delhi, 2000.
31. Ghazi, M.A., *Islamic Renaissance In South Asia (1707-1867): The Role of Shah Waliallah & His Successors*, Delhi, 2004.
32. Graham, G.F.I., *The Life and Work of Sayed Ahmed Khan*, Edinburgh, 1885.
33. Grant, Hope, *Incidents in the Sepoy War 1857-58*, Edinburgh, 1873.
34. Greathed, Harvey Harris, *Letters Written During the Siege of Delhi*, London, 1858.
35. Griffiths, Charles John, *A Narrative of the Siege of Delhi with an Account of the Mutiny at Firozpur in 1857*, London, 1910.
36. Gubbins, Martin Richard, *An Account of the Mutinies of Oudh and of the Siege of the Lucknow Residency; With some Observation on the Condition of the Province of Oudh and of the Causes of the Mutiny of the Bengal Army*, London, 1858.
37. Halls, John James, *Two Months in Arrah in 1857*, London, 1860.
38. Handcock, Arthur Gore, *The Siege of Delhi in 1857: A Short Account*, Allahabad, 1897.

39. Hodson, George Herbert, *Hodson of Hodson's Horse or the Twelve Years of a Soldiers Life in India: Being Extracts from the Letters of the Late Major W.S.R. Hodson*, London, 1889.
40. Hunter, William Wilson, *The Indian Musalmans*, London, 1876.
41. Innes, McLeod, *Lucknow and Oude in the Mutiny: A Narrative and a Study*, London, 1895.
42. Innes, McLeod, *The Sepoy Revolt: A Critical Narrative*, London, 1897.
43. Ishaq, Abdul Hamid, *Ulema of Deoband*, Madarsa Arabia Islamia, Azaadville, South Africa, 2011.
44. Jafri, Saiyid Zaheer Husain, *The Great Uprising of 1857*, Delhi, 2009.
45. James F. Holcomb, and Helen H. Holcomb, *In the Heart of India: or, Beginnings of Missionary work in Bundela Land, with a short chapter on the Characteristics of Bundelkhand and its People, and Four Chapters of Jhansi History*, Philadelphia, 1905.
46. Kaye, John William, *A History of the Sepoy War in India, 1857-58,* Vol. I, London, 1875.
47. Kaye, John William, *A History of the Sepoy War in India, 1857-58,* Vol. II, London, 1874.
48. Kaye, John William, *A History of the Sepoy War in India, 1857-58,* Vol. III, London, 1876.
49. Kaye, John William, *Kay's and Malleson's History of the Indian Mutiny of 1857-8,* Vol. II, London, 1910.
50. Keene, Henry George, *British Administration during the Revolt of 1857*, New Delhi, 1883.
51. Keene, Henry George, *Fifty-Seven: Some Account of the Administration of Indian Districts during the Revolt of the Bengal Army*, London, 1883.
52. Khan Mohammad Sadiq Khan, *Excavation of Truth-Unsung Heroes of 1857 War of Independence*, New Delhi, 2007.
53. Khan, Syed Ahmad, *Asbab-e-Baghawat-e-Hind*, (Eng. Trans.), Patna, 1999.
54. Kim A., Wagnor, *The Great Fear of 1857, Rumours, Conspiracies and the Making of the Indian Uprising*, Witney (UK), 2010.
55. Kofoid, Charles Alwood, *The Story of the Indian Mutiny, 1857-58,* Edinburgh, 1898.

56. Malleson, George Bruce, *History of the Indian Mutiny of 1857-58, Commencing from the Close of the Second Volume of Sir John Kaye's History of the Sepoy War*, Vol. III, (Contemporaneous with Sir John Kay's Third Volume), London, 1878.
57. Malleson, George Bruce, *Indian Mutiny of 1857*, London, 1912.
58. Malleson, George Bruce, *Kay's and Malleson's History of the Indian Mutiny of 1857-8,* Vol. IV, London, 1911.
59. Malleson, George Bruce, *Kay's and Malleson's History of the Indian Mutiny of 1857-8,* Vol. V, London, 1911.
60. Martin, R. Montgomery, *The Indian Empire,* Vol. II, London, 1858.
61. Mead, Henry, *The Sepoy Revolt: Its causes and its Consequences,* London, 1858.
62. Medley, Julius George, *A Years Campaigning in India from March 1857 to March 1858*, London, 1858.
63. Metcalfe, Charles Theophilus, *Two Native Narratives of the Mutiny in Delhi,* (Eng. Trans. Of *Roznamcha Mainudin Hasan Khan* and *Munshi Jeewan Lal*), London, 1898.
64. More, Sheshrao, *The 1857 Jihad,* (Eng. Trans. Bhalchandrarao C. Patwardhan), Delhi, 2009.
65. Mohammad, Shan, *Writings and Speeches of Sir Syed Ahmad Khan*, Bombay, 1972.
66. Naim, C.M., *Urdu Text and Contexts, Selected Essays*, Delhi, 2004.
67. Norman, Henry Wylie Norman, *Delhi - 1857; The Siege, Assault, and Capture as given in the Diary and Correspondence of the Late Colonel Keith Young*, London 1902.
68. Joshi, P.C., *Rebellion 1857,* New Delhi, 2007.
69. Pratap, Mahendra and Jafri, Saiyid Zaheer Hasan, *Region in Indian History*, (*Leadership of Maulvi Liaqat Ali: First Freedom Struggle of Allahabad-* Yusufa Nafees), New Delhi, 2008.
70. Puniyani, Ram, *Communal Politics Facts Versus Myths*, Sage Publication, New Delhi, 2003.
71. Qasmi, Ataur Rahman, *Hindustan Ki Pahli Jang Azadi 1857 Me Musalmanon Ka Hissa*, New Delhi, 2008.
72. Raikes, Charles, *Notes on the Revolt in the North-Western Provinces of India*, London, 1858.

73. Ramchandani, Indu, *Students' Britannica India*, Vol. I, Delhi, 2000.
74. Roberts, P.E., *A Historical Geography of the British Dependencies: India*, Vol. VII, London, 1914.
75. Robertson, Henry Dundas, District Duties during the Revolt in the North-West Provinces of India in 1857*: With Remarks on Subsequent Investigations during 1858-59*, London, 1859.
76. Russell, William Howard, *My Diary in India in the Year 1858-9*, Vol. II, London, 1860.
77. Rotten, J.E.W., *Captains Narratives of the Seige of Delhi from the Outbreak at Meerut to the Capture of Delhi*, London, 1858.
78. Samiuddin, Abida, *Encyclopaedic Dictionary of Urdu Literature*, (Vol. I), New Delhi, 2007.
79. Savarkar, V.D., *The Indian War of Independence of 1857*, London 1909.
80. Sherer, John Walter, *Daily Life During the Indian Mutiny: Personal Experiences of 1857*, Allahabad, 1910.
81. Sherer, John Walter, *Havelock's March on Cawnpore, 1857*, London, 1910.
82. Sieveking, Isabel Giberne, *A Turning Point in the Indian Mutiny*, London, 1910.
83. Singh, Khushwant, *Delhi: A Novel*, New Delhi, 1990.
84. Spear, Percival, *Twilight of the Mughals: Studies in Late Mughal Delhi*, Cambridge, 1951.
85. Stewart, Charles Edward, (Edited by Basil Stewart), *Through Persia in Disguise with Reminiscences of the Indian Mutiny*, London, 1911.
86. Surridge, Victor, *Romance of Empire, India*, London, 1909.
87. Tabassum, Farhat, *Deoband Ulema's Movement for the Freedom of India*, New Delhi, 2006.
88. Tariq, Shamim, *Ghalib aur Hamari Tahrik Azadi*, Mumbai, 2011
89. Tariq, Shamim, *Ghalib, Bahadur Shah Zafar aur 1857*, New Delhi, 2008.
90. Tayler, William, *The Patna Crisis; or, Three months at Patna, during the Insurrection of 1857*, London, 1858.
91. Thomson, Mowbray, *The Story of Cawnpore*, London, 1859.
92. Thurburn, Felix Augustus Victor, *Reminiscences of the Indian Rebellion of 1857-1858*, London, 1889.

93. Tracy, Louis, *The Red Year; A Story of The Indian Mutiny*, New York, 1907.
94. Trevelyan, George, *The Competition Wallah*, London, 1864.
95. Wood, Evelyn, *The Revolt in Hindustan 1857-59*, London, 1908.

Index